The New South Africa

The New South Africa

Guy Arnold

First published in Great Britain 2000 by
MACMILLAN PRESS LTD
Houndmills, Basingstoke, Hampshire RG21 6XS and London
Companies and representatives throughout the world

A catalogue record for this book is available from the British Library.

ISBN 0–333–91887–8

 First published in the United States of America 2000 by
ST. MARTIN'S PRESS, LLC,
Scholarly and Reference Division,
175 Fifth Avenue, New York, N.Y. 10010

ISBN 0–312–23517–8

Library of Congress Cataloging-in-Publication Data
Arnold, Guy.
    The new South Africa / Guy Arnold.
        p.   cm.
    Includes bibliographical references and index.
    ISBN 0–312–23517–8 (cloth)
    1. South Africa—Politics and government—1994– 2. South Africa–
    –Economic conditions—1991– 3. South Africa—Social conditions—1994–
    4. Mbeki, Thabo. I. Title.

    DT1975 .A76 2000
    968.06'5—dc21
                                                                    00–033322

This book is printed on paper suitable for recycling and made from fully managed and sustained forest sources.

10   9   8   7   6   5   4   3   2   1
09   08   07   06   05   04   03   02   01   00

Printed and bound in Great Britain by
Antony Rowe Ltd, Chippenham, Wiltshire

Contents

Introduction

For at least a quarter of a century prior to 1990 observers of the South African scene predicted that apartheid would end in a blood bath; instead, at the eleventh hour, there was an orderly transfer of political power by means of universal franchise elections from the white minority to the black majority and the New South Africa was born. Whatever had gone before, this represented a triumph for peaceful as opposed to violent methods of political change. The problems that faced the new government of the African National Congress (ANC) were – and remain – formidable.

During the apartheid years the white minority in South Africa held all the levers of political and economic power and could be seen as an extension of the rich developed North set down in a poor country of the South and able to control the black majority by means of the apparatus of apartheid. Following the elections of April 1994 this situation was turned on its head: South Africa became (what it always was in fact) a poor developing country with a rich white elite in the middle of it. The majority of those whites, though by no means all, had been either active supporters of the apartheid system or passive recipients of the benefits for whites which flowed from it. The 'trick' for the ruling ANC is how to use this white minority and integrate it into the New South Africa so that its expertise and energies are used to the benefit of the whole population; the success or failure of this integration process will determine the success or failure of the new South Africa.

The adverse economic and social consequences of apartheid will take years to eradicate while, arguably, the psychological scars left by the system will not disappear until the present generation has passed away. One statistic alone points to the extent of the economic problem: only 11 per cent of the population is rated as highly skilled and 53 per cent

1

as unskilled; contrast that to the European Union where 31 per cent of the population is highly skilled and only 16 per cent unskilled.[1] Many other statistics can be adduced to demonstrate some of the world's highest levels of unemployment, gross inefficiency, huge over-manning of the civil service and bureaucracy. South Africa, which sees itself as a putative member of the advanced economies, faces a huge task in modernising its economic structures if it is to be reintegrated into the world economic system.

When, at the beginning of 1995, the civil service advertised 11 000 posts for managers, clerks and cleaners more than 1.5 million applicants applied. Official figures suggest an unemployment rate of 15 per cent; others put it as high as 40 per cent, the vast majority from the black townships. In every direction – housing, electricity, education and jobs – shortages or the absence of anything at all are matched by huge expectations and though the ANC has been exemplary in warning that reforms take time, there is always a limit to people's political patience and the government has a great deal to accomplish in a short time if it is to meet even a fraction of the demands that are being made upon it.

Sub-Saharan Africa represents the least economically dynamic region in the world and, according to the World Bank's 1997 report on 'Global Economic Prospects and the Developing Countries', although the region is on the threshold of a period of sustained growth at 4 per cent per annum this will not be enough to reverse the region's marginalisation. By 2020 sub-Saharan Africa's share of global GDP will only have risen from 1.2 per cent (1997) to 1.7 per cent and will have lost ground to more dynamic countries, especially in Asia. Over the same period sub-Saharan Africa's share of developing world GDP is expected to fall from 7.6 per cent in 1992 to 5.8 per cent in 2020.[2] South Africa may be the largest, most dynamic economy in sub-Saharan Africa but that does not alter the fact of belonging to a region which in world terms is marginal. The new South Africa is only likely to succeed in overcoming the range of problems it has inherited from its apartheid past if it breaks free of the present African mould and ceases to be a marginal economy. And that is a very tall order indeed.

It will not be enough for South Africa to behave as did all other African states on achieving independence, with an African elite replacing a colonial elite and one set of power brokers taking over from another. During the apartheid era South Africa was the most over-bureaucratised country in the world outside the Communist bloc and this does not appear to have changed. In a lecture delivered in August 1995[3] the African scholar Ali Mazrui controversially suggested the creation of an African Security Council consisting of five nations – South Africa, Egypt, Nigeria, Ethiopia and Zaire – to conduct peace-keeping operations. Implicit in this suggestion was that of a new semi-colonising role for South Africa and though on first inspection this may seem anathema to the New South Africa in fact it makes sense for South Africa to pursue conscious efforts to formalise by its actions what it is already in fact, the regional power. By undertaking a role to revitalise the continent South Africa could break away from the endless contemplation of its apartheid past and provide itself instead with a dynamic role that would do more to stimulate economic growth and bring about the consequent solution of internal problems than anything else.

The reconciliation that took place between white and black over the tense four years 1990–94, that saw the replacement of the apartheid system by one of universal suffrage which brought Nelson Mandela to power as the country's first black President, was a remarkable achievement by any standards, and more especially in the light of the country's grim racial history, and South Africans of all races have a right to be proud of such a relatively peaceful transition from minority racial-based rule to majority all-embracing rule. Yet, satisfaction with that achievement should not blind anyone to the race dangers and pitfalls that lie in the future. Centuries of racial divisions may have been glossed over in the euphoria that heralded the appearance of the New South Africa, they were in no sense eradicated, and many years and crises must pass before South Africa achieves true racial integration. Sean Johnson, the editorial director of Independent Newspapers in South Africa, interviewed President Mandela in April 1998 about the peace process in Ulster and asked him whether what happened in South Africa could also happen in Ireland. Mandela replied:

> As long as there are men and women on all sides who are able to rise above feelings for revenge, men and women who can put the future of their children first, who can put terrible episodes behind them in order to move on, this process can work as ours eventually did. ... It will take a long time. There will be many disappointments. But it can be done if the will is unshakeable.[4]

Mandela the 'healer' is right to be optimistic, yet the history of the twentieth century and especially its last 50 years, has shown just how long and bitter racial memories can be and just how determined racial bigots are to remain racial bigots.

South Africa's vulnerability to world market forces, now it has rejoined the economic mainstream, was amply demonstrated in mid-1998 when the rand went into free fall as a result of the financial crisis in the Far East. But the crisis did not simply reveal the country's economic weakness; it also brought into the open the fragile nature of the black–white political rapprochement as white South Africans, whose currency had been one of the world's strongest during the apartheid years, found it (and their savings) battered by world forces quite beyond Pretoria's control. At the time Thabo Mbeki, Mandela's designated successor who was already running the government on a day-to-day basis, faced a 33 per cent rate of unemployment and a 24 per cent prime lending rate while the government's policy of Growth, Employment and Redistribution (Gear) appeared to be coming to a halt. The announcement in August 1998 (during this economic crisis) that Tito Mboweni would replace Chris Stals as Governor of the Reserve Bank led to further white fears which, interpreted, revealed their fundamental racism. These fears were described as follows:

> The coded version goes like this. Stals is politically independent, whereas Mboweni is the ANC's Minister of Labour, and therefore potentially susceptible to political pressure. Decoded, Stals is a white Afrikaner, Mboweni is black, has a not very capitalist first name and calls himself 'comrade' to boot. He has been variously described in the South African press as 'self-confident' and 'arrogant'.[5]

Now, if every time there is a financial downturn or crisis whites are going to quit South Africa in panic as some did at this time, they hardly represent the stuff of the racial partnership that the New South Africa requires. There is, it would seem, too much of a feeling among whites that having made the great gesture by abandoning apartheid there is nothing more that should be demanded of them. In fact, if the New South Africa is to work the whites must be prepared to contribute a great deal more; nor should they expect to escape the effects of many more crises over the next two decades.

South Africa's economic prospects are complex. According to the Washington-based Institute of International Finance (IIF) the restraints imposed by South Africa's Reserve Bank and the governments privatisation programme make it a better candidate for rapid recovery than many other developing countries. Indeed, the IIF praised the South African economic performance in terms of its GEAR programme, in terms of its privatisation, its abolition of export subsidies and lowering of import tariffs at the behest of the World Trade Organization to such an extent as to suggest that Pretoria has already fully accepted the economic orthodoxies which are constantly advocated by the major Western economies, the World Bank and the International Monetary Fund.[6] Whether such orthodoxies in fact represent the best path for South Africa to follow is another question.

There are many questions that the New South Africa must address. Two of the most important of these questions are the following. In its search for capital investment and reintegration into the world economic system is South Africa in danger of accepting uncritically all the Western economic orthodoxies that always work to the advantage of the major Western economies but often spell continuing dependence, if not total manipulation, for developing countries? And, in its desire for racial harmony will Pretoria give way to too many white pressures at the expense of justice for the majority of its people?

1
Setting the Scene

In February 1995, less than a year after becoming his country's first black President, Nelson Mandela ruled out serving a second term after the elections of 1999. For a man of 77 it was an obviously sensible decision to take, yet one has to search a long way to find politicians, however old, who are prepared to stand down after only one term of office, and Mandela at that time was at the height of his popularity in South Africa and acclaimed world-wide in a manner accorded to few national leaders. His decision was not just about his age and health; it was also a statement of confidence in the New South Africa, the African National Congress and Thabo Mbeki, the man designated to succeed him. South Africa was immensely lucky, as commentators have endlessly insisted, to have Mandela as its leader during the crucial transition from minority apartheid-rule to majority black-dominated rule, but as Georges Clemenceau said in the wake of the First World War 'The graves of Europe are full of indispensable men' and the greatest service Mandela can render his country is to ensure a sound basis for the future when he has passed from the political scene.

Speaking in the Assembly at that time Mandela reacted to recent riots that had occurred in Johannesburg, Durban and Cape Town, as well as wildcat strikes by black police officers and civil servants, and those people who continued to use the key weapons the ANC had employed in the fight against apartheid such as refusing to pay bills for rent, water or electricity:

> I would like to address the matter bluntly. The government literally does not have the money to meet the demands that are being advanced. Mass action of any kind will not create resources that the government does not have. All of us must rid ourselves of the wrong

notion that the government has a big bag full of money. It is important that we rid ourselves of the culture of entitlement.[1]

These were brave words; they needed to be said. Later that year, in July, Mandela hosted a remarkable gathering of women from both sides of the former apartheid divide including Adelaide Tambo, Elize Botha, Tienie Vorster, Margot Diederichs, Ntsiki Biko and Susan Strijdom. 'The past is forgotten' he said, 'we must all work together now.' It was part of the healing process at which he excelled. Adelaide Tambo said: 'We've been through the struggle, but we're harbouring no grudges. As the President says, we've got to pull together to make South Africa a nicer place for everyone.' Such sentiments are admirable but they need to be followed by hard, precise actions, and by 1998 the euphoria generated during the first year of the new Rainbow Society had given place to white worries about what they stood to lose and black worries about what they had yet to obtain. The politics of euphoria never last long.

In the immediate aftermath of President Mobutu's exit from Zaire in May 1997 Mandela, who had attempted a mediating role as Kabila's forces closed in on Kinshasa, spoke of an African renaissance. 'It is given that complex problems spanning decades will not lend themselves to easy solutions' he said, but he went on to insist: 'The time has come for Africa to take full responsibility for her woes. ... We are convinced that our region and our continent have set out along the new road to realise Africa's dream of her renaissance.'[2] It is easy to be cynical about such statements but if Africa is to experience a renaissance South Africa must be the leading player; if South Africa can link its own rejuvenation in the wake of the apartheid years with the renaissance of the continent as a whole then the one development will feed on the other to the advantage of both.

The other key player in the transition of South Africa was President F. W. de Klerk. Just as Mikhail Gorbachev embarked upon his *glasnost* and *perestroika* reforms in order to save the Communist system from collapse but found, instead, that he had opened a pandora's box whose contents he could not control, so de Klerk reckoned that by coming to terms with the outlawed ANC and releasing Mandela he could safeguard the long-term future of the white minority whose interests he had been elected to preserve. In 1985 de Klerk had led the hardline members of P. W. Botha's cabinet in opposing any concessions to the black majority in the President's forthcoming Rubicon speech which turned into a disaster. Five years later, after he had replaced Botha as leader of the National Party (NP) and then as President, de Klerk delivered his famous speech of 2 February 1990, in which he unbanned 33 political organisations including the ANC, while a week later he released Mandela unconditionally. The evidence suggests that de Klerk greatly underestimated the strength of the ANC and saw himself holding the ring on behalf of the old white hierarchy between the ANC, the Homeland rulers, Chief Buthelezi's Inkatha Freedom Party and the other contenders for power, rather than presiding over the demise of the NP and the emergence of an ANC majority government, even though the absolute nature of the white loss of political power was temporarily softened by participation in a transitional government of national unity.

Whatever he believed the outcome would be de Klerk's decision to unban the ANC and other banned organisations and initiate a dialogue leading to a one-person one-vote constitution represented a crucial turning point for South Africa. As the country's last white president de Klerk presided over the crucial four year period from his speech of February 1990 to the elections of April 1994; he then became Second Vice-President in the transitional government of national unity before taking the National Party out of it in 1996. In August 1997 de Klerk resigned as leader of the National Party which, already by that time, appeared to be in terminal decline. Since the *raison d'etre* for the National Party was apartheid it seems logical that with the end of the system and the emergence of majority rule the party should largely collapse if not disintegrate and, it can be argued, it was de Klerk's pragmatism which destroyed the party that had brought him to power. He left a party at war with itself, torn between the conservative die-hards and the reformers who were insisting that it should transform itself into a black-led multi-racial mass movement in order to survive. De Klerk failed to please either the right or the left of his party and when he went General Constand Viljoen of the rightwing Freedom Front said de Klerk's departure represented a positive development for Afrikaner politics while a spokesman for the right-wing Boerestaat Party said de Klerk's 'treachery towards his people was unequalled.' Such statements give an indication of racial conflicts to come. On the other hand the NP reformer, Roelf Meyer, who had been the party's chief negotiator during the peace talks, had resigned three months prior to de Klerk's departure in order to create a new more progressive political movement. A week before de Klerk resigned a survey revealed that support for the NP had dropped from 21 per cent at the April 1994 elections to only 12 per cent. President Mandela whose regard for de Klerk had been steadily eroded since 1994, nonetheless, said on his departure that South Africa should not forget his contribution to smoothing the transition from 'our painful past'.

While visiting Britain in 1997 de Klerk defended his record. He claimed that 'Under my leadership, the NP abolished apartheid.' Later, in August of that year, he resigned as leader of the NP leaving a party deeply divided, with half its members regretting the end of white supremacy and the other half believing that the whites still enjoyed too much influence and privilege. When taxed with the policy of the NP over many years, de Klerk denied that he had ever thought Africans inferior to whites, only different: 'The two things are not the same. Times have changed and we now firmly believe in a single, unified state. But 20 years ago the hope was for separate development, parallel improvements for all the races.'[3] However, having carried through his pragmatic task, de Klerk found himself attacked by both the left and the right wings of his party so that his resignation became inevitable. He spoke of a 'quantum leap' towards democracy so that South Africa could assume 'its right place in the world'. Waxing eloquent about the future, de Klerk argued:

> The whole continent needs a success. We can provide it. I don't want to import pollution, but we have vast open spaces. They provide a fine environment for basic industry. We can provide the infrastructure for the whole continent. We can provide the building industry with bricks and not just copper but copper wire and the covering of copper wire. We are going to privatise the mines. The commercial centre of Africa will soon be neither London nor Paris but Johannesburg.[4]

Had the NP had such a vision twenty years earlier the whole unhappy story of South Africa might have been very different. Instead de Klerk came to it when political and economic necessity had forced his and his party's hand. If the New South Africa can assume the industrial place in the world that de Klerk finally came to see as its destiny then it may yet spark off an African renaissance.

South Africa has plenty of able people – in politics, in business, coming up in the wings – to implement its new policies and though for a time after 1994 whites tended to speak fearfully of the AM factor – what would happen After Mandela – that sensibly died away, not least because of Mandela's determination to distance himself from day-to-day affairs and leave these to a younger generation. And though there was also a good deal of speculation about the succession to

Mandela with one party pushing hard for Cyril Ramaphosa as opposed to Thabo Mbeki, that conflict had also been resolved in Mbeki's favour by 1996. There were other fears that Winnie Mandela, the President's estranged former wife, would transform herself into a major political thorn in the side of government, but that threat as well had largely subsided by 1998. Indeed, as 1998 came towards its close the likelihood was that a united ANC would go into the 1999 elections under the leadership of Thabo Mbeki and be returned to power to face the most crucial as well as most difficult five years of its existence, and it is what it does over those five years that will shape the future South Africa and determine whether or not there is to be a South African and a continental renaissance.

2
Racism

The deeply ingrained racism of whites in South Africa and their determination to impose their will upon the black majority lie at the root of
the country's current problems. The injustices of the apartheid system
have finally been admitted by the whites and a new political era has
been inaugurated. Unfortunately, political change on its own is not
enough; emotionally far too many whites, even liberal whites, still
regard themselves as superior to blacks and far too many of them only
accepted the changes that came in 1994 because they could see no
alternative rather than because they actively believed in a non-racial
society. Over the coming years, as South Africa grapples with the
immense range of problems it faces, the attitude of whites to the new
political structures which, inevitably, must lessen their influence,
wealth and power will remain a crucial element in the overall pace of
change. In the four years following the April 1994 elections there was
abundant evidence, despite the euphoria about a Rainbow Society, that
white racism was both strong and active. What has still to be gauged is
whether the outbursts and incidents of racism which regularly occur
are no more than an expected backlash that the circumstances of the
change over were bound to produce or whether they represent a more
sinister long-term determination on the part of a significant and disgruntled minority to fight and disrupt the new system.

In February 1995 white right-wingers wielding whips tried to prevent
children from a Cape Town township enrolling in what had previously
been an all-white school. The children had been bused in from
Khayelitsha township to the Ruyterwacht school in the Epping suburb.
Whites armed with guns, whips, pick handles and dogs attempted to
stop the black students, some of whom responded with stones.
The Conservative Party claimed such troubles were inevitable if the

government attempted to integrate schools forcibly. The behaviour of the whites in an essentially working-class area was reminiscent of whites in the deep south of the USA more than 30 years earlier. This particular incident – and more were to come in relation to school integration – demonstrated that however peaceably the transfer of political power had been carried out the process of redistributing resources including opportunities had hardly begun. Ironically, white schools in the Western Cape where blacks remain in a minority had been forced to close for lack of pupils.

A very different revolt of words occurred later in 1995 as a response to changes in the programmes of SAfm, formerly known as Radio South Africa. The English language programme that had catered for the white middle classes, with its ethnic English voices, now was sending out a different English voice and language to cater for a far larger, mainly black audience. As one irate listener wrote to the *Johannesburg Star*, 'What they have done is impose their will on us. You vill listen to Black music and mangled Black English, ve haf vays and means!' What, it may be asked, do whites expect? They had imposed their will on blacks for so long that apparently it never occurred to this angry correspondent that the converse could ever happen. In response the new head of SAfm, Charles Leonard, defended the changes: 'We are catching a lot of flak from arrogant white English speakers. These people cannot come to terms with the exciting new rainbow society we are trying to create.'[1] That, of course, is the problem: coming to terms with changes that are agreed to as just in theory is very different from doing so when implementation forces people to alter their lifestyles. This was a new kind of quarrel as far as whites were concerned since the changes had been initiated from the top and Govan Reddy, the chief executive of South African Radio, entered the argument to defend the new style programmes and claimed 'Only the English language is positioned to foster mutual understanding among our diverse cultures, kept apart for so long by apartheid.' An even more important comment on the change of programme style came from Ken Owen, the editor of South Africa's *Sunday Times*, who wrote: 'One of the consequences of this shift of power has been to cut English speakers off from Britain as completely and as finally as the British occupation cut the Afrikaners off from Holland.'

Then the game of rugby moved into the limelight. Nelson Mandela's spectacular coup appearing at Ellis Park for the big rugby match against New Zealand wearing the springbok jersey captured the hearts of Afrikaners as few other gestures could have done and the crowd,

95 per cent white, chanted 'Nelson! Nelson! Nelson! Viva Nelson!'. Sadly, most racial reconciliations need more complex tactics. Mandela, of course, was playing politics and in this case the politics of racial reconciliation at which he is a master. Three years later a very different rugby story would mar this brief highlight of the new South Africa.

The need to debate race issues rather than pretend they do not exist until a crisis erupts was recognized by the Institute for Democracy in South Africa (IDASA). The director of IDASA, Wilmot James, held a conference to examine race issues in the Western Cape during August 1995 and insisted it had to be more than a talk shop at a time when racial tensions were surfacing across the political spectrum. The conference was opened by President Mandela and acknowledging the importance of his presence Dr James said: 'He is worried about the sense that people feel marginalised and he has done quite a lot to meet the concern himself. However, we need to go beyond presidential initiatives – and that's what this conference is all about.'[2] It is not enough, as Dr James said, to rely upon presidential initiatives but just how hard those lower down the scale are willing to work at racial reconciliation is another matter.

What became apparent in 1995 was how little the realities had changed: white fears of wholesale nationalisation and redistribution of assets receded as the new ANC policies unfolded and whites remained in their privileged positions while blacks were still dependent upon these same whites for their jobs. As a Mr Tondi wrote to the *Sunday Times*:

> All is being done in the spirit of national reconciliation, preached by President Nelson Mandela with good intentions and hope for a better future. Those who have violated human rights do not show any signs of remorse and would gladly do it all over again. They are happy Mr Mandela is an understanding African, and not a terrorist who belongs in a prison cell, as they always thought.
>
> In work places there is no longer pressure to apply corrective action to open up job opportunities as there was before April 1994. Instead there is a move to reverse what was hastily done in fear of losing business. The good intentions of Mr Mandela are taken for granted and used to turn back to the old ways.[3]

Mr Tondi's sarcasm masked a growing anger among Africans that too many Europeans saw too little need to change their ways.

In his endless search for reconciliation President Mandela met with former president P. W. Botha to discuss the impending trial of the former defence minister Magnus Malan and ten other military officers for 13 apartheid-era murders. Mr Botha who later refused to co-operate with the Truth and Reconciliation Commission, said 'If General Malan ... and others are prosecuted in a wrong way, then things can lead to disaster and I want to stop that road to disaster.' President Mandela rejected Botha's call for a moratorium on the prosecution of apartheid-era leaders prior to the establishment in 1996 of the Truth and Reconciliation Commission. Making clear his own stand, Botha said: 'I am not going to the Truth Commission. I am not going to repent. I am not going to ask for favours. What I did I did for my country, for my God, for my people and for all the people of South Africa.'[4] President Mandela had previously visited Botha privately but this occasion was a public meeting at which an unrelenting Botha showed no signs of remorse for the racism of the past over which he had presided for a decade.

There was nothing really startling about the racial clashes occurring in South Africa at this time; many, such as the argument about the curriculum vitae of Professor William Makgoba at Witwatersrand which 11 senior academics claimed contained lies, could be found in any country with sharp racial divisions. The difference was that for the first time the two sides were operating on a level playing field and whites were being obliged to answer more openly and thoroughly than had been the case in apartheid years: then the law had been on their side, now it could no longer be used in their justification.

Another attempt by Afrikaners to keep their school all-white occurred in February 1996, this time in the rural town of Potgietersrus in the Northern Province, when 200 white parents barred black six year olds from the Potgietersrus Primary School. The parents denied any racist motivation and claimed they were only trying to protect the school's cultural and religious standards from non-Afrikaans speaking children (only three black children were involved at this stage). But a spokesman for the provincial government, Jack Mokobi, said: 'Those three (black) children were enrolled by the school's principal himself. In the past, the school has accepted white, English speaking students without so much as a peep. The excuse now of protecting culture and language is nothing more than a smokescreen for racism.'[5] The row was a test of the government's will to take on entrenched Afrikaner communities and President Mandela was to reassure the representatives of 13 Afrikaans women's groups that Afrikaners had no reason to worry: their rights were protected under the constitution and there was no plan to eradicate their language. However, while schools in

Afrikaans areas could continue instruction in Afrikaans they also had to provide classes in other languages where this was necessary. This did not end the story. White parents continued to maintain a vigil outside the school and in mid-month the Supreme Court ordered the school to open its doors to black students. The provincial authorities saw the action of the parents as thinly-disguised racism and following the ruling of Judge Tjibbe Spoelstra that the school could 'not unfairly on the grounds of race, ethnic or social origin, culture, colour or language, refuse to admit any child' the Education Minister, Sibusiso Bengu, told a news conference 'We saw this as a national case and are pleased that the judgement has come this way.' A week later when the handful of black children entered the school they were forced to run the gauntlet of whites hurling abuse at them, an action which if it demonstrated anything at all showed the low standards of Afrikaans culture that they supposedly had gathered to defend. Although various threats and hints at actions – unspecified – had been made during the month, in the event abuse rather than any other action appeared to be the order of the day. The court judgement and the subsequent acceptance by the school of the black children represented a small advance but later the white parents attempted to set up alternative classrooms in a hostel although they were prevented from doing so by the police. The question remaining was how many other such confrontations would South Africa have to face in the years that followed.

The impact of racist acts is never easy to quantify. By 1996, for example, most South African whites saw the antics of Eugene Terre Blanche and his Afrikaner Resistance Movement (AWB) as an embarrassment, while at the other end of the spectrum evidence of deep resistance to change in the judicial system emerged in September 1996 when 100 judges including 10 out of 11 in the Appeal Court opposed the appointment of the first black judge, Ismail Mahomed, to the Supreme Court. A leading advocate, Clifford Mailer, put his finger on the real issue when he said 'The truth is that few judges on the bench embrace the new culture of human rights and are hostile to change.'

A revolt by the privileged about their privileges rather than about any form of racial incursions upon their shielded lifestyle occurred towards the end of 1996 among the white ratepayers in Johannesburg's most wealthy and exclusive suburb of Sandton. The council for the Sandton area which was led by members of the ANC imposed a 300 per cent rate increase and the wealthy white householders proceeded to mimic African activists of the apartheid era who had refused to pay their rates. The ANC chairman of the regional council said: 'These people have more than everything, yet you go half a mile down the road to Alexandra and everyone is selling a few potatoes to keep body and soul together.' In response, Brian Stolzenberg, acting as spokesman for the rent boycotters, quoted Abraham Lincoln: 'You cannot help the poor by destroying the rich. You cannot help the wage earner by pulling down the wage payer. We want to play our part in the new South Africa. But you cannot kill the goose that lays the golden egg.' Such exchanges will, no doubt, increase as the years pass and greater pressures are mounted by the black majority to even out the glaring inequalities of South Africa's economic extremes.

By the end of 1997 when the ANC met in congress at Mafikeng the issue of race relations looked very different from the temporary happy euphoria which had prevailed in the immediate post-1994 election period when everyone spoke of the Rainbow Society as though a racial fusion had actually occurred and people appeared to assume that racial differences and tensions would somehow disappear of their own volition. Reconciliation cannot be achieved by words alone and the perceived gap between whites and blacks had certainly become more pronounced in the three years since the elections; or, perhaps, the gap which had always existed had simply become apparent again after the brief period of euphoria and healing. What South Africa required at this stage was some blunt debate and a readiness on both sides to discuss the unpalatable before very different emotions took control, for by this time there was a growing sense among the black population that the whites had made no real effort to transform South African society, that they retained all their former privileges and expected to continue to do so, and that they were not prepared to make any material sacrifices to ensure that the New South Africa worked. Thabo Mbeki in a number of speeches has made plain how he sees the problem:

> The white population I don't think has quite understood the importance of this challenge. ... If you were speaking of national reconciliation based on the maintenance of the status quo because you do not want to move at a pace that frightens the whites, it means that you wouldn't carry out the task of transformation.[6]

The theme was hammered home increasingly at this time by the ANC leadership. The whites, on the other hand, argued that plenty of transformation had already taken place and that they had borne the brunt of the costs and would be alienated if the pressures upon them were made too unbearable. As the divide appears to increase rather than diminish

South Africa must ask itself whether a truly multiracial society in which each community has an equally acceptable contribution to make is possible, or whether it will regress into sharply delineated divisions which regard each other with suspicion and downright enmity. If the race divisions cannot be overcome at this particular time in South Africa's history the chances of real reconciliation in the future look bleak.

Three years after Mandela had captured the hearts of Afrikanerdom by appearing in a springbok jersey he was subpoenaed to give evidence in a court case which centred round the fact that rugby had remained almost exclusively white with its hierarchy accused of racism and a national coach – Andre Markgraaff – had been sacked for calling black rugby officials 'kaffirs'. And though President Mandela said he was quite happy to testify many people saw the act of subpoenaing the President as an insult, a last ditch act of racial arrogance and defiance by Louis Luyt, the president of the South African Rugby Football Union (SARFU) who had been accused of racism by a Coloured rugby official, Brian van Rooyen. The government wished to appoint a commission to investigate, Luyt challenged in the court its right to do so.

A quite different aspect of the divide concerns the growing number of poor whites. During the apartheid era the poorly educated, least skilled whites were protected by the system which provided them with jobs or sinecures in government service. This form of relief for the least able whites has now disappeared and jobs which they might have obtained in the past are now competed for fiercely by the far greater number of unemployed blacks, so that a growing number of poor whites, white beggars and increasingly disgruntled whites are becoming a new factor in South Africa's mix of racial problems. Their plight was well illustrated by Kitty van Zyl who cooked nightly for hundreds of poor white children and adults in the Cape Town housing scheme of Sandrift East. She said she had asked the local Kentucky Fried Chicken for its leftovers 'But the manager said he would rather give them to the local black squatter camp.'[7] The people for whom Mrs van Zyl spoke were now among the least favoured in a country where any form of affirmative action is geared to assist the far larger numbers of poor or disadvantaged blacks. And a white person with few credentials and no job is likely to remain unemployed until that person becomes unemployable. Many of these poor whites were the foremost supporters of apartheid in the past because it protected them; now they are desperate and find it hard if not impossible to come to terms with a new order that has already marginalised them. Their inherent racism quickly shows through and as one Sandrift woman said: 'I just don't like blacks. Sometimes I just cry because I cannot take all this. I was not raised for it.' Her last statement goes to the heart of the problem: generations of whites were brought up to be racists and they are unlikely to be able, even if theoretically willing, to change.

Another former whites-only school, this time at Vryburg in the northwest province, was the scene of a racist confrontation in February 1998. On this occasion five black students who had been suspended took hostage the head teacher and two members of the school board. In response some 300 white parents armed with sjamboks and guns converged on the school clearly intent upon teaching the black students a lesson and according to one black teenager the white men sjamboked every black they saw, some of the children subsequently had to be hospitalised. This incident led to four days of rioting in a neighbouring black township. In Vryburg and other similar towns where the whites ruled unquestioned in the past there has been no acceptance of the Rainbow Society. As the head boy of this school, Brendan Gous, said: 'We do not mix. We don't want to mix with them and they don't want to mix with us' and speaking of the community of Vryburg he continued: 'On the streets you never see a white walking with a black. Black pupils have been sent here to disrupt.' The head girl, Martelie Schoeman, said: 'This is our school and they want to make it a black school.'[8] Now, if articulate white youngsters speak in such terms South Africa has a long way to go before any real racial integration is to be achieved.

Even more brutal behaviour reminiscent of the worst days of apartheid occurred in April 1998 when a white farmer, Nicholas Steyn, fired on three black children who were walking through his fields: he killed a baby and wounded the eleven-year-old girl who was carrying her. Their mother worked on the man's farm. The incident highlighted the fact that little appears to have changed in the attitudes of white farmers towards blacks; there had been reports of other such incidents, those responsible excusing themselves on the grounds that they thought the blacks were intruders. This particular incident made the headlines but according to the Azanian People's Organisation 'It is just one example of the way black people are being treated every day on farms by white people.' White farmers, for their part, retort that they are attacked and some of them murdered so that they have come to feel persecuted and some have become trigger-happy. The whites of remote farming areas were always among the most extreme racists in the past and incidents such as this one demonstrate clearly how little they have changed.

In May 1998 the ongoing rugby row came to an end when Louis Luyt finally resigned though only after having forced a bitter racial confrontation with the government. He told *Rapport* that he felt betrayed: 'My people folded, I can't trust them anymore.' The four black members of the rugby board, meanwhile, had also resigned and the whole episode left an unpleasant impression of the deep racialism that lies just beneath the surface of South African life. The Luyt reference to 'my people' really tells the whole story.

These racial outbursts and violent incidents selected from a four year period may be seen as typical of a society that is in the throes of massive social readjustment. No reasonable person could seriously oppose affirmative action in South Africa; the adjustments needed to redress the huge imbalances of the past must take place and are bound to cause resentments and in some cases – like that of the white poor – pain as well. Nonetheless, the sooner the changes are effected the better. The resistance of former hardline supporters of apartheid such as the parents of Vryburg, the farmers or Louis Luyt, for so long the symbol of Afrikanerdom's 'national' game, is hardly surprising; such people must be taught to come to terms with a society based upon different values. Most depressing of all these stories is the rate revolt of the residents of Sandton, protesting that the goose which lays the golden egg should be left in its nest of eggs. These people by any standards, and not just those of South Africa, are among the world's rich elite and possess wealth undreamed of by 90 per cent of their fellow citizens. Their protest at a rate increase as though it would cripple them demonstrated a selfishness and, worse, a blindness to what they ought to be prepared to do for the New South Africa that augured ill for the future. If indeed they are the geese who lay the golden eggs it is time they shared a few with their fellow citizens.

3
Truth and Reconciliation

Even at the best of times truth is at a premium in politics and to ask people who have behaved badly – and in some cases appallingly – to admit publicly to their wrong doings is to ask a very great deal indeed. White South Africans who either committed brutalities under the apartheid system in order to maintain the privileged position of their racial group, or knowingly benefited from such brutalities even if they themselves did not commit them, cannot easily bring themselves to admit that what they did was either brutal or wrong since to do so is to undermine the basis of the lives they lived until the system was brought to an end. As early as October 1994 Archbishop Desmond Tutu was able to say in Cape Town 'It is very difficult now to find anyone in South Africa who ever supported apartheid. Oh no, I never supported apartheid, I always knew it was wrong.'[1] Given the natural reluctance of human beings to admit their wrong doings the astonishing thing about the Truth and Reconciliation Commission is that it obtained as many confessions as it did and even when those that were made in order to pre-empt future prosecution are taken into account, a large number of people did make confessions and some were demonstrably penitent. Whether the truth enshrined in two years of public admissions will promote genuine reconciliation between the races is another question altogether.

Reconciliation is about living together and the Truth Commission was about facilitating this process. When it became clear that the security police had senior Inkatha officials on their payroll as part of the Third Force which was designed to undermine the dominant position of the ANC Mr Buthelezi defended his support for the Third Force in terms of defending the Zulu nation. In fact the Zulu nation was never at risk; what was at risk was Chief Buthelezi's power base. Yet, despite the role he played in the late 1980s and through the 1990s until the elections of April 1994, Chief Buthelezi was then appointed to President Mandela's cabinet of national unity for, though he and his Inkatha Movement were anathema to a large part of the ANC, President Mandela saw quite clearly that it is only possible to resolve intractable conflicts by sacrificing pure principles and accepting political compromises. F. W. de Klerk, who spent the greater part of his political life actively promoting apartheid, ended it as a deputy president to Mandela condemning racial discrimination and though many people must have doubted that his conversion came from the heart it was accepted at face value because it assisted the process of political transition.

The possibility that those responsible for the worst excesses of apartheid might be called upon to answer for their crimes clearly exercised the minds of the National Party leadership during the long negotiations about majority rule in the period 1990–94 and in the immediate run up to the elections of April 1994 a political amnesty was offered to 3500 police officers and others in the security services including the former justice minister, Adriaan Vlok, and the former defence minister, Magnus Malan. In January 1995, however, after long and passionate discussion the new cabinet decided that no indemnity from prosecution had been acquired or granted. These apparent amnesties had only just come to light and outraged the Justice Minister, Dullah Omar. Members of the ANC and liberals saw this offer as further proof of bad faith on the part of the National Party, an effort at cover-up as it lost power. The offer and its would-be beneficiaries also raised, in acute form, the question of the extent to which the new ANC leadership would be able to control the state machinery which was still dominated by hardline Afrikaner elements. The outgoing police chief, General Johan van der Merwe, said he believed he was still covered by the amnesty and claimed he had applied for it in order to give moral support to other applicants who were just obeying orders against 'a revolutionary onslaught'. The Nazi Adolf Eichmann claimed at his trial in Israel that he was just obeying orders.

The trial during 1995 of the policeman Eugene de Kock on more than 100 charges including murder – he was accused of heading a special police unit, Vlakplaas, which specialised in murdering anti-government activists – produced a wealth of revelations at a time when the government was deciding to set up a truth commission which would recommend granting amnesty to people who disclosed full details of their apartheid crimes. The de Kock trial was expected to expose links between the Vlakplaas operation and top officials in the former de Klerk government. At this time (February 1995) Mr de Klerk felt obliged to tell a news conference that the 1982 bombing of the ANC London office was 'wrong and should not have been done' and that he personally had never been part of any decision by an apartheid government to commit a crime. 'I distance myself from atrocities and from assassinations' he said.[2]

The dilemma faced by those who suffered under apartheid and the desire for reconciliation enshrined in the concept of a truth commission was spelt out by Marius Schoon whose wife and six-year-old daughter had been blown up in Angola by a parcel bomb (as was Ruth First) sent by the police unit headed by the former double agent Craig Williamson. Schoon who had been jailed for 12 years for sabotage brought a civil suit against Williamson who in February 1995 had gone into hiding. Schoon asked:

> Are we going to have a situation where people can qualify for indemnity just by saying, as if they were reeling off a grocery list, I killed this one and poisoned that one and beat the shit out of the third one? It seems untenable to me, morally and philosophically. Now there's this little window and I can do something. I can lay charges and assist in the final undermining of the whole apartheid structure, the shitty ideology, the lies, the deceit, the corruption.[3]

Schoon pinpoints the dichotomy in a country where thousands of people suffered from comparable brutalities as he did and see no reason why the perpetrators should be allowed to go unpunished and the arguably more compelling needs of government to reconcile the races for the future good of South Africa. Unsurprisingly, there were differences between rank and file members of the ANC and the general public who wanted justice, and members of the government who did not want attempts at retribution to make more difficult than it already was the task of rebuilding South Africa for the future. As so often in politics the Truth and Reconciliation Commission would bring into conflict the demands for justice and the need for pragmatism and compromise.

Throughout the sittings of the Truth and Reconciliation Commission it was clear that a new non-racial South Africa was an ideal that had yet to be created. The gaps remained – the poverty statistics that separated the majority from the minority – and though black Africans may have gained confidence since the elections of 1994 they have not, in most cases, gained very much else. Whites, who appear to think they have made the supreme sacrifice by the act of rejecting apartheid, behave as though there is nothing else they can do, complaining instead that they are at risk from mounting violence.

The Commission was not the first of its kind in our present brutal age. There had been 15 such commissions in various parts of the world since 1974, in each case designed in theory to heal relations between the extremes in countries which had been divided and morally devastated by former atrocities. Too often, in practice, such commissions have served the more limited interests of the ruling parties enabling them, and therefore the country, to put the past behind them. In countries such as Argentina, Chile and El Salvador such commissions are not seen to have healed. In South Africa there was a major difference: victims groups were established before the Truth Commission and as a result allowed to influence the way it would work and this process alone, at one level, became a healing process while, as a result of their pressures, the original idea of holding the hearings in private was rejected.

At the end of 1995 11 retired officers of South Africa's former military establishment were brought before a judge and charged with 13 apartheid-era murders. Although there were five generals and an admiral among the accused the only one of real prominence was General Magnus Malan, the former defence chief who had been defence minister from 1980 to 1991. After they were released on bail General Malan said: 'What happened here today is causing the biggest crisis that's ever been in the democracy of South Africa. I would like to say I am a moderate...I am a democrat...I am a Christian and I'm very proud of it.' The General did not, apparently, see any irony attaching to his statement about moderation, democracy and Christianity and that inability to recognize the gap between proclaimed principles and past actions lies at the core of the racial chasm that remains part of the South African scene.

In answer to predictable accusations from the white right that the Truth Commission would turn into a witch hunt the then Justice Minister, Dullah Omar, announced in March 1996 that the immunity from prosecution granted by the last white government to 73 ANC members would be withdrawn; originally these indemnities had been granted to enable exiled anti-apartheid activists wanted for political crimes by the former white regime to return to take part in the peace talks and all-race elections of 1994. As a result of the Justice Minister's decision some leading members of the government and the ANC including Thabo Mbeki, Joe Modise and his deputy Ronnie Kasrils would be affected. The decision followed an ANC statement urging members who had past misdemeanours to hide to appear before the

Truth and Reconciliation Commission and meet de Klerk's demand that either the charges against General Malan should be dropped or immunity should be withdrawn from ANC members. Although the party said 'The ANC will never condone any human rights violations which may have been committed by freedom fighters during the heat of the struggle' the general party consensus was that the ANC had been fighting in a just struggle against an immoral system.[4]

At the end of November 1995 President Mandela named the 17 members of the Truth and Reconciliation Commission which was to be headed by Archbishop Desmond Tutu. The Commission had the task of uncovering the truth about the violence of the apartheid era and, in the process of so doing, the aim of healing some of South Africa's deep psychological wounds. As Archbishop Desmond Tutu said: 'I hope that the work of the commission is going to help pour balm on wounds which we will open to cleanse so that they don't fester … so that we can then say let those bygones be bygones and let us now concentrate on … the future.'[5] The sittings of the commission began in April 1996 and at that stage the main questions were whether it would reveal the truth about the past and whether doing so would in fact assist the process of reconciliation.

At one special hearing of the Truth and Reconciliation Commission, speaking on behalf of the National Party, Mr de Klerk accepted responsibility for the conditions which allowed the atrocities of the apartheid years to take place and expressed remorse for them, but he insisted that the National government had never authorised its security forces to commit murder, torture, rape, assassination or assault. His submission did nothing to placate either members of the ANC or demonstrators who asked: 'We want to know how many died. How many did the government kill.' On behalf of the ANC Thabo Mbeki submitted to the Commission a 100-page report which listed 34 members who had been executed in Angola by the ANC and contained an admission that some people had been killed after false accusations of spying had been laid against them. Almost by definition political leaders making such admissions are economical with the truth.

On the other hand, the former police colonel Eugene de Kock, known to his colleagues as 'Prime Evil', was far more forthcoming, confessing to a series of crimes during the apartheid era and seeking to reduce his sentence – he was found guilty of 89 crimes including six murders – by revealing information about the way in which the apartheid security apparatus worked. De Kock was the hit-man while Craig Williamson, who at one stage in his career penetrated the ANC, was the brains, responsible among other crimes for the assassination of the Swedish Prime Minister Olof Palme. Parallel with de Kock's revelations, Magnus Malan and the other security chiefs charged with him, after a seven month trial were acquitted, though whether they were innocent of the charges was another matter entirely. Malan himself had been one of the most hated figures of the apartheid era. Another of the accused, Tienie Groenewald, who had been chief director of military intelligence but had had the charges against him dismissed, claimed the acquittals vindicated the South African Defence Force (SADF) and expressed the hope there would be no more political trials. As almost always in such circumstances, the politicians and those in authority who give the orders or determined the strategy survive unscathed. As a woman in the public gallery said: 'There are plenty of dead and damaged people...but no guilty people. No one supported apartheid. It's denial on a grand scale. Pretty soon we will be talking about alleged apartheid.'[6]

Even so, some truths emerged and deadly and damaging they proved to be. A former police chief, General Johan van der Merwe, told the Commission that he received orders to bomb the headquarters of the Council of Churches, Khotso House, in 1988 and to supply booby-trapped explosives to apartheid activists in 1985. He said the instruction to destroy Khotso House was given by the then minister of law and order Adriaan Vlok: 'According to Mr Vlok, this instruction had come from President P. W. Botha personally.' The general was giving his evidence in support of amnesty applications by five of his former officers who were hoping to pre-empt criminal charges being brought against them.

As Lizzie Sefola, the widow of the anti-apartheid activist Harold Sefola who had been tortured and then killed by the police, told the amnesty committee of the Commission: 'We're still feeling the pain. These people never came to ask us for forgiveness. The government is doing this on our behalf. ... It is people who should forgive each other, not the government.'[7]

Ex-President P. W. Botha, on the other hand, said he would never apologise for apartheid and denounced the assault on the Afrikaner by the country's new rulers. 'I am not guilty of any deed for which I should apologise or ask for amnesty' he said. Going on to the attack he said: 'In many circles the Afrikaner is being isolated to be punished for all the unfavourable events in the history of South Africa' and he then blamed the British: 'The Afrikaner was a victim of (British) colonial greed...the recent conflicts in which we were involved were primarily against Soviet imperialism and colonialism.'[8] A year later Botha was to refer to the Truth and Reconciliation Commission as a 'circus'. Botha was to refuse all chances offered him to appear before the Commission. Eventually, therefore, the former head of state found himself in court; he showed no repentance but in a 40-minute speech defended apartheid as 'good neighbourliness'. Arguing with reporters he said he had tried to save South Africa from the 'Communist onslaught' but when he shouted that 'I tried to protect our fatherland' a young black ANC supporter at the back of the court asked 'Is that the same fatherland as mine?' His question, amid the drama of Botha's court appearance and the ongoing dramas surrounding the Truth and Reconciliation Commission, went to the nub of South Africa's problems and, more importantly, pinpointed the chasm which still divides South Africa's different races.

South African business was accused of making vast profits out of the apartheid system and according to the Minister of Water Affairs, Kader Asmal, the mining industry killed 84 000 while the Dutch Reformed Church, which had provided the theological basis for apartheid in a supposedly Christian country, finally in an appearance before the Commission made a belated apology when its leader, the Rev. Freek Swanepoel, told the Commission 'We confess that great wrongs have been done.' In its own words, the Church had 'not always heard the word of God correctly.'

The former police colonel, Eugene de Kock, whose apartheid crimes earned him a 212-year jail sentence, said in June 1998 in the George Regional Court that he and other security force members had been 'sold out' by the National Party. 'They are cowards. We did the fighting and I am proud of that. The politicians have no pride. They made sure that they only looked after a small five per cent of a little incestuous Afrikaner group.' Speaking of the bombing of the South African Council of Churches head office – Khotso House – in 1988 de Kock said 'The government of the day did not disapprove, in fact they encouraged it.'

As more and more such reactions to the Truth and Reconciliation Commission revealed the extent of the tensions and lies and brutalities that had been axiomatic to the apartheid system it became clear that while those who suffered remembered the past vividly, those who oppressed suggested that the past should be forgotten for the sake of the future. How much will be achieved by exposing 'truths' when Botha insists that he was protecting the Afrikaner nation, and de Klerk denies any knowledge of or responsibility for assassinations and other brutalities carried out on the orders of the government to which he belonged, or de Kock proudly acknowledges his role as a frontline soldier of the apartheid state?

The sittings of the Truth and Reconciliation Commission came to an end in July 1998 and for many who had followed its proceedings there was deep frustration at the National Party's refusal to accept responsibility for the atrocities which had been committed during the long years when it was the government of South Africa. The Commission was mainly a black affair with blacks detailing the brutalities done to them. The whites stayed away and those who did ask for amnesty did so to avert legal action rather than from remorse at their past conduct. By the end of the sittings some 7000 applications for amnesty had been filed though only 125 had been granted; the other applicants had failed to convince the commission that they had revealed all the truth and in many cases court proceedings will no doubt follow. Altogether the commission heard or read reports from 21 000 victims of abuse during the period of white minority rule.

The report was finally ready for release at the end of October 1998 and in an unlikely alliance of former political enemies both F. W. de Klerk and the ANC tried to have sections of the report deleted or withheld before its publication. Mr de Klerk by means of court action forced the commission to remove statements implicating him in state sponsored terrorism. The ANC also launched an attempt to prevent the publication of those parts of the report which implicated the party in gross human rights abuses and with three other political parties deciding to boycott the official handing over of the report to President Mandela it became a moot question as to how much reconciliation the report would achieve. Truth does not please many people and it pleases even fewer factions. The right accused the commission of conducting a witch hunt against the Afrikaner and the ANC accused it of criminalising the movement's struggle against apartheid. But though Thabo Mbeki argued that there was no moral equivalence between the actions of the ANC and the apartheid-era governments, the ANC government, nonetheless, had agreed that the commission should look at atrocities on all sides. This agreement, it must be said, was more designed to ease the process of transition than for any other reason.

When the day arrived on which Archbishop Desmond Tutu was to hand over the report of his commission to President Nelson Mandela, the ANC was attempting to prevent publication in a Cape Town court, prompting the Archbishop to comment: 'Let me say I have struggled against a tyranny. I didn't do that in order to substitute another.' In the event, the court ruled against the ANC, leading Alex Boraine, the deputy chairman of the commission, to call it a 'victory for truth and human rights'. The 3300 page document laid the greatest blame for three decades of brutality squarely upon the National Party which had been in power throughout the apartheid years. The report, however, also identified some non-National Party people as perpetrators of atrocities including the President's ex-wife Winnie Mandela and the leader of the Inkatha Freedom Party, Chief Mangosuthu Buthelezi, and it highlighted white indifference to the work of the commission.

The attempt by the ANC to prevent the publication of parts of the report which accused the party, in the days when it was banned, of human rights abuses (even though these were on a far lesser scale than government abuses) was led by Thabo Mbeki and opposed by Nelson Mandela, prompting Desmond Tutu to say of the ANC: 'The fact that they are the majority party in government does not give them privileges. I did not fight against people who thought they were God to replace them by others. Yesterday's oppressed could become tomorrow's oppressors.'[9] Thabo Mbeki found that many members of the ANC disagreed with his action. F. W. de Klerk made himself even less credible than he had already become when he said: 'The TRC has failed lamentably to carry out its mandate to establish the truth concerning the conflict of the past and to promote reconciliation.' He added that killings and torture carried out by state security forces had been the work of rogue individuals and never state policy. Anyone who believed that after 30 years of systematic state organised brutality would believe anything.

As David Beresford wrote of the report in *The Observer* 'It must rank as one of the great documents of the twentieth century; it may lack majesty of language, but it can only be described as biblical in the wealth of human experience it lays out.' The biggest question of all which is posed by the report is simply whether anything has been changed by it. Will life for the average black South African change? Will whites cease to be racists at heart and work genuinely for a new South Africa? Will the rich be prepared to make any real sacrifices to eradicate some of the desperate poverty of the poor black majority? Or is South Africa, now the report is behind it, simply going to divide into a rich–poor society in which wealth and power remain, overwhelmingly, in white hands?

Whatever the Truth and Reconciliation Commission fails to achieve at least it has made it historically impossible to deny that atrocities took place and that they took place systematically over many decades and were government inspired and directed. And the Commission found that apartheid was a crime against humanity. The greatest lie, consistently advanced by whites who appeared before the Commission, was that gross human rights violations were committed in the context of fighting communism and not in support of a white racial order. Apartheid was a system created to maintain the whites in power; it had nothing to do with fighting communism.

The report of the Truth and Reconciliation Commission provides a benchmark against which future white behaviour as well as the conduct of governments may be judged. It is an historical record of a brutal regime whose primary motive was to maintain a racial minority in power. And it is a reminder of how easily power and the desire to retain it can corrupt and destroy a people's integrity. How much this exercise in exposing truths that a majority of the whites wished only to hide or ignore will assist the new South Africa to forge a racially integrated future remains to be seen.

4
Politics

The African National Congress (ANC) whose foundation in 1912 makes it the oldest political party on the African continent finally came into its own as the ruling party of South Africa after decades of illegality, oppression and persecution. When, in December 1994, after its five-day national conference the ANC declared that it was 'more united than ever' it had good reason to be pleased with its recent achievements. The conference had backed the Mandela government's conservative economic policies and had called for a new constitution that would enshrine 'ordinary democratic majority rule'. The conference called on the government to take urgent measures to improve living standards for the black majority and to restructure the Afrikaner-dominated civil service. As the Justice Minister, Dullah Omar, said: 'Until we transform state machinery as a whole into a loyal instrument of democracy, transfer of power to the people will not be complete.'[1]

In exile, on return to South Africa and in the period 1990 to the elections of 1994 the ANC's principal allies were the South African Communist Party (SACP) and the Congress of South African Trade Unions (COSATU) whose demands on behalf of their supporters would remain close to their positions prior to the 1994 elections, while the government moved into a more centrist position as it was obliged to balance their demands with other considerations. The most important new perspective adopted by the ANC after it came to power was that of promoting a conservative economic policy designed to reassure existing business and attract new business investment. At some point during its transition from exiled liberation movement to ruling party of South Africa the hierarchy of the ANC decided to abandon the Marxist economic rhetoric of its days in exile (as well as its anti-capitalist policies) and instead join the economic mainstream in a capitalist-oriented world in which state economic control was everywhere in retreat. It was not a heroic decision; it was a brave one and especially brave considering the huge pressures to which the party was subject from its allies, from its grassroots supporters and as a result of the huge expectations for change that its victory and the end of apartheid had created. Many members of the ANC and its grassroots supporters found difficulty in accepting such a change of economic direction which went contrary to everything the party had argued during the long years of its exile but as President Mandela said at the 1994 conference:

> We need fresh blood. One problem is that some people have an instinctive resistance to this. Some of us feel threatened by the prospect of being challenged. We cannot survive if we do not change. Some comrades do not welcome opposition and tend to sideline and even slander comrades with an independent view.[2]

In the immediate aftermath of the April 1994 elections the new ANC government had to deal with the very different problems that face any government and party in power: how to treat the President's ex-wife Winnie Mandela, who retained powerful support among grassroots members of the party; what to do over revelations of corruption among popular supporters, such as in the case of Dr Allan Boesak the populist churchman accused of embezzling funds; and most delicate of all, how to treat the leader of the Zulu Inkatha Freedom Party (IFP), Chief Mangosuthu Buthelezi, who alternated between his role as a member of the coalition government in which he was Home Affairs Minister and his IFP role demanding ever greater independence from central government control for his province of KwaZulu-Natal. Mandela alternately tried conciliation with Chief Buthelezi and threatened tough action. In May 1995, reacting to threats against his government by Inkatha, President Mandela said: 'If the situation (intimidatory violence) that is taking place in Natal is allowed to go on, I have no alternative, and I want everyone to know, that I will use everything to protect the lives of innocent people in the province.'[3]

Tom Sebine, who had been the radio 'voice of the ANC' from Lusaka during the 1980s, found both himself and his views less highly regarded by the ruling ANC on his return to the new South Africa in the 1990s. Speaking a language that was already going out of fashion, Sebine said the new revolution would be the people's, 'a revolution of the masses'. He warned of the difficulties in overcoming economic problems:

> Millions of our people are out of work – the poverty of our people stares at you as you drive around Soweto. In fact, the situation is the same everywhere. And it's not that people are out of work because of their own choice. They are looking for work but there is none. People want food in their stomachs. If the ANC government cannot better the people's plight, ... rest assured we will have a new revolution of angry people whose problems emanated from the fact that their lot was not improved by those they trusted and put in power. And mark my words, that danger is looming. The reason is that our people are not going to wait for 10 years to see the fruits of the struggle.[4]

During 1995 the ANC made plain its determination to produce a permanent constitution that would create a system of unfettered majority rule. In response, the National Party expressed its concern that the ANC would eliminate carefully crafted proposals designed to promote white confidence. Apart from this constitutional issue, it was clear by mid-1995 that at least some of the leading members of the ANC government had fallen victim to the temptations of power; they had, after all, taken over intact the all-pervasive administrative machine which their predecessors had created to administer and control apartheid. The dangers for the ANC in power could be traced to the nature of the public service the party had inherited:

> The public service was created, rather like the Soviet public service, to impose on every aspect of society a system that ran contrary to human nature. It required coercion in every sphere of life to determine where people lived and worked, whom they married, how they travelled, what they earned. It sought to regulate sport and theatre, arts and opera; it tried to control speech as well as thought. It intervened in the universities and first overturned, then undermined, the school system.[5]

Revolutionary governments inheriting such means of control do not destroy them; it remains to be seen in the years to come just how authoritarian ANC governments will be.

The power of the ANC became increasingly apparent through 1995 as the National Party destroyed itself in internecine left–right struggles and the other parties were reduced to the role of legitimising what the government did. Real opposition to ANC policies, ironically, did not come from political parties at all but from international business. International business disapproval of the policies it pursued became the most likely restraint upon the government: that, and the skilfully deployed argument (though this would become increasingly less effective) that it should not advance policies which would undermine white confidence. Most political pundits at this time assumed that the ANC was in power for at least ten or 15 years to come and that the greatest strains upon it would come either from its old allies – the Communist Party and COSATU – or as a result of splits in its own ranks. President Mandela constantly demonstrated an awareness of the need for consensus; this awareness was not manifest by his lieutenants.

When some 3000 delegates assembled in Mafikeng in December 1997 for the 50th ANC national conference the party had been in effective power for three and a half years and it was time to take stock of its achievements since the 1994 elections and, still more, to look to the future. The party faced six broad issues: peace and stability; economic transformation; the state and its role in governance; social delivery and transformation; international relations; and building the ANC as an organization.

It had already been accepted that Thabo Mbeki, who was running the government on a day-to-day basis, would succeed Nelson Mandela unopposed as the new president of the party. The issue most likely to cause tensions was that of free market growth and its impact upon the large numbers of unemployed with COSATU attacking the growth, employment and redistribution strategy (Gear) as 'Thatcherite'. The greatest concern of ordinary members of the ANC, its wide constituency throughout the country and its two allies – COSATU and the Communist Party – was how the party would deliver services, shelter, employment, the alleviation of poverty, safety and security effectively. Each of these requirements demand massive government expenditure of a kind seen to be incompatible with the conservative economic policy adopted by the ANC. As part of President Mandela's permanent effort at reconciliation the Inkatha Freedom Party had been invited to send its first ever delegation to the conference.

More ominous for the future was the suggestion advanced earlier in the year by Peter Mokaba, a deputy minister and a member of the ANC national executive committee, that the Communist Party should be dropped from the tripartite alliance and that the ANC should be converted into a party of free market capitalism. Although Mokaba clearly represented only a minority his views could well become far more important in the early years of the new millennium while the Communist Party could find itself bypassed – Mokaba had described it as a caucus within the ANC. At the same time COSATU opposition to the Gear strategy had become so insistent that President Mandela was obliged to tell its September 1997 conference that no policy was cast in stone. Fears of a developing split in the ranks of the ANC between 'haves' and 'have-nots' was set out in the *African Communist* by the Communist Party leader Blade Nzimande who expressed concern at the emerging black middle class: 'Such a scenario could lead to a 30%–70% solution, where 30% of the population is benefiting from a new capitalist order and 70% remain outside.'[6]

Although the leader of the SACP Charles Nqakula could only take 14 delegates to the ANC national conference as non-voting participants, he could take comfort from the fact that many ANC delegates were also card-carrying members of the party. As he said on the eve of the conference,

> We have to ensure the ANC retains its character as a movement of workers and poor people in rural areas and townships. At the same time, we have to jealously consolidate the space the ANC has created in its ranks for other progressive democrats. As party delegates, as members of the movement, we have to make sure the ANC does not veer away from its original mission of raising the standard of living of the disadvantaged.[7]

Nqakula's fears – that the ANC was moving away from the championship of the poor and dispossessed – were shared by others who were deeply disturbed by the party's flirtation with capitalism. Those fears will remain a central problem for the ANC under Thabo Mbeki.

Standing down as ANC president Nelson Mandela endorsed Thabo Mbeki as his – unopposed – successor, guaranteeing that international attention would be focused upon the man destined to lead South Africa into the new century. Aged 55 and seen as a pragmatist, Thabo Mbeki had spent 28 years of exile in Britain, had studied economics at Sussex University and acquired a measure of old world charm that reassured a West still fearful of communism and earlier ANC anti-capitalist rhetoric. At the same time he is reputed to be a ruthless politician and hard on dissenters. His father, Govan Mbeki, was imprisoned on Robben Island with Mandela. After receiving military training in the Soviet Union Mbeki spent much of his time travelling all over the world from his British base to present the ANC case and is credited with masterminding the international sanctions campaign against apartheid South Africa.

The harsh tone adopted by President Mandela in his last speech as party leader to the conference in which he attacked white parties and the white-owned media and lamented the fact that at every turn the ANC was being thwarted by those 'committed to the maintenance of white privilege' gave notice of changes to come. In part, no doubt, Mandela was deliberately taking this hard line to spare Thabo Mbeki from the necessity of doing so in his first speech as party leader but his message was clear enough: talk of the rainbow society was no substitute for a real change of attitude on the part of the whites. In any case, it was widely known that Thabo Mbeki was deeply frustrated by the reluctance of whites to embrace the new South Africa and it was suggested that the speech may have been written by Mbeki rather than Mandela. Subsequently, the government insisted that the ANC's pragmatic free market economic policy would remain in place, although the speech signalled clearly enough that the period of racial euphoria that had followed the 1994 elections had then come to an end. President Mandela also warned the ANC against the spread of careerism, elitism and corruption.

White reactions to Mandela's speech were predictably outraged. The National Party described it as paranoid and unstatesmanlike, while the leader of the Democratic Party – which has traditionally championed rich whites – Tony Leon, said it was 'undoubtedly the low watermark of Nelson Mandela's presidency, it was intellectually dishonest and unsophisticated in its analysis of the political and economic situation facing South Africa.' Elsewhere, and particularly in Britain, reactions were near hysterical with the London *Daily Telegraph* arguing that while South Africa's overseas reputation had been transformed from pariah to paragon Mandela had now presented an ugly, divisive face to the world: 'For a government with a huge parliamentary majority seemingly to seek excuses for its failures (ministerial incompetence, a soaring rate of crime) by casting vague slurs on the white minority is not the action of a statesman.'[8] There was more in this vein. But in Mafikeng the ANC delegates thought Mandela was absolutely right in his criticisms of the whites and saw his speech as signalling that the 'endless pandering' to whites had been abandoned. The reality in South Africa after three years of an ANC dominated government remained, that while blacks ran the government the whites still ran just about everything else, while the gap between rich and poor – which in substantive terms means whites and blacks – remained as great as it had ever been under the apartheid system.

The conference introduced a new rule that a candidate for party office nominated from the floor who formerly had required the support of 10 per cent of the delegates now required 25 per cent; the subject of the change was Winnie Mandela whom the party was determined to sideline and who had been nominated for the post of deputy president of the ANC by the Women's League of the party. When she saw the poor show of support on her behalf she declined the nomination. Thus, perhaps, the 'Mother of the Nation' saw the decline of her influence where it mattered most, in the ruling party hierarchy.

In summary, the ANC gave notice through the conference that its first concern thereafter was to its own constituents and a warning to the whites that it was their turn to make concessions.

If the three years following the 1994 elections saw the ANC consolidate its authority as a party and government, the same period witnessed the disintegration of the former ruling National Party. This was hardly surprising. Ever since its 1948 election victory the National Party had existed to maintain and enforce apartheid, its core belief was the separation of the races – to the advantage of the white minority – and all its actions had been geared to this end. As its more prescient members must have known for many years it had embarked upon a losing battle: numbers were against it; increasingly, the world was against it; and most significant, in the end, capitalism was against it since to operate successfully capitalism requires an open society.

When de Klerk unbanned the ANC at the beginning of 1990 he did so not from any change of heart about the conduct over the years of the National Party in power but simply because the entire political system over which the National Party then presided was becoming untenable. Just as Mikhail Gorbachev, a good aparatchnik communist, saw when he came to power that the Soviet system needed drastic reforms if it was to survive so did de Klerk, a good Afrikaner white supremacist, believed that the future safety of the white minority lay in reforms which he believed he could control. Both men wanted to reform and modernise their systems, not sweep them away; neither was able to control the forces he unleashed. Once the elections of April 1994 had been fought and the nationwide strength of the ANC had been demonstrated at the polls the National Party had to determine upon its future.

Immediately, it was part of the coalition Government of National Unity (GNU) but this was a false position that could not last. The ANC had come to power in order to dismantle everything the National Party stood for and it was unrealistic to suppose that the two parties could remain comfortable bedfellows in a coalition even for a short time.

Given that the white population of South Africa from which the National Party obtained its support represented less than 20 per cent of the total population did the change mean that it would now become the permanent opposition or were there other alternatives available to it?

Brief initial euphoria at the new South Africa was demonstrated during the National Party congress of January 1995 when a mixed race assembly joined in a Zulu melody. The party's spokesman, Martinus van Schalkwyk, was able to enthuse: 'It's totally different, its spontaneous, its wonderful. Afrikaners are usually reserved, but they too got up and sang. It shows there's a new South African culture emerging.' Mr de Klerk told the 1500 delegates that the party had to build up an image as the main opposition party. 'It is our right and duty to promote our policy and to attack, criticise and oppose the ANC as our main opponent in the political arena.' Other speakers pursued this theme of becoming the leading mixed race opposition party. By the middle of 1995, however, this almost euphoric determination to become the main opposition party had given way to brutal infighting, with hardliners determined to oust Roelf Meyer who was seen as the man responsible for selling out to the ANC during the negotiations which preceded the 1994 elections. As Professor Hennie Kotze of Stellenbosch University described the party's dilemma:

> The whole problem comes down to the fact that the NP has still not sorted out the role it should play within the GNU (Government of National Unity). They still don't understand the nature of coalition government. From being top dogs, they've become the total underdogs. A psychological adjustment is necessary. The party's support is broadly spread but they haven't made peace with the new party they are. The whites can't get used to the idea they no longer run the show. There are no signs of any coloured people in the NP hierarchy.[9]

Just before the Democratic Party's federal congress in August 1995 its leader, Tony Leon, rubbed salt into the NP wounds when he predicted that the NP would be 'comprehensively decimated by the truth commission disclosures'. He said the Democratic Party which had lost half its support to the National Party during the 1994 elections was fast regaining it, since the NP had not done as expected and demonstrated that it was the only alternative to the ANC.

> The NP has not performed in any sense as people expected them to. They have not been able to present any alternative to the ANC; they

have been paralysed by their own past, they are going to be comprehensively decimated by the truth commission disclosures and the
Chinese drip torture which is emerging from that.[10]

This was good political rhetoric; it was also largely true.

By August 1995 the NP was in deep crisis and de Klerk was obliged to
call a special meeting of the federal executive, which is the NP's highest decisionmaking body, after the congress to deal with party divisions. The problems faced by the NP were divisions between left and
right, its role in the GNU, its relations with the ANC, its scope, potential or actual, as an opposition party, its future. It was not simply that
the NP was suffering from the aftermath of an electoral defeat after
more than 40 years of uninterrupted power but rather that it was trying to come to terms with the disappearance in April 1994 of its entire
raison d'être. As one MP commented, strong speeches and threats every
few months from Mr de Klerk would not be enough to hold the party
together.[11]

In part the split in the party was a divide between those more progressive members who wished to come to terms with the new South
Africa and those who could not free themselves from the past.
Ministers such as Roelf Meyer, Chris Fismer and Dawie de Villiers
wanted to play a constructive role in the GNU for the national interest
and saw the NP as being in competition with the ANC while others
emphasized a NP opposition role, with Andre Fourie advocating the
formation of an anti-ANC front with the Inkatha Freedom Party and
the Freedom Front. In any case by this time the ANC was making it
plain in the Constitutional Assembly that it would not permit any
entrenched power sharing in the final constitution.

By January 1996, as the political dominance of the ANC became ever
more apparent, there were rumours that the NP was to disband and
then reinvent itself with a new name and image. This was contradicted
by the NP spokesman Marthinus van Schalkwyk who said:

What we are trying to do is realign the South African political scene.
Mr de Klerk has taken the initiative. We now invite other parties
and organisations to react to this. This is not a short-term process. It
will happen over the long term, but we believe it is for the good of
South Africa.[12]

This unconvincing statement did little to set at rest the party's growing
divisions.

At least in May 1996 de Klerk took a logical step when he withdrew the NP from the Government of National Unity. It had never really made sense, except as a short term gesture of unity, for the NP architects of apartheid to be part of the first ANC dominated government. As Mr de Klerk said South Africa needed a strong and confident opposition and the NP would now supply it. President Mandela responded to the NP withdrawal by saying the move represented a 'coming of age' and warned that 'The National Party has a continuing responsibility to contribute to the process of eradicating the legacy of apartheid which they created.' This was the decisive moment when the party might have rallied its forces had it managed to maintain real unity. The previous February Roelf Meyer had resigned his cabinet post in the GNU to become full-time general secretary of the party in order to modernise it and build alliances with the IFP and Democratic Party. The reason for the departure of the NP from the government had been the adoption of the new constitution which de Klerk said lacked commitment both to fiscal discipline and moral values, a curious judgement upon a constitution and even more curious from the leader of the NP whose application of moral judgements over the preceding 40 years had turned the country, over which the party presided, into an international pariah state.

Despite the efforts of Roelf Meyer and the more liberal elements in the party the path upon which it embarked at this time seemed likely to lead the NP into political oblivion. There was no indication that the dramatic move by the NP would have much impact upon the country, although the removal of six NP ministers gave Mandela the chance to bring new blood into his government. As the London *Observer* commented:

The sight of him (de Klerk) now taking the high moral ground verges on the pathetic. His dedication of the National Party to ethical behaviour borders on irony, given that one of its last contributions to the constitutional debate last week was an attempt to entrench the 'right' to double pensions of MPs surviving the old political dispensation. His championship of the 'right to life' sits equally uneasily on the shoulders of a man whose close political colleague – former Defence Minister General Magnus Malan – is on trial for mass murder.[13]

Political turns of fortune can be very dramatic and in the course of the next two years as the Truth and Reconciliation Commission revealed some of the depths of brutality which had been sanctioned by the National Party during the apartheid years its reputation was left in tatters. The chances that de Klerk and other NP leaders could live down these revelations in which, despite their denials, they had been involved seemed remote. In June 1998 the Truth and Reconciliation Commission heard how South African Defence Force scientists had tried to develop a chemical weapon that would be effective only against black people. The Commission was told by a former managing director of a front company, Dr Daan Goosen, how the government had tried to develop a drug that could control the black population so as to allow it to retain white domination. Goosen said that in 1983 the government began a search for a drug that would be effective against 'pigmented people only' and that at first the search had been for a fertility drug that would prevent the black population from increasing. Such revelations deprive the National Party of any effective moral voice in the immediate political arena of the New South Africa.

The ambiguous and dangerous role adopted by the Inkatha Freedom Party (IFP) of Chief Mangosuthu Buthelezi in the period of violence prior to the 1994 elections and in the GNU in which he served afterwards posed a complex dilemma for the ANC and the government of Nelson Mandela. In his capacity as leader of the IFP with its power base in KwaZulu-Natal Buthelezi advanced his claims for maximum provincial power within the new South African system, while as a minister of the GNU (he had the portfolio of Home Affairs) he was an important if not crucial part of the new nation-building operation over which Mandela and the ANC then presided. From the viewpoint of ordinary members of the ANC Chief Buthelezi and his IFP were enemies who had endangered the process of transition and, with covert help from the NP, split the ranks of those opposed to apartheid and in consequence he was bitterly resented. President Mandela and the hierarchy of the party had to treat Buthelezi in a different manner, with kid gloves.

They may have shared the general ANC antipathy to the IFP and Buthelezi but his participation, first in the April 1994 elections and then in the GNU, was crucial to a smooth transition. This fact gave Buthelezi disproportionate influence which he wielded like a bludgeon. He kept everyone guessing until the last moment as to whether the IFP would take part in the elections of 1994; subsequently, as the constitutional talks progressed, he walked out of the GNU in March 1995 to cause the first big crisis for the coalition government. However, after two weeks absence a special Inkatha congress ordered the 48 IFP MPs to return to parliament. Buthelezi had accused Mandela of bad faith in constitutional talks over the future of KwaZulu-Natal. But President

Mandela offered no concessions, instead ordering more troops into the province to prevent further IFP inspired destabilisation. This tough action worked but the brinkmanship was to continue.

In May President Mandela was obliged to leave a May Day rally in Durban in an armoured police vehicle after rival Zulu groups exchanged automatic gunfire. Speaking in the King Zwelithini stadium Mandela had said he was sick and tired of violence; he attacked a 'certain leader' for calling upon his supporters in KwaZulu-Natal to 'rise and resist' central government following the rejection of Buthelezi's demand for international mediation of the constitution. Yet only three days later Mandela and Buthelezi shook hands and the President declared Chief Buthelezi to be 'my traditional leader, my chief and my prince' while paying tribute to him as one of the people who had worked hardest for his release from 27 years in prison. Mr Mandela then said of the violence in KwaZulu: 'There is a problem, but there is no crisis.' Chief Buthelezi for his part declared 'I am a loyal member of the President's cabinet.'

Such public posturing by the two men may make sense in terms of political expediency though many observers found such kowtowing to Buthelezi's threats hard to take. On the other hand, Mandela appeared to believe that by such tactics he could eventually persuade Buthelezi to accept the inevitable without too much loss of face. A report on the violence in KwaZulu released later that May by the New York-based Human Rights Watch Africa group warned that the continuing violence in KwaZulu-Natal had the potential to derail the South African democratic process.

> Although the monthly death toll has declined from the catastrophic heights seen before the elections of April 1994, the figures remain high enough to undermine the process of national reconstruction. While the report blamed both the ANC and IFP for committing atrocities it blamed senior Inkatha members for promoting the violence for their own political benefit.[14]

Confrontation with central government continued to be the IFP policy through July 1995, with Buthelezi apparently becoming frustrated by those of his own supporters who were not prepared to be sufficiently confrontational with the ANC whether or not they agreed with ANC policies or decisions. Essentially, the argument was about the degree of autonomy the IFP could obtain under the new constitution for KwaZulu-Natal and this was part of a wider argument about a highly centralised state, which was favoured by the ANC, or a more federal state in which substantial powers remained with the provincial governments. However, the IFP hold over KwaZulu-Natal was never as strong as Buthelezi claimed or, perhaps, believed and according to a survey of June 1995 the ANC said it had just over 60 per cent of support in urban and peri-urban areas in the province, while IFP support among whites had declined from 28 per cent in April 1994 to 15 per cent in June 1995. Africa Watch claimed that the IFP was fighting to preserve 'undemocratic and probably unconstitutional' traditional powers under a new system of local government.

On 20 August 1995 Chief Buthelezi called on the Zulus to adopt a new covenant to unify the divided Zulu nation and demand self-rule. It was another step in his political war with the ANC, another pressure for greater Zulu independence from central government control. The division he referred to was that between Inkatha as represented by the KwaZulu-Natal Premier, Dr Frank Mdlalose, and the Zulu King Goodwill. In an address to some 40 000 people in the King's Park rugby stadium at Durban, Buthelezi said:

> We must now more than ever demand the right to govern ourselves within the parameters of a broader, federal relation with the rest of South Africa. Today, August 20, will be remembered in history as the day of the Zulu covenant in which the people of the kingdom have become one. We are now moving towards our liberation as one nation with one kingdom and one purpose. Today is the day of unity and the beginning of our liberation.[15]

Such language could not endear Buthelezi to Mandela and the ANC coming, as it did, little more than a year after the historic elections which marked the end of the apartheid era and the emergence of the new united South Africa.

The end of the year was marked by a brutal massacre of ANC supporters in the village of Shobashobane on Christmas morning when 600 Zulu warrior supporters of the IFP cheered on by accompanying women shot, stabbed and burned to leave 19 dead, 22 wounded and scores more homeless; they razed 87 huts and houses and ransacked many more. By this time it was reckoned that over a decade of Zulu–ANC slaughter 13 000 people had been killed.

This, surely, represented more than just the 'problem' Mandela had described it as being earlier in the year. And so in January 1996 Mandela and Buthelezi held a meeting in Pretoria to discuss how to stop the escalating bloodshed. President Mandela proposed the holding of an *imbizo* or traditional gathering of Zulu leaders from both the ANC and Inkatha; he was backed by King Goodwill Zwelithini. At that time it was at least possible that the violence could escalate into a full-scale civil war. But while Mandela behaved as a conciliator, in part blaming the violence on the 'third Force', Buthelezi behaved more as though he represented an independent state rather than a long-standing component part of South Africa.

The next crisis occurred in April 1996 when President Mandela suggested that local government elections in KwaZulu-Natal might have to be postponed because of the widespread violence and intimidation taking place in the province. Then it was suggested that evidence of massive fraud had surfaced prior to the 29 May elections although Chief Buthelezi rejected charges that Inkatha was involved in fraud. Crises came and went. The problem was the unwillingness of Chief Buthelezi to accept a subordinate role in the new South Africa and his determination to use his IFP both to stir up trouble for the government (of which he was a part) and to prise from it maximum independence of action for KwaZulu-Natal province. If one approach did not work he turned to another and the threat of violence remained just below the surface when it was not actually being employed. President Mandela alternated between conciliation and toughness though without ever surrendering the crucial Buthelezi demand for greater autonomy. When the twice postponed local government elections were finally held the Inkatha Freedom Party won the most votes in KwaZulu-Natal, but the ANC won control of governing councils in the main cities including Durban: Inkatha received 44.5 per cent of the votes cast, the ANC 33.2 per cent. Both sides claimed a victory. These elections (the rest of the country had held local government elections the previous November) completed the transformation of South Africa to a regime of democratic government.

By the end of 1997 the KwaZulu-Natal premier and IFP national chairman Ben Ngubane claimed that the peace process between the IFP and ANC would be expedited in 1998 and spoke of steadily marching towards the goal of 'harmonious co-operation' between people of different political persuasions. He was far more emollient than Buthelezi usually managed to be but also made plain that the IFP intended to increase its majority in KwaZulu-Natal during the 1999 elections. During much of 1998 South Africa's attention was focused upon the proceedings of the Truth and Reconciliation Commission and relations between the ANC and IFP in KwaZulu-Natal were less explosive and violent than had been the case in the previous three years. However, the issue of provincial powers had not gone away.

Part of the South African political story from 1994 to 1998 was the search for a viable opposition to the African National Congress which was the sole ruling party in all but name. Since, moreover, it was expected to continue as the ruling party for at least ten years after the 1999 elections where did this leave the National Party, the Inkatha Freedom Party, the Democratic Party, the Pan Africanist Congress and any other party or group that did not see itself belonging to the ANC juggernaut? As the ANC moved to occupy the centre ground and where possible achieve consensus politics, hoping to attract the IFP into its ranks, two scenarios began to emerge.

The first scenario concerned its allies COSATU and SACP: would they find themselves torn between their loyalty to the ANC from the days of struggle and an increasing need to oppose government policies when these failed to deal adequately with the demands of their own con-stituents – the poor underclass created by the apartheid system. Already over this period both COSATU and the Communist Party have expressed deepening concerns at the business-oriented policies of the ANC which they see as a prelude to the abandonment of its earlier socialist policies. And though the demand of Peter Mokaba that the Communist Party should be dropped from the tripartite alliance was seen as the view of a small minority, that could change quite rapidly as a significant proportion of ANC supporters become affluent in the new South Africa. Will COSATU, the SACP and the more radical elements in the ranks of the ANC become the real opposition to the government during the first decade of the new millenium?

The second scenario concerned the white parties and most notably the disintegrating National Party and the Democratic Party. Will the whites they have traditionally represented find any real crossover into a genuinely multiracial society too hard to make and will they, in conse-quence, despite all their rhetoric find themselves coalescing into a hard core white opposition? Should this happen, and there are plenty of indications that it might, it will only serve to perpetuate the race divi-sions that created the apartheid system in the first place. Of course white leaders will deny that any such development will not take place but as of 1998 the omens were not good. The great achievement of the four years 1994 to 1998 was to narrow the political middle ground and this was occupied by the ANC. The great danger for the next 20 years will be that the ANC develops into a monolithic centre party that brooks no opposition or, rather, sees opposition as unpatriotic and such a tendency would be all the more likely if the whites combine to form an opposition representing dwindling racial privileges. Burying the past on all sides may well turn out to be the hardest political act of all.

In an upbeat article published in the South African *Sunday Times* the political–cultural choices facing South Africa were set out succinctly:

> After generations of humiliation, brutality, fear and oppression, black South Africans glory in freedom, and express themselves vigorously and articulately in the great debate about where we are going and how we will get there. They hold in their hands the reins of power of the continent's most virile, sophisiticated economy. They take their rightful seats in assemblies around the world where their views are canvassed and respected.
>
> No nation has a leader of whom they can be as proud of as we can be of Nelson Mandela. No nation has ever had, in its enormous dimensions, the historic opportunity we do to prove that black and white, Indian and coloured and people of all races, creeds and philosophies can co-exist peacefully and prosperously.[16]

The euphoria may strike some as excessive but the opportunity is there; whether it is properly grasped remains to be seen.

Corruption and political expediency often walk hand in hand. There was massive evidence of corruption in the old National Party whether about money, about office or about cover-up when corrupt practices were discovered. It is not to be supposed that the ANC will be any more free of this universally endemic political disease than any other political party anywhere else in the world. What is important is the manner in which the party and the government deal with corruption once it has been uncovered. The omens are not good.

Early in 1995 scandal broke round the charismatic figure of Dr Allan Boesak, then South Africa's ambassador-designate to the United Nations, who was accused of embezzling funds from his own charity; thousands of pounds were diverted from needy children (victims of apartheid) apparently to pay for Boesak's wedding and to settle his wife's debts as well as for ANC election funds. At the ANC conference of December 1994 President Mandela had warned the leadership to guard against the corruption of power. He said he saw a parasitic class emerging in the ranks of the ANC and pointed out how often freedom fighters in other African countries entered government and then became unaccountable to their people.

By February 1995, only two months after he had delivered that warning, a number of senior ANC officials were facing charges of mismanagement or impropriety: those involved included the former youth leader Peter Mokaba then chairing the parliamentary committee on tourism; Major-General Bantu Holomisa, the former ruler of the Transkei and then deputy minister of the environment and tourism; and Winnie Mandela, then deputy arts, culture, science and technology minister. The slowness to act at this stage did damage to the ANC image. Mandela and other ANC leaders have impeccable personal records but if the ANC is to stay clean the leadership must be ruthless in rooting out any forms of corruption once these have been exposed. The three people named above came from the populist wing of the party and that being the case it would require a bold man to act against them. As Steven Friedman, head of the Centre for Policy Studies, said, corruption is a great threat to both the political system and stability: 'A corruption-free society is a myth, but at the very least it is necessary to treat corruption as if it is not the norm – to take action when it is exposed.'[17] Unfortunately for South Africa at this time in its history, the main opposition in parliament, part of whose natural role would be to point out corrupt practices in the government, consisted of the National Party whose own record for corruption in government destroyed any credibility it might otherwise have exercised in this respect.

In July 1995 it was disclosed that 40 MPs had accepted a two-night lobbying excursion on the expensive Blue Train from Transnet and that many of the MPs saw nothing wrong in the exercise. Transnet argued that the Eastern Cape excursion which included the Grahamstown Festival was simply a marketing exercise and that as MPs received many overseas visitors these could be potential customers. But though Transnet insisted that no government money was involved this was not true since as a state enterprise all its activities involve state money.[18] Perhaps it was not very important but the sight of 40 MPs travelling the country in luxurious conditions is hardly an inspiring one for a country which suffers from as much poverty as does South Africa.

By early 1998 corruption and the maladministration of state assets had reportedly reached such staggering proportions that the head of South Africa's crack anti-corruption unit was experiencing difficulty in preventing the haemorrhage of public funds and, Judge Willem Heath told *The Sunday Independent*, 'What we have managed to reveal so far appears to be just a tip of a problem that has taken root through the entire administration.' The Judge, who had been appointed to head the

Special Investigating Unit set up at Mandela's insistence in 1997, said that despite recovering R10 billion in state assets over 18 months another 90 000 cases awaited investigation and these involved a further R6 billion. He said 'The level of corruption and maladministration is much more serious than even politicians and government officials expected.'[19]

An expedient dishonesty occurred right at the beginning of ANC rule over the report of the European monitors of the April 1994 election results. No copy of the 134-page report was given to the South African government; instead, it was decided not to examine the flawed details of the election since it produced the results everyone wanted to see. It seems almost certain that the results obtained in some areas of KwaZulu-Natal were simply fixed so as to ensure that Buthelezi's Inkatha Freedom Party secured sufficient votes to enable it to participate in the government of national unity. Pragmatists will argue that in terms of the volatile situation in KwaZula-Natal at the time it was more important to fix things and bring Buthelezi into the government than not to fix the results and have him a danger outside it. The difficulty, as always, with such a proposition is that once a new era is launched with the help of fixing, however apparently justifed it may be, fixing subsequently becomes the norm for a precedent for it has been set.

5
Problems and Expectations

The range of problems facing the post-apartheid government were by any standards daunting. A census of mid-1997 shocked South Africa by revealing that its total population at 38 million was four million less than previously estimated, although this might have been seen as a relief in terms of development needs since most of the 'lost' four million had been assumed to be blacks. The new count classified 77 per cent of the population as black, 12 per cent white, 9 per cent coloured and 2 per cent Asian. Of the whites 2.6 million or roughly 60 per cent were Afrikaners. Possessed of the fifth largest population on the African continent and endowed with major resources South Africa will require all these resources and all the energies and co-operation of its people if it is to tackle effectively the mammoth tasks of reconciliation, reconstruction and development that face it.

The first problem facing the new Mandela government in 1994 was simply that of expectations: how quickly could the government meet the economic and social needs of its supporters – if at all? Political discussions about priorities make no impact upon the very poor; as one member of Alexandra township said in response to a question about the new government's record in December 1994: 'Satisfied? How can you ask if I am satisfied with this government?' And as another said: 'The government must start doing something concrete.'[1] President Mandela who earlier in the year had made a tour of squatter camps in the Johannesburg area warned that it would be years before the government could deal adequately with the problems of unemployment, housing and education and most of his audiences understood him well enough. At the same time there was criticism that he pandered too much to the concerns of the white minority and that ministers drew huge salaries when millions of South Africans live in poverty.

As Nkele Ntingane, a founder member of the Alexandra Civic Organisation, a pro-ANC community group, said: 'If a section of society has been excluded for so long, it is not feasible to make it up, even in five years. Just because we voted for the ANC, it does not mean that everything will change.' Such a sensible response to events denies the underlying desperation of people who expect that at least some things will change to their advantage and do so quickly. In Alexandra township at this time unemployment was running at 65 per cent.

Part of the initial problem was simply that of adjustment: the ANC in 1994 had yet to make the transition from liberation movement to party of government and though its supporters had voted for it on a great wave of hope, that could rapidly turn sour if expectations for change were not quickly met. The three primary demands were – and remain – for houses, education and jobs. According to a Central Statistical Service (CSS) survey of October 1995 rich households in South Africa spend an average of R13 000 a year on food and poor households only R2000, and the poorer the household the higher the proportion of income spent on food. The survey did little more than confirm disparities which have become all too familiar. Two reports released in mid-1998 drew a grim picture of the country's poverty; both reports put the blame for widespread poverty among the black majority on apartheid social engineering.

The first report which had been commissioned by the UNDP was published by the National Institute for Economic Policy and called 'Poverty elimination, employment creation and sustainable livelihoods in South Africa'. Its principal message was to mainstream the reduction of poverty into national policy and it argued that failure to invest in human development resources fast enough contributed to an increase in overall poverty. Lack of social investment led to underskilling, lack of access to basic social services and lack of access to essential economic assets such as land and credit. If the majority of the population cannot actively participate in the consumption of goods and services this in turn must adversely affect the development of South Africa's home markets. In many rural areas the poor depended upon remittances from working family members in the towns. A second report commissioned by Deputy President Thabo Mbeki – 'Poverty and inequality in South Africa' – said the reduction of poverty and inequality must depend upon government spending targeting the poor: 'The richest and middle income groups have been largely the beneficiaries of public spending in the past ... to address inequality policies must target the poor, as well as address racial, gender and spatial imbalances in access to basic services.'[2]

However, the report also admitted that the government was uncertain how best to tackle poverty and inequality, and expectations had not been met. The poorest 40 per cent of households accounting for 19 million people had a monthly expenditure of only R353 and South Africa remains one of the most unequal societies in the world with the gap between rich and poor second only to that existing in Brazil. Furthermore, a relatively new problem, the growth of inequality between rich and poor blacks was near to the national average. If the poor are to break out of the poverty trap economic growth and redistribution must go hand in hand.

A statistical summary of the country's poor shows that 50 per cent receive only 11 per cent of total income, that 72 per cent of these live in rural areas, that 61 per cent of Africans (as opposed to one per cent of whites) are poor and that three children in five live in poor households.[3] The report became the basis for debate in mid-June at a conference on poverty and inequality in Midrand. The report estimated that 1.2 million people eke out a living in the informal sector and of these 86 per cent were Africans and 7.6 per cent coloured. The rural areas had the most poor and the poverty rate was highest in the Eastern Cape and lowest in Gauteng.

The UNDP's *Human Development Report 1998* included a special box – 'The new South Africa – ending apartheid in consumption' – which bore out the above conclusions. Apartheid separated black and white consumption patterns both by the unequal distribution of income and also by unequal access to basic services and by the suppression of living standards. Government house building had come to a halt in the early 1980s at a time when the housing backlog was estimated at 600 000. By the mid-1990s the housing backlog had soared to 2.5 million units. As the report argued 'Among the top objectives for the new South Africa is to meet basic meeds for all – housing, water, transport, electricity, telecommunications, a clean and healthy environment, nutrition, health care and jobs.' Nonetheless, some major advances had been achieved and in 1995 alone black households enjoyed a marked increase in their access to services including households with electricity jumping from 37 to 51 per cent, those with telephones from 12 to 14 per cent, those with piped water from 27 to 33 per cent, those with flush toilets or latrines from 46 to 51 per cent and those with refuse removal by the local authority from 37 to 43 per cent.[4]

Education lies close to the centre of any long-term development improvements while also focusing attention upon the huge differentials between blacks and whites that were deliberately fostered during the apartheid years, when ten times as much money was allocated to the education of an individual white child as was allocated to an individual black child. Unsurprisingly in the years immediately following the 1994 elections a number of ugly confrontations took place between white and black, where the government insisted upon black–white integration in schools which formerly had been reserved for white pupils only. Furthermore, many of these confrontations took place in schools which had catered for poor whites, as in the white working-class district of Ruyterwacht, 10 miles from Cape Town. The end of segregated schools for poor whites, arguably, spelt the end of the last differential between themselves and the black majority, hence their bitter resistance. These confrontations, similar to those that took place in the American 'deep South' in the 1960s, will be a passing phenomenon. Much more important, in the long run, must be South Africa's capacity to compete in a ruthless world economic system and that will depend upon the speed with which education is upgraded and made available at all levels – primary, secondary and tertiary – to the whole population.

The South African Institute of People Management (IPM) warned at the end of 1997 that the country would fail in its drive to become a world class player in the global economy unless companies took serious steps to develop their personnel. According to Tiisetso Tsukudu 'South African companies are experiencing more competition than ever before. We have to jack up our systems at home and put people at the core of our organisations' drive for competitiveness. We can't be world class without developing people.' According to the World Economic Forum's latest global competitiveness report South Africa was ranked 52 out of 53 industrialised countries in terms of skills and productivity. The IPM has 8500 members of whom 40 per cent are corporations, 35 per cent students and the balance small businesses. Prodding by such organisations will be crucial to South Africa's management performance.[5]

Another body – the Foundation for Research Development (FRD) – said in 1997 that the government-inspired programme for technology and human resources for industry should be spending R500 million by the end of the century as more industries tapped into its research facilities to enhance their competitive edge. Its major objectives, according to the director of academic–industrial co-operative research Tjaart van der Walt, were to provide appropriate technology and managerial skills for industries and to encourage students to follow technical careers, as well as stimulating the discovery of new products and enterprises.

If such organisations are to succeed in promoting greater skills for industry they must be able to rely upon a steady and increasing stream of students coming up through the schools but problems in the educational field which surfaced in 1998 were hardly encouraging. They reflected the limits to resources (money) at the disposal of the government; they also arose out of past political attitudes, especially in the case of student fees, and the poverty of too many students. At the financial level the government decreased expenditure on school books from R851 million for 1995–96 to R381 million for 1996–97 and down to R226 million for 1997–98. At the university level about 20 000 students faced the possibility of being excluded from their universities or technical colleges by the end of 1998 for not settling their fee accounts. The decision to expel students followed six months of talks between universities and students on how to accomodate poor students and how to distinguish between poor students and those who could but would not pay.

In May 1998, for example, universities had only recovered R100 million of R500 million that had been owed to them at the end of 1997. Part at least of the problem is the culture of non-payment that arose in the days when students were defying apartheid regulations. As Wanga Sigila, the chairman of the students representative council of the University of the Western Cape, argued (at a time when 2000 students faced the possibility of being expelled), 'If it is the remains of a culture of non-payment, then they must be deregistered. This kind of culture has to be removed, while truly needy students have to be helped.' Amounts owing varied enormously between universities. Debt at the University of the Free State had increased from R11 million to R15 million; the University of Zululand claimed it had recovered R14 million of debts but was still owed R41 million; Fort Hare University said it had signed agreements with parents to ensure that R26 million in fees would be settled; while Technikon Witwatersrand had handed over unpaid accounts to lawyers and debt collectors. These university debts were one of many facets of an educational system under severe strain.[6]

Many of the problems afflicting the educational sector are the direct legacy of the apartheid years, whether as the result of the inequalities of the former system and the huge amounts of money that will be required to bring black education into line with white education, or because of the attitudes imbued by black students from the time of the Soweto uprising onwards. During the last 15 years of the apartheid era thousands of black students accepted the slogan 'Liberation first, then education' and those who did so had, by the 1990s, become the 'lost generation' who were both unemployed and unemployable. At least that generation, in theory, had fought for a proper education that was untainted by racism. By the late 1990s the education system was seen to be beset by drugs, teenage pregnancies and lack of funds and though in 1998 education received nearly 30 per cent of budget funds this was not sufficient to meet educational expectations without the government being forced to cut back teacher numbers so as to release funds to spend on books and buildings. As a result it faced a new prob-lem – the threat of a national teachers' strike because of the cutbacks, the first such threat in the country's history. As a teacher from Orlando West High School in Soweto, Veli Ndhlovu, explained: 'The problems we have had over the past decade result from a total breakdown of the culture of learning and teaching… In many ways, education in the townships is starting from the beginning, and we are no further than we were in 1976.'[7]

Inequalities and gross inadequacies in the health system parallel those in education while statistics released in 1995 alerted South Africa to the additional problem of a massive Aids epidemic. An estimated 850 000 people – just over 2 per cent of the population – were believed to be HIV positive and this level doubles every 13 months according to the director-general of the Ministry of Health, Dr Coenraad Slabber. Although the South African figure was well below those for the urban areas in Uganda, Zambia or Zimbabwe, it was much higher among high risk groups such as pregnant women. About half those reported to be infected are likely to die within eight to 10 years and as Thabo Mbeki said when he opened the 7th UN Conference on Aids in Cape Town in March 1995, 'The impact has begun to cut deep. Those affected are from the young and able-bodied workforce as well as young intellectuals.'[8]

Another aspect of the health scene concerns recruitment to medical school. The University of Cape Town announced that it was willing to test for entrance to medical school the top 10 per cent of students from any high school. In practice this would mean that a C-aggregate from one local township school would not be a lower qualification than five distinctions from another top school. Such students would then undergo extended degree courses which would turn their potential into actual ability. However, this approach raised the bogey of applying racial quotas to medical entrants regardless of real abilities. The medical uni-versities appealed to the government to fund bridging programmes so as to boost the intake of black students in order to make the student popu-lation representative of the races rather than penalising institutions which did not have enough black students. The health department had told parliament that it planned to draw up a racial quota system for the university intake of first year medical students.

Predictably, a row about standards developed between the department of health and the universities. The director-general of the health department, Olive Shisana, said that while no quota system would be enforced, state subsidies to the universities would be in proportion to the enrolment of black medical students. In reply, the dean of the Medical Faculty at Stellenbosch University, Jan Lochner, said the health department was insinuating that there was something wrong with the university selection process when the problem lay with the school system: 'Politicians should spend money to get the level of schooling up instead of promoting the lowering of standards. Universities have to admit students most likely to succeed. They owe this to the taxpayer and to the government.' E. T. Mokgokong, the principal of the Medical School of Southern Africa, said that if the government wanted to introduce quota systems, it should fund bridging programmes so that the universities could tap into the potential of black students who showed signs of being academically gifted. And William Saunderson Meyer, spokesman for the University of Natal, argued that there was no point in pulling in a huge number of black students who could end up failing their first year. He said that while universities were trying to redress the racial imbalance, 'there are only so many students who are suitable and other universities are chasing the same students.'[9] As with so many of South Africa's problems of adjustment and development the race issue lies just below the surface and a fine line has to be drawn between the ideal as far as good medical students are concerned and the desperate need to bring on black medical students commensurate with the size and requirements of the country's total black population.

Housing is highly visible and the government can only claim success when it can point to houses on the ground. Under the government's housing policy low-income earners qualify for subsidies from R7500 to R15000. But as the Minister of Housing, Sanki Mthembu-Nkondo, pointed out shortly after succeeding Joe Slovo in the job, a housing programme needs land, water, sewerage and a developer. However, in mid-1995 it was clear that housing policy was in crisis when the minister indicated that she was unhappy with the policy she had inherited from Joe Slovo. After holding major consultations and taking account of demographic realities and fiscal restraints including widespread poverty, the huge housing backlog to be eliminated, rapid urbanisation and population growth, Slovo's approach aimed to provide people with a serviced site, basic top structure and basic services which would ensure that residents had support for their own upgrading efforts. His approach was highly politically sensitive because in many ways it was akin to the schemes which had been advocated during the apartheid era. Slovo, however, saw as the overriding need housing the population as quickly as possible – improvements could come later. He opposed the policy advocated by provincial housing ministers, who wanted to build houses of between 40 and 50 metres square, simply on the grounds of cost – the money was not available and the construction industry would not be able to cope. In addition, Slovo worked to bring in the banks to provide 50 000 loans for low cost homes. There were other elements in what was a highly complex and ambitious plan that might have worked, despite its political unpopularity, had Slovo lived. On his death, however, he was succeeded by Mthembu-Nkondo who had neither his political clout nor his drive as well as facing provincial housing ministers who wished to pursue a different path. What was also apparent in mid-1995 was the fact that housing was possibly the ministry above all others that would determine how the voters at large would judge the government's performance.

Following the launch of the government's mass housing programme on 5 June 1995 the banks had announced stricter lending criteria for low-income home buyers because of the risks attached to such loans. However, in an effort to revitalise the government's programme banks, builders and the housing ministry reached a joint agreement in July to postpone the implementation of stricter lending criteria, making possible 200 000 housing subsidies approved by housing boards. The joint statement added that stricter criteria would eventually have to be applied. Problems in the housing sector simply reflect the poverty of those who seek new housing and they regard housing as either the top priority or one of the three most important basic needs. Research revealed that at least 40 per cent of urban African people had a monthly income of R800 or less while an additional 30 per cent received between R801 and R1500 and 20 per cent between R1501 and R2500 so that only 10 per cent received more than R2500 a month. Roughly 40 per cent of households have incomes between 50 per cent and 20 per cent below the subsistence level. These are the people demanding housing and requiring loans.

Yet within a month of the agreement between the housing ministry and the banks Gauteng's Premier Tokyo Sexwale accused the banks of betraying their agreement with the government on the provision of low-cost loans. He said the National Housing Accord had failed because banks refused almost 90 per cent of all bond applications at the lower end of the market. In the first quarterly political review of the South African Chamber of Business (SACOB) for 1995 Professor Lawrence Schlemmer argued that the minister's support for complete houses for all was a 'totally impossible challenge' and that there was widespread disillusionment with the government's Reconstruction and Development Programme (RDP). Few homeless people could actually afford a built home when interest rates on loans were up to 22.5 per cent and that of the 581 000 households who wanted and needed to buy formal low-cost homes only about 166 000 could afford the repayments. The argument was to continue, but as with all the problems to do with expectations, the political desire to meet the demands always outruns the capacity to achieve the targets and the people's ability to meet even minimal costs.

In April 1998, speaking at the first annual conference of the South African Residential Developers Association, the housing minister Sanki Mthembu-Nkondo claimed that the government had provided shelter for 3.3 million people since 1994 but that the housing backlog still amounted to 4 million units if informal dwellings were excluded. A month later the minister addressed the National Assembly in Cape Town in the debate on the R3.6 billion allocation to housing when she announced that subsidies had by then been extended to rural communities occupying communal land. She presented statistics of units constructed or under construction since 1994: 47 901 in the Eastern Cape, 36 646 in the Free State, 144 120 in Gauteng, 29 345 in Mpumalanga, 39 599 in the North West, 14 658 in the Northern Cape, 25 254 in the Northern province and 67 811 in Western Cape. The needs remained as great as ever but there was a 7.1 per cent cut in the budget allocation for the year.[10]

According to a report by the Development Bank of Southern Africa (DBSA) entitled 'Infrastructure: A Foundation for Development', South Africa's infrastructure facilities such as telecommunications, electricity, railways and roads are on a par with those of high income countries despite the fact that the country's per capita GDP is only a sixth of those countries. On the other hand, the huge income disparities between rich and poor mean the latter benefit little from the infrastructure advantages. In the case of schools, for example, 83 per cent lack libraries, 61 per cent are without telephones, 24 per cent do not have water, 52 per cent lack electricity and 12 per cent lack toilets. As the Finance Minister, Trevor Manuel said, the report

> focuses the collective mind on where we have come from, where we are, and where we need to go. We cannot rest until all South

Africans enjoy access to decent housing, safe water and sanitation, reliable energy and the many other services that underpin a life of quality. There is a vast apartheid-inflicted backlog to overcome and a great many serious economic and financial problems we must tackle.[11]

Another set of telling statistics appeared in the 1998 World Competitiveness Report which ranked South Africa's infrastructure as 35th out of 46 countries for its overall ability to satisfy business needs. South Africa stands in the top 25 per cent of countries surveyed for transport but ranked 40th for telephone lines per 1000 people; it ranked 38th for computers per capita, 30th for its share in computer usage world-wide, 33rd for cellphones per capita and 13th for investment in telecommunications as a percentage of GDP. On infrastructure maintenance it came in 30th place. Thus, the country is well endowed with its capacity to produce the necessary infrastructure, especially to service the business community but household access to infrastructure is low. Infrastructure on its own does not mean development, however; it depends upon how it is used and who benefits from it. Overall in 1997, 58.1 per cent of households had access to electricity, 59.3 per cent of the population had access to water, 46.9 per cent of the population had access to sanitation, and 71.4 per cent of households to telephones.

A major problem that has only begun to be tackled concerns the restitution of land to people who were forcibly removed over the apartheid era. The government set a deadline of April 1998 for claims to be lodged and by mid-1997 16 500 land claims had been lodged – 13 358 in urban areas and 3110 in rural regions and by that time only one case had been concluded. These claims followed the passing in 1994 of the Restitution of Land Rights Act whose purpose is to redress the injustices of forced removals. However, despite the admirable purpose of the act, claims were standing in the way of other developments where they conflicted with housing or road building programmes.

A quite different problem relates to the large number of immigrants coming into South Africa. Many of these are refugees from violence as far north as Algeria or the Horn of Africa; others are economic migrants coming from South Africa's neighbours to seek better opportunities than exist at home. Given South Africa's range of problems, deep poverty and unemployment even bona fide refugees are regarded with suspicion if not open hostility which, for example, often erupts between street traders. The Department of Home Affairs has to process thousands of applications for asylum each year. The other side of this problem concerns white emigrants, especially from the professional and managerial classes. President Mandela referred to such migrants as cowards and rats deserting a sinking ship. And Deputy President Thabo Mbeki objected to 'business confidence figures' released by the South African Chamber of Business (SACOB) which he described as white scare tactics. At least part of the problem arises from the fact that there are three business groups – Afrikaner, English-speaking and black, and each is represented by its own organisation – the Afrikaanse Satekamer, SACOB and the National African Federated Chambers of Commerce (NAFCOC) which each put out their own figures and appraisals of the state of the economy.[12]

Faced with this background of problems, South Africa, if it is to find adequate solutions quickly enough, must achieve a series of economic miracles as it enters the twenty-first century.

6
Mechanisms

Assessing the impact of development policies is never easy and what benefits one group may work to the disadvantage of another. Business, for example, despite constant warnings about its plight must have been amazed at how well it did in the aftermath of apartheid. Between 1976 and 1995 corporate tax contributions fell from 35 per cent to 12.5 per cent although in the eight years prior to the 1997/98 budget taxes on individuals increased by 17 per cent. With the disappearance of exchange controls companies will be able to move their money out of South Africa if it suits them to do so. Mounting business profits have pleased both business and its shareholders but what of the other end of the scale? How under the government from 1994 to 1998 did the unemployed or ordinary workers fare? Approximately 116 000 workers were made redundant during 1997 while the growth, employment and redistribution (Gear) policy was to slash 300 000 public sector jobs by the year 2000. Income redistribution as envisaged by the Reconstruction and Development Programme (RDP) had not taken place and though advances had been achieved in a number of sectors poverty remained widespread.

When business argues that it requires more freedom and minimum controls if it is to create more wealth for the country this sounds logical. The question at the end, however, is who then enjoys the extra wealth business creates? If, at the other end of the scale, workers and the unemployed find more of them are being made redundant, wages have to be held down because business has to remain competitive and the standard of living remains static what, they must ask, is the extra wealth about? It was inevitable that a conflict of interests would arise between business on the one hand and organized labour on the other. This is inherent in the capitalist structure of South Africa and by 1998 there was every indication that such a conflict would worsen. The Confederation of South African Trade Unions (COSATU) rejects the Gear policy on the grounds that it limits the government's capacity to deal with the social deficit. Studies of the South African tax system suggest that the country is undertaxed by about 3 per cent of GDP. Moreover, COSATU argues, taxes on business are not high as the business community insists for, whereas in 1970 company taxes yielded half the total government tax take, by 1995 they only yielded 14 per cent while, over the same period, the proportion of personal tax to government revenue rose from 18 per cent to 42 per cent and this before VAT was taken into account. As a consequence of this trend, according to COSATU, there was a cut of between 4.5 and 5 per cent in government social spending in the 1997–98 budget.

Such arguments will certainly influence the government of Thabo Mbeki after he takes full control in April 1999. Disparities of wealth in South Africa mean that the vast bulk of the country's wealth is controlled by only a handful of people and companies or corporations, with an estimated 10 per cent of the population enjoying 95 per cent of the nation's GDP of $106 billion.[1] Such comparisons should always be treated with caution yet if these figures are only approximately correct they provide cause for profound disquiet. How can the new South Africa (which in economic terms continues to look remarkably like the old South Africa) mobilise its wealth to solve its problems?

The one macroeconomic decision the government has taken since 1994 is to follow a capitalist-oriented open market system as favoured in the West on the assumption that this will create wealth more efficiently than any other system and that it will also gain or retain the confidence of the world business community and, therefore, persuade it to invest in South Africa. Assuming that this decision was the correct one and that it will create more wealth than could be created in any other way, the next macroeconomic decision to be taken is what to do with the extra wealth that is created and this will be fully answered when the government works out a new tax regime to take account of the post-1994 changes and opportunities.

The Reconstruction and Development Programme (RDP) was the result of much consultation within the ANC and with its Alliance partners (SACP and COSATU) as well as other mass organisations in civil society. It was published in 1994 to provide the new government with 'an integrated, coherent socio-economic policy framework' which would mobilise the people and the country's resources toward the final eradication of apartheid. The RDP laid down six basic principles which together present a political and economic philosophy. These are enumerated as follows: an integrated and sustainable programme; a people-driven process; peace and security for all; nation-building; linking reconstruction and development; and the democratisation of South Africa. As the RDP states, the first priority is to begin to meet the basic needs of the people – jobs, land, housing, water, electricity, telecommunications, transport, a clean and healthy environment, nutrition, health care and social welfare.[2] Essentially the document is a blueprint for action, guidelines for the implementation of a better more equitable society.

It was inevitable, both from the nature of politics as well as resulting from the huge pressures for action from every kind of interested group, that within a short space of time the RDP would be attacked for failing to answer the needs or expectations of many sectors in the society. By mid-1995, for example, it was attacked because of the slow pace at which funds were allocated for job-creating projects such as building houses, schools, hospitals and clinics, and for not closing the gap between the haves and have-nots. The RDP's apparent inability to deliver money allocated for development projects was in part because of the inadequacy of government structures. As Professor Willie Esterhuyse of Stellenbosch University said, preventing the RDP from becoming 'a romanticised economic blueprint, controlled by bureaucrats and technocrats' would be a challenge. There were fears that the RDP would spawn a new bureaucracy and that there would be an over-emphasis upon consensus by the ANC, both of which trends slowed down decisions about projects or their implementation. As Brian Kantor, professor of economics at the University of Cape Town and chairman of the Victoria and Alfred Waterfront Development, said 'all sorts of new political entrepreneurs' were finding a niche for themselves in the bureaucracy.[3] Such developments are hardly surprising. Whatever else the development needs of South Africa achieve they will create a commensurately large bureaucracy.

A survey conducted in July 1995, 15 months after the new government came to power, showed that two-thirds of those who had heard of the RDP had not benefited from it, although expectations that it would deliver – eventually – remained constant with 47 per cent of blacks saying they had high expectations for the future. And at the end of July 1995, frustrated at the failure of the government to deliver on election promises, President Mandela instructed the cabinet to abandon its obsession with grand plans and give top priority to economic growth. He set up a special cabinet committee over which he would preside to decide upon the actions to be taken to stimulate growth, and his Deputy President, Thabo Mbeki, said that these priorities would focus on 'key critical issues that, if properly implemented, would make a significant difference.' The committee concluded that focusing upon delivering basic services as outlined in the RDP would not succeed unless the government first concentrated upon stimulating growth. The new initiative also had the effect of demoting Jay Naidoo, the minister responsible for overseeing the implementation of the RDP. By the time this new committee was created there appeared to have developed a mounting gap between the promises of the RDP and what was actually happening on the ground. This was hardly surprising and represented no more than the crisis of expectations that had been predicted.

An article in the *RDP News* of August 1995 admitted that implementation of the RDP programme had been slow and suggested that this was the result of delays in the process of identifying projects and ensuring the flow of financial backing for those projects which had been approved. There were few delivery mechanisms which, the article argued, was why in its first year the RDP had failed to spend nearly half the funds allocated to it. The article claimed, unsurprisingly, that 'Nearly everyone concerned with the future of South Africa believes that the future of democracy in the country will be best assured if all the aims of the RDP are achieved'. Few would argue with the sentiment; the question, however, was whether the RDP was the best instrument for achieving those aims.

The next instrument for development was that enshrined in the government's growth, employment and redistribution (Gear) strategy. Gear projections announced in June 1996 were seen by many economists to be too optimistic; they depended upon a GDP growth rate of 2.9 per cent for 1997 and a 3.8 per cent rate for 1998, figures that were later revised downwards. Gear projections for the economy over the years 1996 to 2000 suggested an average GDP growth rate of 4.2 per cent, inflation of 8.23 per cent and new job creation at an average rate of 270 000 jobs each year.[4] Gear projections were seen to be too business-oriented by organised labour whose first priority was job creation. The labour movement as a whole saw the government as central to job creation and at least some members of the most powerful of the union movements, COSATU, wished to challenge the approach to development laid down by Gear, claiming that South Africa needed a fundamentally different growth and employment path. The three labour federations – COSATU, the Federation of South African Trade Unions (FEDUSA) and the National Council of Trade Unions (NACTU) – rejected any linkage between wages and employment and claimed that job creation strategy had to address the quality of jobs.

The Gear strategy was attacked in 1998, both for strangling job creation and for its inability to curb rising poverty, in a report prepared for the United Nations Development Programme by the National Institute for Economic Policy. The report – 'Poverty Elimination, Employment Creation and Sustainable Livelihoods in South Africa' – tackled the Reserve Bank's emphasis upon zero inflation which, it said, ignored the macroeconomic and social costs associated with the policy and argued that South Africa's monetary policy had remained unchanged since 1980 despite changes in government priorities since 1994. It argued that the Reserve Bank's high interest rates harmed investment, consumption and the government's debt repayments. Most damning, it claimed that Gear closely resembled an IMF structural adjustment programme because it gave priority to budget cuts, liberalisation, deregulation, privatisation and tight monetary policy. It added that the 'trickle-down theory of economic development' that underlay Gear was an inappropriate framework for South African economic transformation. Gear, it went on, ignored the important link between better income distribution and growth, and had not explored the development of the domestic market in achieving sustainable development because its emphasis was upon an export-oriented economy. Moreover, Gear envisaged a lesser role for the government and over-emphasized the private sector in the achievement of transformation in South Africa. Gear was too anxious to incorporate South Africa into the global financial, production and distribution markets. It also criticised the government's agricultural policy on the grounds that it was particularly damaging to small farmers.[5]

Such an attack upon the Gear strategy naturally provoked a defence, especially from cabinet ministers who claimed that it helped stave off a monetary crisis in May 1996 at a time when a rumour that there was something wrong with Mandela's knees could lead to trouble in the bond market. By the end of 1998 the Gear strategy was due for a major overhaul, however, as the ANC looked to the 1999 elections and sought both to stimulate growth and appease its alliance partners. As a result, any further moves towards either privatisation or the deregulation of the labour market were unlikely to be implemented. Nonetheless, an ANC official said the party had no intention of dumping Gear: 'We can say the overall framework in the GEAR strategy will remain. The principle that you cannot rely on borrowing to fund social investment remains sound.' In the course of this debate over Gear, Blade

Ndzimande, the secretary-general of the South African Communist Party (SACP), said the aim was to resolve differences within the alliance: 'It would be premature to say that GEAR has run its course, but the SACP and COSATU have said they are not happy with it and the president himself has said that no policy is cast in stone.'[6]

By October 1998 the government had to admit that its Gear policy was not meeting its targets and that South Africa would have to rely more on fiscal revenue than direct foreign investment for economic growth. South Africa had suffered the 'knock-on' effects of the Asian financial crisis which had led investors to withdraw their funds from emerging markets at a time when such investment was most needed in South Africa. The secretary-general of the ANC, Kgalema Mothlanthe, said the failure of Gear was forcing the government to make 'carefully considered adjustments' to its policy: 'The NEC (national executive committee) agreed that detailed work needed to be done to address these changed circumstances while retaining the coherence and strength of our policy.'[7] According to the economist Jac Laubscher the Gear policy had failed because unrealistic targets had been set while it had also suffered from non-implementation and lack of focus. The core of the policy had been based upon boosting gross domestic fixed investment which relied on business confidence, domestic savings and capital inflows. In other words, the Gear strategy had relied upon an orthodox approach to investment that was highly dependent upon international confidence which had not been forthcoming in the circumstances then affecting South Africa.

Another development instrument, the National Economic Development and Labour Council (NEDLAC), had by 1998 become increasingly important in setting national policy without, according to its supporters, engendering conflict. The NEDLAC Act which was passed in 1994 required NEDLAC to:

(a) strive to promote the goals of economic growth, participation in economic decisionmaking, and social equity;
(b) seek to reach consensus and conclude agreements on social and economic policy;
(c) consider all proposed labour legislation relating to labour market policy before it is introduced in parliament;
(d) consider all significant changes to social and economic policy before they are implemented or introduced in parliament;
(e) encourage and promote co-ordinated policy on social and economic matters.

At its third annual summit held at Midrand in May 1998 speakers in the plenary session agreed that NEDLAC had created an effective mechanism for participation and put in place a system that had created a high level of peace and stability and had had a positive impact on the core social and economic issues. Addressing the summit Tito Mboweni, the minister of labour, said:

> NEDLAC strives to promote economic growth, participation in economic decision-making, and social equity. While NEDLAC as an institution could not directly ensure higher rates of growth and economic development, we are convinced that by promoting social dialogue and consensus on many economic and social issues, this institution has contributed indirectly to the growing confidence in the South African economy.[8]

As another speaker pointed out finding solutions to such problems as the low level of savings, the high rates of crime and the need to restructure the labour market were the *raison d'être* for NEDLAC and as a forum NEDLAC clearly had a contribution to make even though it had no power.

By 1998, with an election looming for 1999, pressures mounted upon the government to explain, against a background of growing discontent, why the pace of 'transformation' was so slow. As Thabo Mbeki argued, reconciliation was impossible unless there was a redistribution of resources to correct the unfair distribution of resources that had taken place under apartheid. According to a Johannesburg businessman, Ian Mann, successful transformation depended upon a deep respect for people. He was addressing the subject of affirmative action and argued that if the attitude was that a business had to 'get this bloody affirmative action' on the road such an approach showed no real commitment to change; he also suggested that companies deliberately sabotaged the process by, for example, hiring a (black) person in an affirmative action position and then giving no support and waiting to see a mess occur. There must be support, he argued, for when people are put into an environment they perceive to be hostile they are likely to perform badly. As Mann also said:

> There is now legislation that people have to start transforming their organisations. So it's not a matter of whether you want to or don't want to, you have to do it. It's about time people stopped complaining about the Equity Bill and get on with the business of implementing it.[9]

Whatever mechanisms for development were used the government had to operate against the realities of a harsh international environment and respond to a variety of pressures not of its choosing. It had to come to terms with the increasing trend towards globalisation, arguments that privatisation is an essential prerequisite for attracting international capital and the constant complaints of international business that it could not or would not invest in South Africa just yet because government social policies or violence or the uncertain state of developing markets made such investment too risky. When, quite rightly, the government showed caution at accepting international aid it was accused of being awkward by donors whose primary concerns were their own political agendas rather than South Africa's development. In 1995, for example, the then finance minister, Chris Liebenberg, said that South Africa had a reputation for being difficult about foreign aid and explained: 'Donors often insist that aid is used to build something like a hospital or township but forget that the government is left to put in the infrastructure and maintenance which puts a tremendous strain on the Budget which is struggling to meet basic needs.' Such a cautious approach to aid made sense, especially when the huge indebtedness of half Africa can be seen as the direct result of accepting aid of this sort too readily and without understanding the long-term consequences.

Aid and debt go together. Public debts are one of the main challenges facing the economy and debt servicing by 1998 had become the second largest call on the budget amounting to R43.7 billion which was equivalent to 21 per cent of total expenditure and 6.2 per cent of GDP. That figure was expected to rise to R48 billion by 2000 although total debt at 55 per cent of GDP compared favourably with most other developing countries. The greatest part of the country's debt – 95 per cent – is domestic while foreign debt is modest. In general, the less South Africa borrows from international donors, whether on a bilateral country-to-country basis or from multilateral institutions such as the World Bank, the better its development prospects.

In 1998 the government clearly remained in two minds about privatisation. On the one hand, it claimed to be committed to what it called restructuring while at the same time considering creating new parastatals, including one for housing and a state oil company. As proponents of privatisation point out, the essence of the policy is the acknowledgement that a government should not be involved in running business enterprises. This may make sense in countries like the USA or Britain but does it also make sense for South Africa? Given the skewed economic legacy of apartheid and the urgent need for various forms of affirmative action, government has to intervene: the question is how much, when and where? As of mid-1998 state spending accounted for 13 per cent of the economy, parastatals such as Telkom and Eskom for a further 15 per cent and the private sector for 72 per cent. By September 1998 privatisation of state assets appeared to be speeding up despite growing opposition from organised labour with COSATU demonstrating against the planned privatisation of municipal services and demanding a moratorium on the sale of parastatals.

Meanwhile, under another kind of mechanism, the government had created eight spatial development initiatives or SDIs. These had been launched jointly in 1995 by the departments of transport and trade and industry and expected to attract to South Africa investments worth R60 billion. The SDI co-ordinator of the trade and industry department, Paul Jordan, said R30 billion of investment had already been secured by three SDIs. These were the Maputo development corridor which had attracted R20 billion worth of investment, the Fish River SDI and the Wild Coast corridor in the Eastern Cape. The Maputo corridor was the most attractive such development and included the upgrading of Maputo port and the railway link which would tie in the economies of South Africa and Mozambique more closely. The centre of the Fish River SDI would be a R2.5 billion zinc smelter by Gencor and a R1.5 billion port at Coega which would be surrounded by a 10 000 hectare industrial development zone. These and other industrial developments were going ahead, while arguably the most important development of all was the launch of the trans-Kalahari highway that would link Walvis Bay in Namibia through Botswana and South Africa to Maputo in Mozambique. These SDIs are a mixture of manufacturing-based public and private sector partnerships which aim to create jobs, boost exports and contribute to black empowerment while developing specific regions with a range of new enterprises and infrastructure. At this time all eight SDIs had been started on the coast. According to Alec Erwin, the trade and industry minister, the 'government's spatial development initiatives in the west coast region links to a series of projects with neighbouring southern African states.' The aim was to open up the entire southern African market which is rich in natural resources.[10] Black empowerment is the objective of all these policies.

One of the great ironies of post-1994 South Africa is the extent to which arguments are advanced which insist that business must be unfettered by state intervention, if it is to produce the wealth the country requires and work efficiently on behalf of South Africans as a whole. Such arguments were almost never heard during the apartheid years. Approximately 60 per cent of employed Afrikaners were employed by the state and, apart from the Soviet Union, South Africa was then the most over-bureaucratised state in the world. Parastatals abounded, exchange controls were operated and the government was prepared to interfere directly or indirectly in most aspects of business in order to ensure the continuing grip upon affairs of its white minority. Moreover, international business did not argue, as it has done since 1994, that it would be difficult or impossible to operate under such conditions. It invested in South Africa to take advantage of the apartheid laws which, by depressing wages, made such investments immensely profitable. The switch in business attitudes – from what it was prepared to accept under the apartheid system and is apparently not prepared to accept in the new South Africa – should act as a constant reminder to the government that business is actuated by only one code – profit. If it is profitable to invest in the new South Africa then companies will do so; otherwise they will stay away. And this will remain true whatever policies the government pursues.

Mohil Bandulal, an investment analyst in Frankel Pollak Vinerine, has argued that with black business aggressively on the acquisition trail all deals have a potential black empowerment aspect which means that 'Effectively the established listed companies are going to have to consistently source new markets and become far more dynamic and entrepreneurial in management styles and acquisition philosophies.' He also argued that 'Black business groups can look at businesses which they can acquire now and gain in-roads into strategic markets by filing anti-trust representations to the Department of Trade and Industry.' Such activities will certainly increase over the next few years and one strategy for white business will be to maintain as much of its market share in South Africa as it can manage, while also developing business in the rest of Africa or elsewhere in the world. As Bandulal also said: 'As far as they are concerned, big business is there to make money for itself and not to share it among the workers. That philosophy has to change. I think big business recognises this and is willing to make sacrifices.[11] Bandulal's belief that big business will change is probably more the projection of a wish than an estimate based upon evidence.

A study by the Black Management Forum which was launched in 1995 received wide acceptance from several sectors of South African industry. Its primary aim was to establish affirmative action practices and identify the most successful ones. At the time some 80 major companies agreed to take part in the survey. What appeared to be emerging at that stage was the fact that those sectors which responded most enthusiastically to black empowerment were service-oriented, suggesting that customer service and affirmative action could be closely linked. At the 31st annual conference of the National African Federated Chamber of Commerce (Nafcoc), held in July 1995 at Sun City, reference was made repeatedly to 1948 when the National Party came to power and set out to empower Afrikaner business so as to redress the balance as against the then dominant English-based business. It was suggested that now was the time for an ANC-led government to do the same thing for black business.

Cyril Ramaphosa, one of the most able South Africans of his generation who may well return to the political arena in the next century, made himself less than popular in 1997 with his comments upon what constituted black empowerment. He was then the chairman of the industrial holdings group Johnnic and the National Empowerment Consortium as well as deputy executive chairman of Nail. He suggested that it was not a question of equity ownership in such groups as New Africa Investments Ltd (Nail), Real Africa Investments or Johannesburg Consolidated Investments. As a result of the unbundling of some white conglomerates and new partnerships between white and black businesses, the number of black controlled companies on the Johannesburg Stock Exchange (JSE) rose in five years from five with a market capitalisation of R1.8 billion to 16 with a market capitalisation of R36 billion. He said:

> The real empowerment is taking place elsewhere. It is taking place not in the boardrooms of formerly white-owned conglomerates, nor in the large finance houses. Black empowerment is taking place on the streets of South Africa, in makeshift workshops in Soweto, or small accountancy firms in Mamelodi or in the kitchens in Mdantsane.

A counter view was advanced by Thami Mazwai, publisher and journalist, who argued that the mere existence of high-profile multi-billion rand 'black empowerment' ventures such as Nail had had a significant psychological effect: 'They changed the mindset of people. Now blacks know they can own major companies.' Both viewpoints have their own significance but underlying them is the growing gap between rich and poor which emphasizes the anger of the majority against the conspicuous wealth of the few. As Rams Ramasha, head of the Southern African NGO Coalition, argues:

> This growing gap between rich and poor is going to result in a class struggle which will no longer be defined in terms of race and colour

but in terms of the haves and the have-nots. I think that the poor may have no option but to wage another form of struggle. And, if they do, their struggle will be of the kind that no political rhetoric or military might will be able to quell.[12]

Black empowerment for the poor means getting a job.

How much black empowerment policies are gesture politics and how much they really represent a shift of economic power remains to be seen. Many businesses felt the need to be seen to adopt black empowerment policies in the years immediately after the 1994 elections; they are only likely to continue to do so in the future under substantial government pressure and this will depend upon the extent to which the policy remains at the top of the ANC agenda. The debate continued through 1998 but black empowerment gains also noticeably increased. In 1995 only 20 empowerment transactions were recorded; by 1998 the figure was 20 a month. In September 1995, 11 black-owned companies with a combined market capitalisation of R4.6 billion were listed on the JSE; by February 1998 the JSE had 28 black-owned companies listed with a market capitalisation of R66.7 billion.

In August 1998 a number of leading black businesspeople decided to launch a Black Economic Empowerment Commission, to be headed by Cyril Ramaphosa, to evaluate and plan empowerment initiatives. As the executive deputy chairman of Nail, Ramaphosa heads the largest black business group in the country which by then was one of the top 20 companies on the JSE. Of 68 black-influenced companies listed on the JSE in August 1998 a number had links to trade unions, including COSATU, the National Union of Metalworkers, the National Union of Mineworkers, the Clothing and Textile Workers Union and the Railways and Harbour Workers Union.

As with all the other moves to redress the balance from the apartheid past, black empowerment has a vital role to play in shaping the new South Africa; in the long run it will only make sense if those whom the process empowers demonstrate their capacity to perform as business leaders and, despite some early disasters and collapses, on the whole the omens at the end of 1998 appeared reasonably good.

7
Labour and Unemployment

At the present time in South African history the need to create jobs is more important than any other of the country's compelling needs. In August 1995 an ANC MP, Saki Macozoma chairman of the parliamentary standing committee on information and telecommunications, challenged the business community to help bring the 50 per cent of the population presently outside the market economy back into the formal sector. He said:

> In practical terms, this means job creation in all parts of the country, the rendering of service to all South Africans, the provision of educational facilities to all our people and enabling entrepreneurs to get the loan finance and advice they need to start their own business.[1]

At the same time the Reserve Bank's annual economic report warned that South Africa needed strong and sustained economic growth, a reduction in labour unrest and a more flexible labour market to counter growing unemployment. Business often argues for a flexible labour market; it does not explain how this reduces unemployment.

In 1996 the idea of a presidential jobs summit was floated and in 1997 Sipho Pityana, the director-general of the department of labour, argued sensibly that disagreements between labour and business on job creation should not be allowed to block progress: 'We must not be too ambitious about getting agreement on everything. ... We must agree on some policies and create space for further discussions.'[2] Arguments about job creation, understandably, became a permanent feature of public debate in the mid-1990s and all too easily such debates ignored or at any rate discounted factors over which South Africa had little control: the globalisation of the world economy, how safe would-be investors perceive the South African market to be, the knock-on effects of the Asian crisis and so on. Painfully South Africa had to learn that just as it had returned to the international fold in a political sense so it had also become a full member of a rapidly changing world economy at the very time when that economy was exceptionally volatile, so that even the leading economic players were often less than sure of the direction it was taking or the extent to which they could influence it.

Peter Fallon, the director of the World Bank's human development department, said in April 1998 that South Africa had to get both its macroeconomics and its social fundamentals right together if it was to tackle the unemployment crisis. He argued that public works programmes and market-based land reform were stop-gap measures and that

> Ultimately, employment growth has to come from sustained growth in South Africa's private sector. That growth has to be more labour-demanding than it has been in the past years; that is basically the bottom line and what people have to work towards.

With unemployment variously estimated at between 12.3 per cent and 29.8 per cent it was one of the most serious problems facing policymakers. Fallon argued that the labour market was further distorted by wage inequalities that were 'extremely severe by international standards, and a massive disparity in the incidence of unemployment by race' which was at the rate of 33.6 per cent among black men as opposed to 3.6 per cent among white men and that 'The differences in what we call the probabilities of being unemployed and in unemployment rates are extremely large in terms of current statistics such as race, gender and location by international standards.' He concluded by saying what everybody knows that there are no quick fixes.[3] On the other hand, what labour constantly asks is whether the fixes that are being applied are coming too slowly.

The World Trade Organisation (WTO) now entered the South African debate to argue that the South African import tariff regime contributed to unemployment by encouraging capital intensive industries rather than labour intensive ones. Responding to these arguments, Dr Zav Rustomjee, the director-general of the department of trade and industry, said such criticisms assumed that South Africa was a normal developing country that should focus all its attention on labour intensive industry when South Africa's industrial strategy was based on the fact that the country possessed certain strengths which other developing countries lacked.

Light was thrown upon the relationship between unemployment and informal sector earnings by the Central Statistical Service (CSS) in a survey of households in October 1997 which found that in the year 1994 to 1995 unemployment had fallen from 32.4 per cent to 29.3 per cent, indicating that the rate of unemployment in South Africa was still among the highest in the world. According to another survey by the South African Institute of Race Relations (SAIRR) 'At least 20 per cent of the people who claim to be unemployed were found to have various kinds of *ad hoc*, informal or casual employment, and stated they would not accept formal employment below R760 per month among Africans and coloured people and R1300 to R1400 per month among whites and Indians.'[4]

Yet another study threw doubts upon the accuracy of CSS statistics. This was conducted by Stephan Klasen, a research fellow at Cambridge, and Ingrid Woolard of the University of Port Elizabeth. In its 1996 country review the International Labour Organisation (ILO) commented upon the poor quality of South African statistics and methodology and identified a number of problems: undercounting in mining; the omission of small-scale agriculture and small self-employed manufacturers; underestimating employment in a number of sectors such as construction, trade, transport and finance, where the trend has been to employ contract workers; the omission of new firms from the sample; undercounting of rural employment; and undercounting of the informal sector.[5]

Deep-rooted mistrust between COSATU and the government over the latter's Gear strategy was exposed during the sixth national congress of the labour movement held during September 1997 and even those who had been prepared to give Gear a chance now became firmly opposed. Although President Mandela twice attempted to persuade COSATU to give Gear a chance he was openly snubbed by delegates who believed the strategy marked an ideological shift to the right by the African National Congress. The government however did not budge.

COSATU threw its weight behind a campaign spearheaded by non-government organisations and some of the churches to have debts incurred by the apartheid regime written off or restructured. The campaign based its arguments on a report by the Alternative Information and Development Centre (AIDC) *A Strategy for Challenging the Apartheid Debt* which argued that government debt accumulated before the democratic government took power in April 1994 should be cancelled. The argument was a familiar one used in relation to debt elsewhere in the Third World. Government debt, the argument ran, was a major obstacle to the country's growth prospects since debt at R311 billion equalled about 56 per cent of GDP and the cost of servicing it absorbed 21 per cent of the budget, the largest single expense after education. COSATU's main argument was that servicing this debt jeopardised the implementation of the RDP and other programmes designed to meet the needs of the poor. According to the South African National Non-governmental Coalition (Sangoco) writing off the debt would make available to government an additional R39 billion a year for people who had laboured so long under an oppressive regime. There was no possibility that the government would jeopardise its international relations by adopting any such policy.

COSATU agreed at this time to provide both financial and political support to the South African Communist Party (SACP) rather than see the emergence of an independent workers' party, an idea first advanced by the National Union of Metalworkers' of South Africa (NUMSA) in 1993. The plan was welcomed by the SACP while NUMSA's secretary-general Mbuyiselo Ngwenda said 'There is a specific goal for a transformation to socialism.' Other unions supported the initiative although both COSATU and the SACP were quick to point out that the move did not represent any ganging up on the ANC. The fact they felt obliged to make such a statement indicated the extent of the division that was developing.

It became increasingly plain during 1998 that differences between COSATU and the government were fundamental and increasing, even though rarely tackled openly since neither side wished to damage the alliance or the show of public unity. Growing opposition to Gear whose macroeconomic policies include a wide measure of privatisation was highlighted by the South African Municipal Workers Union (SAMWU) which launched a major anti-privatisation offensive in 1997, concentrating its pressures upon Nelspruit, the provincial capital of Mpumalanga, which put out to tender its water and sanitation services. Gear policy is based on the premise that redistribution can only be achieved through economic growth and that this requires the state to relinquish as much control of the economy as possible. This approach fits in with the wider economic orthodoxy of the West generally and understandably raises the hackles of organised labour in South Africa. The ironies are considerable. The West which did so little to bring an end to apartheid and made such large profits out of it is not seen as a friend of South African labour. Moreover, since through the apartheid years state controls or state enterprises were largely used to safeguard the jobs and livelihoods of the white minority why should they not continue to be used in the post-apartheid era to do the same for the black working majority?

During March 1998 COSATU circulated a discussion document outlining key components of an employment strategy which identified the public sector as a critical employer and engine of job creation, a view that went in the face of recent government statements that the state was not an employment agency. The document called for a demand-led growth strategy to create jobs. An employment strategy, the document argued, had to help eliminate poverty, inequality and unemployment. It had to examine the quality of jobs created and distribute economic resources to reduce poverty and inequality, and a broad job creation strategy would have to examine a range of policy areas including macroeconomic policies, investment and industrial policies, productivity, the role of the public service, state asset restructuring, public works programmes, a social wage, hours of work, a social plan and job security. COSATU denied that it intended to boycott the coming jobs summit.

Meanwhile, unions insisted that wages should keep pace with the level of inflation. As Nowethu Mpati speaking for COSATU said in April 1998

> First, COSATU is still running a living wage campaign. We have been fighting for a living wage since 1987 and we are still fighting. Second, we are fighting a campaign to close the wage gap between workers and managers. At our congress last year, delegates voted that we should continue both these campaigns. So we will go on fighting for good wage increases regardless of lower inflation.[6]

COSATU proposals for the jobs summit included a social wage package to be financed by higher income tax, a payroll tax or tax on monopoly profits, and massive state-sponsored infrastructure and public works programmes as a solution to the unemployment crisis. In essence COSATU was arguing that the government's macroeconomic policies had to go further than only satisfying investors and had to gain the support of the general public and organised labour. It also argued that the state should play a role in encouraging and directing investment so as to increase employment; unproductive or speculative investment as well as capital outflows should be limited. Criticism of the government's Gear policy continued in the months prior to the jobs summit with COSATU demanding an interventionist state policy as opposed to the Gear strategy which focused on high interest rates, preserving the value of the rand and defending foreign exchange reserves.

During 1998 the presidential jobs summit became the focus of attention for both sides of industry. As Tito Mboweni, the minister of labour, said in May:

> At the jobs summit in particular, employers, the trade union movement and government will meet to hammer into shape a common strategy to attack the problem of unemployment. This common strategy should be based on alignment of existing initiatives and introduction of new ones.[7]

At the end of the month Mboweni defended his forthcoming Employment Equity Bill which aimed to redress historical workplace inequities and avoid chaos in future race and industrial relations. The minister argued that there was widespread misinterpretation of the bill. As he said: 'There are all these inequalities in our society, most of them historical, that we have to address now if we are to avoid chaos in future.' The minister did not accept that the bill was a retrogression towards apartheid laws; he argued that 'Racial and other prejudices still prevail in many sectors of business. If we do not deal with this now, then these historical inequalities will linger with us for a long time.'[8]

By mid-1998 it was predicted that at least 67 000 workers from the formal sector would lose their jobs during the year. The Stellenbosch University economist Pieter Laubschert forecast that unemployment would continue to rise until the year 2000; the figure of 67 000 represented one per cent of total employment for 1998 nationwide. Already by May 1998 an estimated 15 000 miners had been made redundant. According to the University of Cape Town economist, Professor Brian Kantor, many companies were out-sourcing to small- and medium-size black enterprises while many employers had little flexibility. He said:

> The unwillingness of employers in the formal sector to provide employment has more to do with protection of the workers for which COSATU is responsible. Companies are not going to hire if they cannot fire workers who do not perform.

But a contrary view was expressed by the COSATU spokesperson Nowetu Mpati who said: 'We feel it is the attitude of business towards workers that is the major problem. They blame the lack of productivity on workers alone.' She added that the process of transformation was proving very difficult for business and said companies needed a vision that was also shared by workers.[9]

The employment trend through 1998 remained negative and in September 1998 the Unemployment Insurance Fund (UIF) asked the national treasury for an immediate bailout of R350 million as rising unemployment and retrenchment spurred by deteriorating economic conditions had led to a rapid depletion of its reserves. In September the UIF put in force new tougher rules for those claiming benefits, aimed at eliminating fraud, as pressures for assistance mounted. As the time for the Job Summit, scheduled for October, approached a number of undertakings aimed at arresting the country's growing unemployment were advanced. Business pledged R1 billion for job creation and the government budgeted R800 million for infrastructural development. Two weeks before the Job Summit was due to take place the South African Reserve Bank issued figures which showed that 100 000 jobs had been lost over the previous year while Statistics SA (the former Central Statistical Service) estimated that the economy had shed 500 000 jobs over four years.

Just prior to the presidential Job Summit Alec Erwin, the summit co-ordinator and minister of trade and industry, appealed to labour and business to use their organisations to double government efforts to create jobs: 'The real challenge for its success will be if there is a new concerted, collective effort that doubles government's resources, because everyone is pulling in the same direction.' Government estimates suggested that the economy had to generate 250 000 new jobs a year to keep the unemployment rate from rising and another 350 000 jobs a year to absorb new entrants into the labour market. The chances of meeting such requirements did not seem very encouraging against the background of rising unemployment worldwide. The ILO, for example, had just reported that another 10 million people had swelled the ranks of the unemployed as a result of the Asian economic crisis and its director-general Michel Hansenne, speaking at the launch of the ILO's annual *World Employment Report* had said 'The global employment situation is grim and getting grimmer.' According to ILO figures 150 million people world-wide were unemployed, of whom 60 million were aged between 15 and 24, while another 900 million were in part-time work but either wanted full-time employment or were not earning sufficient to live on. And worse, the ILO estimated that by the end of 1998 one billion people or a third of the world's labour force would be unemployed or underemployed, 170 million of them entirely without work.

The presidential Job Summit, it was hoped, would yield at least 35 initiatives worth between R2 billion and R3 billion to boost employment levels. In the wake of the global financial crisis South Africa was facing a further loss of jobs with attendant massive social consequences. Just prior to the summit the government admitted that the targets it had set out in its 1996 Gear strategy had not been met; these were a growth rate of 6 per cent and the creation of 400 000 jobs a year by 2000. Instead, growth was down to 1 per cent and unemployment was rising. Despite these disappointing results the government remained committed to its Gear strategy which included tight fiscal controls. One Summit initiative that seemed likely was to improve the lot of people struggling outside the formal sector by making the state's small business support organisations more effective and accessible to 'survivalist' business.

The summit produced a 94-page declaration signed by all parties although tensions between the rival groups – labour, government and business – were palpable. The deputy president Thabo Mbeki said

> The predominant feature reflected in the declaration is not dissonance but a united voice on the truly extensive programme of action on which we have agreed.... We have created a situation where we have pooled our different views.[10]

Yet, despite such emollient words deep divisions remained, especially over the issues of macroeconomic policy and labour market flexibility. As the president of COSATU, John Gomomo, said, it was not enough that the government was thinking of 'carefully considered adjustments' to the growth, employment and redistribution (Gear) strategy; rather, the framework and structure of Gear had to go. Labour had called for a basic income grant for the unemployed and a moratorium on retrenchments during the implementation of Summit projects to be launched in the country's poorest regions, but these requests were ignored. Business, on the other hand, demanded a legislative and regulatory environment that fostered growth. According to Dorian Wharton-Hood, the president of Business South Africa,

> Too many restrictions remain and insufficient attention is being paid to developing a culture of enterprise to allow both the new and established business to create wealth and employment.

As President Mandela summed up,

> The mass of South African people are perfectly correct in expecting a ray of hope from our deliberations and decisions. They know that

the summit will not produce miracles. But they do expect leadership on matters which are to millions, a matter of life and death.

Initiatives arising out of the Summit included: a Buy South Africa Campaign; strengthening customs and excise; a trade policy review; small business promotion; tourism marketing; and R2.56 billion earmarked for low cost housing. On the labour front there was a social plan to avoid job losses and a focus on special groups – youth brigades, women and the disabled; and special employment programmes. There were a number of regional and provincial projects. A range of other initiatives was also proposed. Like other such initiatives taken against grim economic conditions some will no doubt bear fruit, others will achieve little and be abandoned, others again will not take off at all. The Summit did not really even dent the opposed objectives of business and labour, while none of its initiatives could do more than scratch the surface of the formidable economic problems the country faces.

As the trade union movement discovered in the new South Africa which emerged from the April 1994 elections, it was one thing to fight alongside the ANC in its battle against apartheid, but something very different to expect to be at one with a subsequent ANC government that had to cope with many demands other than those of organised labour. As other African labour movements have found, most notably for example that created by Tom Mboya in pre-independence Kenya, once independence had been achieved they were more likely to be seen as threats to government strategies and power than as its natural allies. In post-apartheid South Africa the labour movement soon discovered, despite the tripartite alliance between the ANC, COSATU and the SACP, that a cosy relationship with the government was never a practical possibility. Already, by mid-1996 COSATU was spurning appeals by the ANC government and pressing ahead with strike action and Sam Shilowa, its general secretary, insisted that COSATU was opposed to constitutionally negotiated positions on the employers' right to lock out workers, and in June of that year thousands of workers marched and rallied throughout the country demanding that the new leadership should increase workers' rights.

There is always a conflict between labour and employers, just as there will always be a conflict between labour and the government, for each has its own agenda. In South Africa where labour suffered under the added disabilities and distortions of apartheid there is a special need to right the wrongs of the past, as well as creating a level playing field for the normal bargaining that the trade union movement exists to conduct. As Sam Shilowa the COSATU general secretary said in 1994 'Workers expect to see political democracy translate into economic democracy at the workplace. They don't just want to hold a ballot paper every five years.'[11]

The political battle to end apartheid may have been won; as COSATU and the other union movements saw things in 1994 and 1995 the labour battle for greater equality had only just begun. Labour unrest was bound to follow the sense of release that came in the wake of the April 1994 elections and the year that followed witnessed demands for wage increases and an end to on-the-job racial discrimination while frustration was apparent at the slow rate of change. As Sam Shilowa put it, 'In a country like South Africa, with obscene disparities, where workers have been denied their basic human rights, current developments are hardly surprising.' Another labour leader, Tom Phalama, secretary-general of the 8000 strong Banking, Insurance, Finance and Assurance Workers' Union, claimed that widespread discrimination remained in the financial sector against black employees many of whom earned only R800 a month. There was a substantial increase in labour unrest and strikes during 1995 (over 1994) much of it related to expectations for change that were not being met.

The labour movement which emerged in the new South Africa after the 1994 elections had its roots in the struggle against apartheid and that fact will colour its actions for years to come. It is not just a movement concerned with the rights of labour; it is also a movement concerned with bringing an end to racial discrimination in the workplace and in this regard it has a long way to go. COSATU is the largest labour federation with a membership in 1998 of 1.7 million, but it is not the only such umbrella organisation. The National Council of Trade Unions (NACTU) though much smaller with 18 affiliates and some 200 000 workers also rose to prominence as a militant anti-apartheid organisation. Unlike COSATU which is in the tripartite alliance with government and SACP, NACTU is not politically aligned, although as its secretary-general Cunningham Ngcukana says 'We will support policies of political parties which benefit workers.' The two groups discussed amalgamation but though NACTU did not see COSATU's membership of the Alliance as a stumbling block to an amalgamation the Federation of South African Unions (FEDUSA), with its more conservative background, did. FEDUSA in 1998 had a membership of 27 unions and 515 000 members.

Two labour bills – the Employment Equity and Skills Development bills – were passed by the cabinet in May 1998; they were described by the labour minister Tito Mboweni as victories for the millions of workers still struggling to overcome the unjust employment practices that had been inherited from the past. The low level of skills of African workers, a major inheritance from the apartheid era, was the target of the Skills Development Bill under which it was proposed that 20 per cent of levies raised from industry should be channelled into a national training fund that would also be supported by government. The European Union made a grant of R250 million to the fund although the levies were only due to be collected in 2000. Many in the labour movement object to what they see as the government's slavish acceptance of globalisation and the rapid tariff reduction programme advanced by WTO. However, Alec Erwin, the trade and industry minister, argued that government industrial policies had not led to a growth of unemployment. Erwin, a former trade unionist, said:

> We have the worst poverty in South Africa and that is in wage employment, suggesting that there is something seriously wrong with the lower wage levels paid in certain sectors. What we are looking for in the labour market is a well streamlined process where business and labour can resolve the problems themselves while government facilitates. This is designed to create labour stability.[12]

In August 1998 the government announced it would spend R150 million over the next five years to enforce the new employment equity law. A study which had been commissioned by the Department of Labour showed that only 29 per cent of 455 businesses surveyed had established employment equity policies and that only 20 per cent had established equity goals and timetables. The study also revealed that most organisations had only implemented formal policies and that progress, at best, had been inadequate. The Equity Bill was passed by Parliament despite objections from the Democratic and National parties; it would compel businesses employing 50 or more people with an annual turnover of more than R10 million to submit within 18 months their plans for employment equity: how they would remove discrimination and ensure the creation of a more diverse and representative labour force.

It was clear that achieving employment equity would take a long time and face formidable hurdles and much opposition. The study of 455 organisations with 173 828 employees demonstrated just how difficult achieving employment equity was likely to prove. Although 6000 organisations were approached only 455 responded and of these only 430 provided detailed analyses of employee conditions according to groups and occupational categories. The survey suggested that affirmative action was stalling. At the date of the survey only 11 per cent of senior management was black and a further 25 per cent were in junior or middle management positions, while white men and women still made up 73 per cent of all professional workers and African men and women accounted for 87 per cent of all labourers. Large corporate employers, many of which had been involved in affirmative action, nonetheless appeared to have made little progress. As Labour Minister Shepherd Mdladlana said of these findings: 'When South African employers are judged against the backdrop of international best practice, our situation can only be described as abysmal.'[13]

8
Crime and Violence

Since 1994 under the terms of its new constitution South Africa has abolished the death penalty; many people, both black and white, who have suffered through the country's violence and the soaring rates of crime would like to see the death penalty restored. Apartheid bred violence and during the apartheid years the statistics for physical punishments, whether capital or corporal, were grim. In February 1995 the country's new constitutional court began a debate on whether or not to abolish the death penalty and Justice Albie Sachs said the debate represented the beginning of an era in which laws and justice were allies. The 11 judges of the court who had been at the forefront of the anti-apartheid campaign considered capital punishment to be an unwelcome legacy of the old regime; they also had to take into consideration the emotive demands of groups who supported the death penalty. Prior to the 1994 elections violence could always be ascribed to apartheid or the political turmoil that had been released, especially in KwaZulu-Natal, in the period following the unbanning of African political parties in February 1990; after the elections violence did not have the same excuses. And though ANC–Inkatha violence continued in KwaZulu-Natal, elsewhere political violence had all but disappeared with the result that non-political violence was much more obviously apparent.

Estimates for the second half of 1994 suggested that a serious crime was being committed every 17 seconds, a murder every half-hour, a housebreaking every two minutes. Moreover, a new factor had entered the crime scenario with the appearance in South Africa of big crime syndicates often with international links. White reactions to the growing crime wave were predictable and in Sandton, Johannesburg's richest white suburb, residents established a 'Citizens Countering Crime' group and provided the money for a police precinct and mounted police unit.

Much crime is attributed to the huge unemployment figures and lack of opportunities, but that is only part of the problem. A culture of violence grew up in South Africa during the apartheid era and especially after the Soweto uprising of 1976 when young people turned away from education to fight apartheid instead. As Johannesburg's deputy police commissioner, Brigadier Jac de Vries, said in May 1995 'Carjacking is a profession for many of these people.' De Vries was then in charge of Operation Safety which covered five of the worst affected neighbourhoods with helicopter overflights and increased police controls.

An article in the South African *Sunday Independent* of July 1995 began as follows:

> Like the nobles of feudal Europe, white South Africans are retreating behind fortifications. In the leafy avenues in Johannesburg's richer suburbs, defensive walls around the houses are climbing upwards, usually topped off with what South Africans call siege architecture: crenellations, electric fencing or just plain razor wire.[1]

Prior to the 1994 elections a majority of whites saw violent crime as a black political problem largely confined to the townships, but since that time they have seen the pattern alter radically and even the most fearful whites admit that the gap between themselves and the poor black majority is vast, greater in fact than in most other countries in the world so that, racial antagonisms apart, whites represent natural targets for criminals. However, underlying economic disparities and the legacy of apartheid there is another legacy. Lloyd Vogelman, director of a centre studying crime at the University of Witwatersrand, argues that 'There is a moral sanctioning of violence. [In the apartheid era] The government used it for repression, the liberation movements used it as a means of liberation.' As a result a generation was raised which regarded defiance of the law as a badge of respect.[2]

Other factors also contributed to a growth of crime. The end of the civil war in Mozambique meant the release of large quantities of weapons, many of which have found their way into South Africa and in Soweto, for example, guns can be rented by the hour, while more open borders have given an impetus to drug smuggling. Johannesburg has developed into both an internal drug market and a transit point for cocaine and heroin from Central America *en route* for other parts of Africa or Europe. The Government announced in July 1995 that it had knowledge of 1155 organized drug syndicates and another 278 syndicates concerned with other forms of crime.

Endless argument about violence and crime rates, and a constant stream of new statistics became a feature of political debates in the new post-1994 South Africa. Whites spoke fearfully of the escalating risks they faced; the ANC, at first, dismissed talk of violence as a legacy of apartheid while business people and foreigners spoke of confidence and the need to reduce crime so as to attract foreign investment.

Opening the annual congress of the Democratic Party in August 1995, Tony Leon said that unless South African streets were reclaimed from the criminals who had seized them the country did not have a future. Over the top, perhaps, but he expressed a viewpoint that was enthusiastically received by his audience. The Democratic Party leader claimed that over the preceding ten years 140 000 South Africans had been murdered, which was a greater number than those killed by the Hiroshima atomic bomb and three times the total number of American casualties in the Vietnam war. He made the point that in a year in which President Mandela had allowed the release of 15 000 criminals from prison 789 000 violent crimes had been committed against South Africans.

Government figures released at the end of 1995 revealed that a serious crime was committed every 17 seconds, more than 50 people were murdered every day and a robbery occurred every six minutes, earning South Africa the unenviable reputation of being the most dangerous place in the world outside a war zone. The Police Commissioner, George Fivaz, warned that violent crime was threatening the country's democracy:

It is not an understatement to say that crime has reached such pro-portions that it is becoming a grave threat to democracy. If not dealt with more efficiently, our people will become disillusioned with the fundamental rights which underpin South Africa's miracle democ-racy … resulting in mob justice, hysteria and unleashing an even greater cycle of violence.[3]

New figures released in January 1996 by the Police Service's National Crime Information Management Centre revealed that in the first seven months of 1995 10 000 people were murdered and 1 126 101 serious crimes were reported across the country (excluding the former home-lands). These included 46 752 armed robberies, 55 890 car thefts, 18 684 rapes, 96 391 aggravated assaults, 90 410 common assaults and 10 161 murders which averaged out at one in every 29 minutes. In 1995 the World Health Organisation named South Africa as the world's murder capital. Despite the prominence given to white fears of crime and violence blacks are significantly more affected by crimes than are whites. Perhaps this relates to the fact that an estimated average of 15 per cent of disposable income is spent on security measures and most of that would be white rather than black expenditure. Violence is given as a principal reason for white emigration from South Africa.

The rate of crime will not be reduced as long as it pays, and the evidence suggests that it does pay and pay well, for the simple reason that a majority of offenders escape capture. The police reckon that they only solve a quarter of all reported robberies, only 15 per cent of car thefts and only 19 per cent of house burglaries. But it is worse than this because a large number of those arrested in the end walk free, because of poorly prepared cases, weak or incompetent prosecution and a grossly overworked court system. Such failures lead us back again to the legacy of the apartheid years when the police were trained first and foremost to maintain state security – which meant security for the white minority – and in the process paid little attention to proper or just procedures. And this police culture was matched by a liberation culture of making the country ungovernable. The one culture fed on the other and the result for the new rainbow society has been an unprecedented level of crimes and violence, which will only be reduced when the police have been retrained and have also become more efficient and more trusted by the black population. In the meantime both whites and blacks are moving towards vigilante tactics to protect themselves and their communities.

In such circumstances it was inevitable that crime and racism should become intertwined and the term crime used by whites all too often means blacks. In response to such attitudes the ANC and blacks generally excuse crime and violence – or at least a substantial proportion of it – on the grounds that the townships lack recreational facilities, that young people do not have jobs or opportunities for jobs and so turn to crime as an escape from both poverty and boredom. Thus, crime becomes an expression of economic, social, political and racial ills. There may be a great deal of truth in such claims and levels of crime will only be seriously reduced when major economic improvements work their way through the system as a whole, but in the meantime South Africa is acting as a magnet for organised crime from outside the country. Nigerians appear to have taken control of the drug trade in downtown Johannesburg and early in 1996 the police estimated that about 500 criminal networks were operating through Johannesburg dealing in cocaine, heroin, mandrax, diamonds and ivory. South Africa is an attractive destination for international criminals: its financial infrastructure is sufficiently large and varied to allow easy money-laundering; its borders are extensive and inadequately controlled and large numbers of illegal immigrants are coming into the country. Moreover, there are a wide range of international airflights from South Africa to destinations in the Americas, Europe and the Far East. A high proportion of the contraband that passes through Johannesburg is not destined for the South African market but is in transit for Europe or the United States and, according to the United Nations, Lagos crime groups are at the heart of the new international criminal activities.

Carjacking has become the most blatant and apparently profitable crime in South Africa and in an effort to combat it the government has introduced a high-tech satellite tracking system to disable and recover stolen cars. Increasingly, carjackers and armed gangs force drivers to hand over a still running car, sometimes shoot them or take them with them in case the car engine cuts out after a short distance. In mid-1996 units from the army and air force were brought into Johannesburg to spearhead a drive on crime. It was yet another of the many ironies that the country constantly produces, that two of the men leading this Operation Anvil were former leaders of South African interventions in Angola. Colonel Buks Pietersee had been second in command of the notorious 32 Battalion which earned an evil reputation for its part in the Angolan civil war while Colonel Theunis du Toit had headed the South African air operations in Angola; now they were deployed to fight crime in Johannesburg. For many South Africans the military are seen as less objectionable than the police who were always regarded as the spearhead of the apartheid state.

In May 1997 a civilian, Meyer Kahn, became the head of the police force at a time when it was deeply demoralised and corrupt and losing personnel precisely when it urgently needed new recruits. He took on the job when public concern with crime was sometimes close to hysterical and seemed to rate it above most other of the country's many problems. What was needed was a transformation of the police. In 1996 73 policemen were killed on duty, another 211 after hours and a further 160 committed suicide; many police officers simply wanted to leave the force and some police stations were unable to function for lack of officers. Admitting that a crisis of lawlessness threatened the country's democracy and economy the Deputy President, Thabo Mbeki, caused controversy by claiming that a key factor in the crisis was sabotage by former and current security force members who remained loyal to the old apartheid government, and that some were reviving the 'Third Force' activities they had used against the ANC to destabilise the new South Africa. At the same time the safety and security minister Sydney Mufamadi claimed that international crime syndicates had infiltrated government departments and were being aided by disloyal officials. He compared South Africa to Russia after the collapse of the Soviet Union and communism and said the country was being targeted by crime rings from Nigeria, Yugoslavia, Russia and China. Mr Mufamadi also suggested that intelligence networks set up under the old government might be operating as crime organisations. Although much of this might have been true a National Party MP, Andrew Fourie, pointed out that 'The ANC conveniently forgets that organised bank robberies formed part of the fund-raising efforts by the liberation movements.' However much truth lay in such accusations against the past the problem lay in the present.

A number of daring hold-ups in which security guards were shot dead took place during January 1998 and set the tone for the year, finally forcing the government to admit that former ANC guerrillas were behind the attacks; Sydney Mufamadi then warned former cadres that the government had 'no sentimental attachment' to them and that they would be hunted down. Problems in the police services were duplicated in the prisons which were overcrowded and unable to carry out any sensible programmes of re-education. In May foreign diplomats presented an urgent appeal to the Foreign Affairs Department to improve security arrangements following several attacks on diplomatic personnel. In Parliament Sydney Mufamadi gave figures for prosecutions and convictions for 1997: of 24 684 murder cases reported, 11 352 were prosecuted and 3609 convictions (14 per cent) were obtained, while in the case of hijackings the police had won convictions in only 205 (1.6 per cent) of 12 895 cases reported. Then, of 52 110 rape and attempted murder cases reported, 22 255 were prosecuted to obtain 3532 (6.7 per cent) convictions. Of 243 639 reported burglaries from residential properties, only only 30 548 resulted in prosecutions and only 10 845 (4.4 per cent) of these resulted in convictions. And finally, of 86 454 burglaries from business premises only 12 885 came to court and only 4865 (5.6 per cent) resulted in convictions. Such figures made gloomy reading for both government and public.[4]

Through four years of argument and debate about the levels of crime in the country and the ability or failure of the police to cope with them what emerged again and again was a distrust of the police who were seen as not only corrupt but unchanged from the apartheid era. Apologists for the government who attempted to explain away the rising crime rates might argue that the police remained imbued with the attitudes of the apartheid era when they were trained to safeguard the white minority and repress opposition rather than fight crime – and might be correct to do so – but to do so did not solve the problem. As the new police chief, George Fivaz, said at the beginning of 1995 when he took on the job 'The police service must make a clean break with the past.' And as President Mandela said in Durban in mid-1995, emphasizing the distorted way in which the police had been used during the apartheid years:

> Were you aware that in this country, where whites only constitute 14 per cent of the population, 82 per cent of the police were deployed in white areas and only 18 per cent in the rest of the country? Were you aware that most vehicles of the police were concentrated in white areas and in black areas only a few vehicles?[5]

In August 1995 the South African Police Service announced a new form of police training 'in tune with the changes within the country'. The head of the police human resources division, Neels Steenkamp, said officers would be the product of a new community oriented police training programme: 'The distinguishing features of this training are, among others, a culture of human rights, community relations, accountability and transparency' and trainees would have to complete 22 weeks theoretical as well as 22 weeks practical education. At the time some 1700 trainees had been deployed at training stations throughout the country. It is likely to be a long time before the police have been fully transformed into a force whose ability to fight crime and maintain law and order is in accord with the new South Africa.

Meanwhile, Johannesburg has earned an unenviable reputation for violence. At one end of the scale is the black-on-black violence to be found in the huge African town of Soweto which was long regarded by the apartheid regime as a ghetto which could be sealed off and controlled by the police and military. At the other end of the violence scale are the northern suburbs of Johannesburg where the rich or well-to-do whites live. Here, the quiet residential streets are guarded by high walls and other devices, and very few houses do not have signs warning of 24 hour patrols, bearing the names of security companies on call and depicting a dog's head (of the Rottweiler variety) or a hand holding a gun. Such security conscious houses are still regularly robbed. One of South Africa's largest and fastest growing 'armed response' security companies, Paramed, is ready through every twenty-four hours to respond to the panic button and scarcely a home does not have some kind of 'Immediate Armed Response' warning. Johannesburg most obviously displays the huge gap that exists in what are becoming two-ghetto cities – one ghetto for the rich that sports every kind of security device and another for the poor which does not – and this huge disparity provokes the general problem of mounting crime. Meanwhile, protecting the well-being of the 'haves' who remain overwhelmingly white, has become a major new business estimated at more than 13 billion a year.

Two events early in 1999 again drew attention to the fragility of law and order in South Africa. In January President Mandela was obliged to cancel a trip to Uganda following a political assassination and massacre in KwaZulu-Natal Province. Sifiso Nkabinde, the leader of the United Democratic Movement (UDM), was shot dead in Richmond and shortly afterwards in what appeared to be a revenge massacre 11 people were killed and eight wounded in attacks upon members of the ANC. Then in early February the head of the South Korean Daewoo car giant, Yong Koo Kwon, was shot dead in a Johannesburg suburb; as a spokes-person for the South Korean Embassy said subsequently: 'We are worried about the crime situation in South Africa. This murder can affect the business community.' Quite apart from the impact at home, violence on the scale that occurs in South Africa with such monotonous frequency does great damage to the image the country is trying to project on the international scene.

9
The Economy

The South African economy is one of the most widely developed and sophisticated in the Third World and in the long run it should more than meet the needs of its people. Immediately, however, its growth is likely to be inhibited by a range of problems arising out of the political choices and priorities which will be made in the post-apartheid era until a balance between economic objectives and political imperatives has been achieved.

Agriculture contributes under five per cent to GDP, yet South Africa is both self-sufficient in food and a substantial food exporter as well, although in drought years it faces shortfalls in maize, the principal staple. Meat, fruit, wines and fish are all exported and agricultural products together account for just under eight per cent of exports. The country has long been a storehouse of minerals with gold, diamonds, the platinum group and coal dominating the sector and of 26 leading minerals South Africa is a leading producer of 14 (chromite, copper, gold, iron ore, crude steel, lead, manganese, nickel, silver, uranium, diamonds, phosphate rock, elemental sulphur and coal). It is in the top ten world producers for nine of these minerals and in the top 20 for the remainder. Minerals account for slightly under eight per cent of GDP and about 55 per cent of all exports. Manufacturing contributes approximately 25 per cent of GDP and, with Egypt, South Africa has the most advanced manufacturing sector on the continent. Finally, the infrastructure – roads, railways, ports, air transport – is well developed and South Africa has the best overall telecommunications system in Africa while its main cities – Johannesburg, Cape Town and Durban – are geared for international business.

Addressing the ANC conference at the end of 1994 Thabo Mbeki detailed the problems the government had to tackle: corruption, unemployment at 40 per cent, seven million people without proper housing and an economic growth rate that was slower than the rise in population. Only efficient government spending and management, a disciplined labour force and a stable investment climate would promote the growth needed to uplift the poor, he said on that occasion. The debate has been going on ever since. During 1995 when South Africa was the recipient of much international good will, only rarely was this translated into actual investment in the economy. In general, the international business community and especially that of the West adopted a wait and see attitude: would the Reconstruction and Development Programme (RDP) work; would disappointment at the slow rate of meeting popular expectations lead to political unrest; would continuing white control of the greater part of the economy perpetuate racial suspicions and divisions; what would happen after Mandela passed from the political scene? The RDP enumerated accurately enough many of the country's economic shortcomings: repressive labour practices, neglect of training, isolation from the world economy, low investment in research and development, outflows of capital and talent, low exports and high imports.[1] One obvious indicator of change was the rapid increase in airlines operating to South Africa and the forecast of a 50 per cent rise in passenger traffic over five years. On the other hand, South Africa found out just how vulnerable its market was to events outside its control; the Mexican market collapse and two years later the Asian crisis both drove home the lesson that South Africa was seen from outside as a fragile Third World economy which had to be approached with care.

When the finance minister, Chris Liebenberg, introduced the budget in March 1995, the emphasis was upon attracting foreign investment. A spokesperson for Sanlam, one of South Africa's biggest financial institutions, said: 'Sanlam feels very positive about it. The budget seems aimed at growing the economy. This budget is very foreign-investment friendly.' Foreign investors would benefit from the abolition of the non-resident shareholders' tax while a substantial proportion of the budget deficit was to be financed by foreign loans. A spurt of confidence followed this budget and Britain, which is South Africa's biggest investor, planned to spend half its export promotion budget for 1995 on encouraging trade with South Africa. Businessleaders applauded the budget for the emphasis it gave to fiscal stability but Chris Liebenberg warned:

> This is but the beginning of a long and arduous road and we cannot afford the luxury of complacency. People out there are rooting for us

to succeed. Internationally, they look to us as an example – we owe it to Africa and specifically our region. We cannot afford to fail them.[2]

In response to the new optimism the American investment company, The Calvert Group – which had been one of the first US companies to pull out of South Africa in the troubled 1980s – announced its return to the Republic to invest in firms listed on the Johannesburg Stock Exchange or in multinational companies that do business in Africa. Calvert's New Africa Fund was the first open-ended fund to invest in South Africa since the election of Nelson Mandela as president a year earlier. The Calvert decision was taken as a sign of a slow but steady return of American investment to South Africa.

A worker management conference held in Durban during August 1995 considered the role of the special cabinet committee appointed to deal with economic matters. COSATU warned against a 'neo-liberalist policy'; Sam Shilowa, the COSATU general-secretary, said that while the movement supported the cabinet committee as a possible vehicle for economic reform business should not seek to steer the committee towards 'failed' economic policies. He said COSATU was weary of policies which favoured 'short-term growth spurts' at the expense of long-term socio-economic upliftment and argued that there should be a radical departure from policies of the kind pursued in the 1960s when South Africa enjoyed rapid economic growth but did not secure sustained growth. He pointed out that 'The number of investors investing internally are a drop in the ocean compared to those taking money out.' Further, he argued, business should not behave as though South Africa could be internationally competitive 'with just about anything under the sun' but should aim at niche markets. If it was to compete on the international market business would have to change its business practices fundamentally.[3]

In a well-reasoned appraisal of economic problems the South African *Business Report* of August 1995[4] argued that while over the preceding 20 years the world business community had changed out of recognition, with the adoption of information-age technology at the same time that foreign exchange controls and trade barriers were being dismantled so as to globalise the world economy, South Africa had proceeded in a disastrously wrong direction. In its determination to uphold the apartheid system which in the end proved unworkable, it had spent billions on ultimately artificial political solutions such as the unviable Homelands and had done so without any semblance of fiscal or monetary discipline. In the ten years 1981 to 1991 employment in the formal private sector had decreased by one per cent while over the same period the public service had increased from 1 377 000 to 1 610 000, while of 3 327 000 people who reached an economically viable age over these years only 186 000 found work in the formal sector. As in the old communist countries South Africa had created an artificial economy. It argued that

> Governments and union leaders will soon have to realise that it is only in establishing the right climate for the private-sector risk takers that we can hope to have sufficient economic growth. Investors demand a well-schooled, disciplined, productive labour force.

Early in 1998 South Africa was adjusting to the Asian economic crisis which had sent shockwaves through the world system. The South African equity market, for example, suffered an initial decline of 22 per cent in dollars but then recovered to the equivalent of a 15 per cent loss with the Johannesburg Stock Exchange (JSE) showing greater resilience than other emerging stock markets. Two years earlier, in 1996, the currency collapsed following a tightening of monetary and fiscal policy. As the Asian crisis took hold the South African stock market with a capitalisation of US$245 billion moved to the top of the investible indices for emerging markets. In part this reflected the country's relatively favourable external debt position. At the end of 1996, for example, the debt-servicing to export–earnings ratio for South Africa was 6.8 per cent as opposed to 17 per cent for all developing countries while the figure for South Asia at that time was 24.6 per cent and for Latin America 26.1 per cent. Total foreign debt amounted to 26 per cent of GDP and 96 per cent of export earnings at the end of 1996 while the average total debt–export ratio of all developing countries was 151.6 per cent; for South Asia 218.7 per cent and for Latin America 212.3 per cent.[5]

Understandably, much concern often tinged with apprehension on the part of business, has been voiced at the process of black empowerment. Speaking at a *Société Générale* investment conference in February 1998 Cyril Ramaphosa, the chairman of Johnnic, tried to put the process into perspective. The huge political changes the country has undergone in the 1990s were bound to be accompanied by equally unsettling economic ones, as well with the idea of black empowerment being a firm part of the total agenda. As Ramaphosa argued:

> Contrary to conventional wisdom, the political transition does not provide us with the motivation to pursue black economic empowerment. The motivation was always there. Instead it provides the

opportunity. And the opportunity is being exploited. Four years ago black people owned and controlled only 0.3 per cent of the market capitalisation of the stock exchange; they now control and own 10.3 per cent.[6]

Later, he said that

black economic empowerment is still in its infancy and perceptions about the capacity of black business people are not always flattering. As black South Africans enter the economy as owners in greater numbers, there is a need to demonstrate that they are bringing more than the colour of their skins to the economy.

The deployment of black skills would best be achieved through corporate restructuring. Most important, restructuring should be done, not for reasons of political expedience but because 'the economy stands to benefit from the development of black business as part of a broader process of black economic empowerment.'

At the end of 1998, as South Africa approached closer to the 1999 elections, so economic arguments about priorities became more overtly political while growth figures were severely affected by a return of emerging market jitters. Economists downgraded forecasts for 1999 GDP growth with 1.5 per cent being an optimistic figure. Most depressing was the fact that even in a growing economy South Africa had failed to generate anywhere near the number of new jobs required to address unemployment while another depressing factor was the extremely low level of domestic savings which had declined from 18 per cent of GDP in early 1993 to 13 per cent at the end of 1998.

Both government and the private sector put emphasis during this period upon encouragement to small- and medium-sized business growth. According to Nicky Oppenheimer, the deputy chairman of Anglo American, links between small and big business needed to be developed to create a dual economic structure while Trevor Manuel, the minister of trade and industry, told the 31st NAFCOC annual conference: 'Our mission to create an environment to support small and medium business can never be about the creation of five or six black billionaires.'[7] He went on to say that legislation would remove barriers and punish the anti-competitive behaviour which still dominated the South African economy to maintain the exclusive position of the old business establishment.

The government was then in the process of creating a small and medium business agency. At the same conference Thabo Mbeki argued that government would sometimes have to play an interventionist role to promote the economic empowerment of disadvantaged communities, though without displacing individual initiatives: 'Throughout the world, the small-enterprise sector is playing a critical role in absorbing labour, penetrating new markets and expanding the economy in creative and innovative ways.' People from both extremes of the business spectrum constantly reverted to the same themes: the need to develop human resources; the implementation of modern management techniques; the formation of alliances with foreign countries; the acceleration of black economic empowerment; the creation of a stable labour environment; and the combating of crime.

A different problem facing the government in the mid-1990s concerned the major South African conglomerates. During the apartheid era leading companies such as Anglo American, Rembrandt, Liberty Life, South African Breweries, Old Mutual and Sanlam were forced by exchange control regulations to plough their profits back into South Africa; they did so by acquiring other companies, which in a more open system they would have ignored, to become sprawling conglomerates. During the 1980s when many international firms pulled out of South Africa these conglomerates were able to purchase bargains, which they did in large numbers. The result of this process was a growing antagonism on their part to competition, for the country had over many years become used to the operation of cartels. What Trevor Manuel highlighted in 1995 was the need to encourage the unbundling of these conglomerates without overtly attempting to break them up since this would send out the wrong signals to the international business community.[8]

A surprise for South Africa came in early 1998 when a survey of 23 African nations by the World Economic Forum and Harvard University ranked the country as the seventh most competitive after Mauritius, Tunisia, Botswana, Namibia, Morocco and Egypt although its businessleaders were seen as the least optimistic. South Africans, the Forum found, expressed 'tremendous concern over crime and the instability associated with the transition to democratic rule.' South Africa ranked bottom of the list for personal security, organised and petty crime. Where South Africa scored in the rating was for infrastructure, telecommunications, financial services, commercial law and the availability of capital. There was considerable evidence to suggest that flows of foreign direct investment had moved to South Africa from countries which had been more favoured when the apartheid system was in place. Where South Africa should be most concerned was over the poor supply of properly trained workers and in the failure of the secondary school system to produce people with rigorous training in languages, maths and science.[9] However, three months after this report a global survey by accountants Ernst and Young showed that South Africa had the second highest rate of fraud in the world, after the United States.

Many of these problems which were debated *ad nauseum* during the years 1994–98 were an understandable aspect of the search for a working and workable new South Africa. What still needed to be achieved and, arguably, will not be resolved until after the Mbeki government gets into its stride is a sense of business ease. There will always be conflict between business and labour, the big and the small, and that is to be expected. What is also needed is the sense that whatever the differences everyone is working towards the same end and given the long shadow of the apartheid years, that sense has as yet, perhaps, only been partially achieved.

10
Catching Up

In 1995 there were more telephones in Manhattan than in the whole of sub-Saharan Africa and a majority of Africans had never made a telephone call. Such statistics illustrate both the problems and the opportunities South Africa faces. We now live in an 'information age' and the capacity to progress and develop adequately depend more and more upon the mastery of information technology. Speaking at the opening of the four-yearly International Telecommunications Union (ITU) conference in Geneva in 1995 President Mandela said:

> One gulf will not be easily bridged – that is the division between information-rich and information-poor. Justice and equity demand that we find ways of overcoming it. If more than half the world is denied access to the means of communication, the people of developing countries will not be fully part of the modern world. In the 21st century, the capacity to communicate will almost certainly be a fundamental human right.
>
> Eliminating the distinction between information-rich and information-poor countries is also critical to eliminating economic and other inequalities between North and South, and to improving the quality of life of all humanity.[1]

In a world where the gap in communications access and technology is actually widening between rich and poor South Africa, which in technological terms lies halfway between the two, has immense possibilities for rapid technology improvements for itself while also being in a position to become a principal source of such telecommunications advances in the rest of Africa. A country that does not have a proper command of modern telecommunications will find it also lacks access to the rapidly developing information markets upon which, increasingly, world business depends.

South Africa's ports began to feel the strain in the mid-1990s, as a rapid increase in trade put pressure upon a system that was both old-fashioned and inadequate. Cargo passing through Cape Town was growing at such a rate that the port required major expansion to cope not only with the country's own growth in imports and exports but also with the fact that Cape Town has developed into a transit port for cargo bound for West Africa and South America. Many of the port's facilities still reflect the past age of steamers; now it must handle a different class of ship and the exploding container business. Tankers carrying crude oil come into the port and for such potentially hazardous cargoes the port authorities are examining the practicality of an off-shore buoy system and a pipeline to bring oil ashore. In addition, the port has to create specialised terminals to handle different cargoes. The total container traffic in and out of South Africa grew by 20 per cent during 1994/95 over the figures for 1993/94 and by more than 30 per cent the year before that while comparable figures occurred for 1995/96.

The statistics of growth in trade were encouraging but increasing port congestion pointed to the urgent need for both expansion and modernisation of handling capacity. As Albert Schuitmaker of the Cape Town Chamber of Commerce pinpointed the problem: 'very strong signals' had been received from customers abroad that unless South Africa was predictable in its delivery, custom would be redirected elsewhere.[2] Ports were just managing to cope, but without massive investment in modernisation, would soon fall behind. Pressure upon the ports signalled a welcome growth in South Africa's trade and economic expansion yet should the expansion outstrip the ability of the ports to handle the trade then development could be stymied, just as it made a real impact upon the country's many problems. The dilemma was emphasized in May 1998 when foreign buyers of raw materials threatened to go elsewhere because of port delays and inefficiencies at Durban, with customers from the Far East complaining they could no longer rely upon Durban for turnround efficiency. As a result they were threatening to pull out and purchase their raw material requirements elsewhere.

But if there were problems there were also new opportunities. Thus, in 1995 Safmarine, in conjunction with other members of the South African Ship Owner's Association (SASOA), began work on a project which aimed to make South Africa a 'Maritime Business Location'. A report published under this title emphasized the need for South Africa to be internationally competitive and the advantages that should enable it to develop the shipping industry. Three areas for improvement were identified: ship registration, the fiscal environment and crewing; their development in an integrated way, it was suggested, would enable South Africa to become an international maritime centre. The country is in an advantageous position for such a development. It could become an important source for marketing seafarers. What is required first is major restructuring of crew training; should this be done adequately, South African seafarers could be a source of hard currency and bring a measure of skilled employment into the economy. If in addition South Africa embraced a new tax regime acceptable to shipowners world-wide it could develop as a centre for shipping registration. Apart from efforts to create an acceptable seafarering industry, South Africa enjoys several obvious advantages as a shipping centre: these include its geographic position on the Asian–European/American sea route and its proximity to cargoes – that is, its capacity to handle many cargoes from the continental hinterland as well as from South Africa itself.

By 1998 the government had made commitments to improve the delivery of infrastructure to all South Africans at an estimated cost of R170 billion over ten years. At the same time, in order to do this while also exercising fiscal constraints, the government was forced to examine alternative ways of funding infrastructure improvements. What this meant in practice was following the world-wide trend of purchasing from the private sector services that formerly would have been provided by the government. As the head of investment banking for Deutsche Morgan Grenfell, Martin Kingston, put it:

> Government is changing its philosophy from being a provider of a service (in particular through government ownership) to becoming a purchaser of services. It is increasingly prepared to consider allocating the responsibility for design, development, construction, operation, financing and ownership to the private sector and then entering into a contractual arrangement to purchase the service, whether it be water treatment, prisons or the development of private toll roads.[3]

Such an approach represents a major departure from former South African practices. It is, however, a trend that began in the USA and Europe during the 1980s and subsequently spread to South East Asia, China and India. By 1998 the practice was being developed in South Africa, bringing the country into line with modern world practices. An important step forward was made in Johannesburg on 12 December

1997, when the financing of the N4 Maputo Corridor toll road project was finalised as a mix of public and private finance, the first of its kind in the new South Africa. Other proposed toll roads were expected to be financed in the same way.

In its determination not to incur large foreign debts for development purposes the government, instead, is turning to the private sector. The director of the South Africa Foundation, Paul Runge, argues that private funding will lead to better managed projects: 'At the same time, governments do not have to relinquish their control over infrastructure. They can, for example, take a toll road back after, say, 30 years and can limit how much is charged to use the road.'[4] Kobus Viljoen, the director of the project finance division of the Standard Corporate and Merchant Bank expected a rise in the size and level of sophistication of development projects in Southern Africa:

> There is so much scope for vast infrastructure creation and improvements beyond the fiscal constraints of governments that the private sector must play a pivotal role in these developments. Africa continues to be an important provider of mineral resources, but with a few exceptions has historically not been strong on the beneficiation of raw material. These activities require fairly sophisticated infrastructure and we believe the long-term project finance probabilities are legion.[5]

The construction industry also faced a shake-up in the 1990s as the implementation of the RDP led to a building boom. Italy, where construction has always been a lead industry, sought ways to cash in on the huge demand for low cost homes in South Africa and, for example, one of its construction companies, Technopref, worked out new techniques for constructing cheap bungalows. The firm sought joint ventures with South African companies and, no doubt, such European expertise will soon enough be assimilated by the venture partners for few developing countries offer so many opportunities for the construction business as a whole. Similarly, British architects and construction companies moved sharply into South Africa to benefit from the expansion of activity envisaged under the RDP. Such expansion included offices, hotels, sports centres, the amenities of any modern city.

One area in which South Africa fell behind quite drastically during the isolation of the apartheid era was in tourism. The country's new acceptance meant two kinds of catching up to be done: first, it required new hotels, cafés, cinemas and leisure facilities to cater for an increased flow of tourists; and second, it needed new attitudes to visitors. South

Africa has much to offer the tourist but during the apartheid era came increasingly to adopt a take-it-or-leave-it attitude and became dependent upon tourists who came to visit relatives and accepted the system as they found it without asking awkward questions. In the post-apartheid era South Africa has to attune itself to one of the most competitive industries in the world in which the customer is always right and, moreover, if unsatisfied simply heads for a different destination. It is likely to be some years before South Africa has become sufficiently tourist friendly that it will compete on equal or better terms with other major tourist destination countries.

The telecommunications market is expanding at an enormous rate world-wide and by the early 1990s South African companies were seeking major new outlets on the continent as a whole as restraints upon their activities outside South Africa disappeared. According to the ITU to increase teledensity (the number of telephone lines per 100 population) in sub-Saharan Africa to one line per 100 people would cost about US$ 28 billion and in terms of current economic conditions in Africa such a sum can only be raised from the private sector. Here was an area where South African companies could make a huge contribution to continental growth and in the process put themselves at the top end of the market. Competition between African companies for new business has become acute and the South African state-controlled Telkom has been pushing for new business throughout the continent.

In March 1998 the black empowerment group, Vula Communications, signed a R600 million telecommunications satellite deal with the US Mobile Communications Holdings (MCHI) and the company then invited South African institutional investors to invest in Vula. The chief executive of Vula, Mark Mathule Headbush, said: 'Vula is committed to opening the gateways of communication for Africa and empowering Africans to own and operate their own high-technology companies.'[6] At the same time the European commercial space transportation company, Arianespace, moved into South Africa hoping to establish the country's first satellite-based telecommunications system. As Claude Sanchez, the company's spokesman, said:

> Africa's economy is beginning to grow, and with it comes the need for telecommunications. If there is a need for telecommunications, there is a need for satellites. The continent's geography and its economy is characterised by wide spaces with isolated pockets of economic activity, making it highly suitable for satellite telecommunications systems. Because South Africa is the continent's dominant

economic power with a well-developed infrastructure, the development should start from here. There is no satellite system serving only Africa at present.[7]

It did seem that during the 1990s Africa's long delayed telecommunications revolution was about to take off; the process was assisted by growing privatisation and deregulation moves in an increasing number of countries which together attracted much needed foreign investment and technical know-how. The process has a long way to go. In 1994, for example, there was one telephone line for every 235 people in Africa as compared with one line to every two or three people in the industrialised world. Africa had been held back mainly through lack of investment but in this area, at least, it seemed that a new take-off for Africa (as envisaged by Thabo Mbeki) was at last underway. South Africa should be in the forefront of such developments if it is to partake of the new international information economy. An ITU report of 1998 showed that Africa had achieved an annual growth rate of new telephone lines of 10 per cent and that the 1996 figure of 13.7 million main telephone lines for the continent could double by 2003. At the same time the mobile cellular market was rapidly increasing with most of that increase in South Africa.

In an upbeat address to the World Economic Forum's Southern Africa Economic Summit held in Windhoek, Jay Naidoo, the minister of post, telecommunications and broadcasting, said that Telkom was exploring possible investments in the rest of Africa, apart from those it had already embarked upon in Uganda and Mauritius. However, he insisted that the drive to invest in Africa would not be at the expense of the company's commitment to extend telecommunications into South Africa's rural and poor areas. He said the drive to invest outside South Africa was part of Telkom's obligation to form strategic partnerships in Africa so as to pool the technology, expertise and capital of the private sector so as to get the continent connected. He said that

> By June 1 2000, we will have a framework in place that will be attractive to foreign and local investors. It will include a data bank of African expertise, human resources and capacity building in information technology and telecommunications. We have to develop regional markets and regional frameworks as many of our countries are too small to negotiate individually (with investors).[8]

South Africa, by implication, was not too small to negotiate and should take the lead. South Africa had the fastest Internet growth on the continent with 600 000 users, Egypt came in second place, followed by Morocco, Kenya, Zimbabwe, Ghana and Tanzania.

Sophisticated developments go hand in hand with huge gaps in the provision of the most simple technology, in part of course a legacy of the double agenda of apartheid. Thus, on the one hand Eskom (the state electricity utility) announced in mid-1998 that it was about to deliver safe 'pocket-sized' nuclear power stations whose reactors would fit on the back of a truck with one station able to generate enough power for a medium-sized town; on the other hand, nearly half of South Africa has yet to be electrified with 23 million South Africans in 1998 who still had to experience the benefits of domestic electricity.

South Africa has no oil of its own, a fact which proved a major headache during the apartheid era when governments were fearful of sanctions. In fact South Africa developed oil-from-coal technology through its SASOL plants and stored large amounts of fuel in its dis-used mines, Iran (more of a pariah state in the West than South Africa) being its principal supplier. In 1997 South Africa concluded a major arms sale with Saudi Arabia in exchange for oil and the Foreign Ministry identified Saudi Arabia as a strategic partner in the Middle East. South Africa has many international readjustments to make in political as well as economic terms. In May 1998 Sasol Petroleum International, the company's oil exploration and production subsidiary, announced that with a Mozambican partner it was to spend R50 million on drilling and gas exploration on the Mozambican Temane gas field. The previous year it had announced the start of development at the 4000 barrel-a-day Djambala field 55 km offshore from Congo. Penuell Maduna, minister for minerals and energy, gave his support in 1998 to the exploration activities of Soekor, the state-owned exploration company, and Mossgas, the state's oil-from-gas producer; Soekor was about to bring its Oryx oil field off Mossel Bay into production and Mossgas wanted to expand its offshore gas production. The minister signalled his intention to deregulate at least parts of the liquid fuels industry although he defended continued state support of Mossgas. The fuels sector which was tightly controlled throughout the apartheid era for strategic as well as economic reasons is one of a number of sectors that would benefit from at least some deregulation so as to attract investment capital and know-how. In mid-1998 SASOL, which produces the equivalent in synthetic fuels of 200 000 b/d of oil, had talks with the government about its subsidies since world-wide low oil prices made its products increasingly uncompetitive. The government promised to continue the subsidies though at a reduced rate.

Whether in the future, except for strategic reasons, it will make sense to continue producing oil from coal in an over-supplied world oil market is another question altogether. In any case, a shake-up of South Africa's monopolistic oil industry was threatened by the black empowerment company Worldwide Africa Investments which was negotiating a deal at the end of 1998 with Malaysia's state-owned Petronas. Engen, South Africa's second largest integrated oil company after SASOL, has interests in 20 African countries and it, too, was contemplating a tie-up with Petronas. Like many other players in the South African economy which had enjoyed a monopolistic position for years, the oil industry was beginning to look for outside partners and regear its activities to the continent as a whole.

11
Investment

The willingness of international business to invest in South Africa under Mandela's presidency became both the touchstone of the country's new acceptability and the measure of its economic success. To what extent, the government wanted to know, was South Africa able to attract back the old investors from Britain, the United States and other European countries; and, perhaps even more important for the future, to what extent could it also attract investment from the rising economies of Asia. In July 1995, hopefully a sign of the new times, the Indian conglomerate UB Group which operates in 21 countries and is one of India's ten leading companies, invested in South Africa's tourist industry and property, and announced an interest in taking a 30 per cent stake in National Sorghum Breweries. These were hardly major investments but they were in industries on the ground as opposed to portfolio investment which can be withdrawn as fast as it can be invested. Any such investment was considered newsworthy.

At the same time the National Economic Development and Labour Council (NEDLAC) proposed to establish a national investment promotion agency for South Africa. This, however, did not receive any enthusiastic support from the business community which argued that such an agency would merely duplicate the work of existing bodies such as the South African Chamber of Business (SACOB) or the Afrikaanse Handelsinstituut (AH). However, despite misgivings, the business community finally endorsed the idea though without making any promises of financial support. Opposition was in terms of such a body being an expensive bureaucracy, that the government should concentrate upon other priorities and that it would duplicate the work of existing bodies. There was, though unstated, the usual business opposition to government interference. At this stage in South Africa's international business rehabilitation there was growing private-sector confidence, following agreement on labour legislation between business, trade unions and government, although foreign investors remained wary and Julian Ogilvie Thompson, the head of Anglo American, argued that vital investment would only be forthcoming if there were a reform of the domestic labour market.

After visiting South East Asia Stanley Subramoney, a partner of Price Waterhouse, said Malaysia was prepared to invest billions of rands in South Africa but first the country needed an economic vision. This was on the eve of a visit by some 200 Malaysian businessmen to South Africa. He said: 'Attracting foreign direct investment requires a creative, simple and deliverable system into which capital can flow. South Africa does not have this facility – the current system is outdated, and internationally uncompetitive.'[1]

At the same time an argument was developing in business circles between those who wanted incentives to be provided to attract foreign investment and those more concerned to protect home industries, who feared that such incentives would give foreign investors an edge in the home market. As South Africa still had to learn, perhaps, there was plenty of available capital for investment but it would go where conditions were most attractive. Where there is competiton between two or more markets for investment the capital is likely, other things being equal, to go where the tax incentives are best, but not otherwise. In contrast to the late 1980s when virtually every tax incentive had been scrapped in an effort to enervate a stagnating economy that was hit by sanctions, labour problems and political instability, by the mid-1990s South Africa was desperate to increase the flow of inward investment. The question was how, at a time when South Africa had high taxes but almost no incentives. As the chief economist of the Reserve Bank, Ernie van der Merwe, argued, tax incentives do not work but distort the economy while other economists argued that political and labour stability were far more important. This view was advanced by Ben van Rensburg, the director of economic policy of SACOB: 'If sound political and macroeconomic policies are not in place, foreigners will not even think of investing in South Africa.'[2] And as the chair of the American Chamber of Commerce (and managing director of Ingersoll Rand in South Africa) Walter Mallory pointed out, American firms that inquired about investing in South Africa did not ask about incentives but were concerned with other issues such as the availability of labour.

At the same time the ANC announced its intention of breaking the stranglehold on the economy of five or six large conglomerates on the grounds that they were blocking foreign investment, hampering growth and frustrating black business ambitions. There was obvious ANC frustration at the slow pace at which economic benefits were filtering through to its supporters in the wake of the 1994 elections. Cyril Ramaphosa, then secretary-general of the ANC, said that these monopolies had become a problem both for the economy and for the democratic movement. The companies referred to were the giants – Anglo American, Sanlam, Rembrandt Group, Old Mutual and Liberty Life. In a hard-hitting speech the ANC secretary-general said:

> International companies are concerned by the lack of opportunities that exist for entering the economy. It is, of course, well known here the economy is tightly controlled by these monopoly companies. In addition, the closed shop they are operating means black business cannot get access to the economy because the monopolies have such a stranglehold.[3]

Estimates by McGregor Information Services claimed that 85 per cent of capitalisation on the JSE was held by the largest six conglomerates with Anglo-American accounting for 40 per cent although the company said it accounted for no more than 25 per cent. There were some sharp reactions to Ramaphosa's speech by the conglomerates. Anglo American director Michael Spicer replied that the big companies were among South Africa's best ambassadors and were not to be 'cowed by populist rhetoric'. 'We have been the best salesmen for South Africa for many years, and in terms of investment we have put our money where our mouth is' he said.[4]

Incentives are relative and in 1995 when there was a building slump in Britain a number of British architects and construction firms were attracted to South Africa to participate in the huge public and private building programme which was trying to satisfy the demands of a rapidly expanding tourist industry and the need to meet post-apartheid housing requirements. Thus Broadway Malyan, Britain's fourth largest architectural firm, opened a Johannesburg branch after it had secured three design projects worth R640 million. As Broadway's senior partner, Brian Relph, explained: 'Tourism has been ignored over the past several years in South Africa and now there is a drive to build hotels and leisure sites. There is also a tremendous drive to replace township accomodation.'[5] Other construction-related companies from Britain such as Bovis or Turner & Townsend also moved into South Africa at this time.

Much interest in investing in South Africa was shown during 1995 and some substantial investments came too. Corovin, the world's fifth-largest manufacturer of non-woven textiles, invested R55 million in a joint venture with the South African textile manufacturer Industex. Corovin was the first new German company to invest since the 1994 elections. A total of 25 options for possible joint development of the petrochemical industry were identified by South African and Taiwanese investors. The South African Foundation restructured itself during 1995 to focus upon business rather than political affairs and aimed to provide a forum in which South African corporations could formulate a co-ordinated view on macroeconomic and other issues. Members included 50 of the country's largest companies. South African businesses believed there was a need for a non-statutory, non-political body to represent their interests and uphold certain fundamental values:

These values include sound economic management, fiscal, monetary, manufacturing and trade policies, free enterprise, effective competition, effective and affordable government, healthy and balanced international trade, and an independent central bank.[6]

A list that amounted to a form of business leader's charter.

Malaysian interest in South Africa was strong at this time. The leisure group Landmarks Berhad looked at links with Grinaker Construction and Stocks & Stocks in a move into the black-controlled low-cost housing sector. The Malaysian companies made plain they wanted to link with South African groups where there was a minimum of 30 per cent black ownership. South East Asian interest in South Africa as a new and acceptable emerging market continued into 1996 and though it was inevitably set back by the 1997 'Tiger' crisis this is unlikely to affect the long-term trend of Asian investment in South Africa. It will probably also act as a stimulus to renewed European investment in the region as well.

In late 1997 British Airports Authority (BAA) put in a bid for a strategic equity stake in the Airport Company of South Africa (ACSA) and, according to director Richard Jeffrey,

There is enormous potential at South Africa's major airports and our extensive experience in managing international airports, both large and small, can help to realise that potential for the benefit of the airports themselves, their customers and staff, and the local and national communities which the airports serve.[7]

Other bidders for a stake included the Malaysian Airports Authority, Vienna Airport and Singapore Airport. Such interest may appear flattering but bidding for a stake in a profitable and expanding airport management business is not the equivalent to investment in production on the ground and too much of the external interest in South Africa at this time was in terms of portfolio investment or management rather than in the more traditional form of setting up new enterprises.

At the end of 1997 General Motors (GM) returned to South Africa after 11 years absence to take a 49 per cent stake in the Delta Motor Corporation in Port Elizabeth. GM claimed it saw strong growth potential in the South African motor sector but though the return of GM was seen as a positive move it also raised fears that the introduction of new GM models onto the South African market would act to fragment the industry. A month later, in January 1998, Fiat Auto announced it was about to invest R250 million in order to produce new models in South Africa. The investment followed an agreement with Automakers, the holding company of Nissan South Africa. The R250 million investment was in preparation for the production in South Africa of the '178 family' of cars. This 'invasion' by major car manufacturers could be seen in two ways: as the opening up of the South African market to major car industry investment; or as the inclusion of South Africa on an auto globalisation map. Fiat, for example, had already invested in Brazil, Turkey, Argentina, India, Poland, Russia and Morocco as promising outlets for its Palio and Siena models, and now it was South Africa's turn. The Fiat investment, however, was also the type of investment the government most desired; it would create between 800 and 1000 jobs. By May 1998 BMW South Africa announced the completion of a R920 million expansion to make the company one of the country's largest exporters (and its biggest vehicle exporter).

Part of the attraction of South Africa for foreign investors is as the jumping off board for business to the north. As the president of Coca Cola Southern Africa, Charlie Frenette, explained the company was targeting an African volume growth of between 15 and 20 per cent a year over the long term and he described South Africa as the 'wellspring for the growth of our business in Africa'. He said that in 20 years the population of the African continent would have reached 1000 million and that would be equivalent to 15 per cent of the world's population and 22 per cent of its teenage population. He saw South Africa as a high growth market and believed that Coca Cola could double its business over five years.

Foreign direct investment in South Africa during 1997 grew by 65 per cent to R14 billion although a great deal of this investment was in terms of acquisitions rather than new investments while many investors, especially those from the United States, saw South Africa as the centre of a wider regional market. However, 1998 got off to a bad start as the repercussions of the Asian crisis worked their way through the global economy. The result for South Africa was a renewed wariness about investors as well as a hiatus in Asian funds as countries such as Malaysia had to re-examine their strategies. There was no lack of economic experts telling South Africa what it had to do. As Joel Stern, the chief executive of a New York consulting firm Stern Stewart, lectured there was great concern around the world that South Africa had not achieved what it might have done during the euphoria generated by Mandela's presidency and that foreign investors were concerned about the investment climate and exchange controls:

> They believe that when a country has controls, it's an indication of what is acceptable. Governments can mistreat their population by having controls. A sign of confidence that the government has in its own policies is the freedom to move capital elsewhere.

He went on to suggest that investors could not earn sufficient returns in South Africa when compared with alternatives.[8] Stern's advice consisted of the familiar litany of business strictures aimed at achieving a more open market.

In the first months of 1998 the Asian crisis had the effect of pushing South Africa up the emerging market table although later in the year the rand was to be adversely affected and weakened substantially. According to the World Bank South Africa's attraction for portfolio investors increased markedly as a direct result of the Asian crisis but this represented a doubtful advantage with South Africa, for the time being, representing the upbeat side of the world's financial volatility. Merger and acquisition activity rather than direct foreign investment were the order of the day. The major conglomerates which had been forced by the control structures of the apartheid era to acquire more and more companies now needed to unbundle. At the same time, there was a new danger that the black empowerment groups would, in their turn, create new monoliths to replace the old ones. Yet, despite these up-and-down estimates, Alec Erwin, the trade and industry minister, was able to claim in May 1998 that South Africa had moved into the top ten developing country investment destinations and was becoming increasingly competitive in the global market. In 1997 some 398 projects had received investment worth R82 billion and created 77 000 jobs. However, he argued that South Africa had no option except to open up its economy: 'You will not get sustainable employment if you are not capable of competing on world markets.'[9]

Yet another survey of prospects for business in South Africa was released in September 1998 by the Southern Africa service of the US Investor Responsibility Research Center which had polled more than 2000 companies with either business in or exports to South Africa. The companies polled included 751 from the USA, 288 from Britain and 245 from Germany. The report suggested that perceptions of South Africa had become less favourable with only 28 per cent of the respondents saying that government policies were better than those of other emerging markets. Companies complained of the employment legislation and the quotas in the Employment Equity Bill. Labour was seen as a key problem: 51 per cent of respondents saw the local labour as less productive than elsewhere and 41 per cent said labour relations were worse in South Africa than elsewhere. Such complaints must be seen against the history of labour relations in South Africa and the urgent political need to redress a balance that had long worked to the absolute detriment of labour. At the same time 40 per cent of respondents said they planned to invest in South Africa with mining and manufacturing the most likely target sectors. However, of the firms polled only 35 per cent of American firms intended to invest as opposed to 53 per cent of British firms, 89 per cent of German firms and 98 per cent of Swiss firms.[10]

By 1998, indeed, a kind of dialogue had grown up between the South African government on the one hand and the multinational companies which by mid-1998 had become cautious of further commitments – or any if they were not already in the country – as they expressed concern over the slowdown of the economic policy and the rising rate of crime. They were worried that the government's growth, employment and redistribution (Gear) programme appeared to have stalled – it had not remotely achieved its targets of six per cent growth or the creation of 400 000 new jobs a year. More worrying for South Africa, of the R40 billion of foreign capital flows into the country between 1994 and 1997 only 25 per cent had been in the form of direct fixed investment while the rest was mainly portfolio investment. Large scale foreign investments remained as the exception rather than the rule at the end of 1998. The doubts expressed by would-be investors were hardly surprising. The post-1994 election euphoria was not going to be sustained. The huge demands of organised labour and the political need to meet a range of priorities that were opposed to a free market system were bound to make investors wary while the business expectation that once full democracy was in place everything else would also fall neatly into place as well was always naive. Critics of the South African labour movement suggested that the unions were too slow in evolving from being a revolutionary force to adopting a more pragmatic mode in dealing with management and, it was suggested, 'The movement here is like Europe during the late 1970s and early 1980s.' This may be true but it is unrealistic of business to expect either labour or management in South Africa at once to equate with that of Europe in the mid-to-late 1990s. There exists too much historical baggage which has to be cleared away first.

Billions of investment are required if the country's impoverished majority is to be employed and the gap between the rich and poor created by apartheid is to be even partially overcome. Investment from Britain ought to make a significant impact upon these problems. In July 1996 President Mandela led the largest ever South African business delegation to London in the hope of building upon the wide-ranging British business interests that already existed in South Africa. Britain, with its long historical connexion, is South Africa's top investor with (mid-1996) over 500 companies accounting for more than 12 billion worth of investment while two-way trade in 1995 amounted to 4 billion. Although many US corporations such as IBM and Coca Cola had been forced out of South Africa by anti-apartheid activists during the 1980s, the majority of British companies had never left though both Barclays and Standard Chartered banks had withdrawn. President Mandela and the business leaders who accompanied him were well received in London but they faced a formidable list of objections to overcome before they could expect to attract the investment they so urgently sought. These included the usual litany by then associated with South Africa: militant labour unions, escalating violence, uncertainty as to the future economic direction and the need for a firm fiscal policy that would 'favour' international investors.

Despite its ample resources and huge potential, investment since 1994 was still only a trickle while most of the funds that had been transferred to South Africa were in the form of portfolio investments. What South Africa needed, according to one business analyst, was more business-friendly policies. As President Mandela was to tell his London audience, Britain was of key economic importance to his country: British investments stood at R12 billion while nine of the country's top 20 employers were British. As Mandela said:

The central message I bring to you this morning is that we should build on what exists. It is a message infused with urgency precisely because beyond the profound political changes, the iniquitous system that we set out to destroy is still alive and well. The poverty, decay in the social fabric and profound inequality that are the product of the past can only be eradicated with your co-operation.[11]

The message was well enough received but perhaps of greater interest to business leaders was the President's announcement that his government had embarked upon the sell-off of R173 billion worth of assets in the state sector. There were plenty of pledges of investment from the 400 business leaders gathered to hear Mandela; how soon these would be turned into reality was another matter.

By the end of 1997, according to Britain's consul-general in South Africa, Peter Longworth, British companies had invested R6 billion since 1994, nearly all of which had created real businesses. This was on top of the R12 billion that already existed in the country. Britain was both the biggest investor in South Africa and the largest foreign creator of employment. In May 1998 a trade promotion campaign called 'Britain and South Africa: partners in opportunity', was launched with the British government funding the campaign to the tune of R17 million over three years. Meanwhile, South African companies were beginning to examine the possibility of flotations on the London Stock Exchange; the first to do so was the South African mining conglomerate Gencor and this led to the later listing of Billiton. The South African government was described as privately unhappy about the Gencor decision to seek primary listing outside South Africa and the move raised another problem that the opening up of the economy was bound to face, which was the difference between South African companies investing outside South Africa and South African companies moving out of South Africa. As other major companies examined the possibility of moving their headquarters and primary stock exchange listings to London it was unclear whether they would be granted automatic permission to do so by the South African government.

The largest foreign investor after Britain was the USA, whose investments were a mixed blessing. A classic example of American bullying came with Merck, the US pharmaceutical corporation, which in 1997 warned that it might pull out of South Africa to the detriment of thousands of jobs if the health minister Dr Nkosazana Zuma did not withdraw plans to import patented drugs. The threat was clearcut and arrogant: with 12 American pharmaceutical companies with a combined revenue of R705 million operating in South Africa, the US ambassador called for the removal of a clause in the health legislation that aimed to curb health costs even though it complied with free market principles. The US ambassador, James Joseph, said the reform would override the 'universally accepted principles of patent protection' and he warned that the new legislation would send a negative signal about intellectual property rights to companies that otherwise might play a crucial role in South Africa's development. While the drug companies insisted that the move violated WTO agreements, Dr Zuma disagreed. South Africa could save many millions by purchasing cheaper drugs (than the American ones) on the world market. The row was a warning to South Africa of the pressures that could be exerted upon it by international business and as Charles Medawar, an expert on the pharmaceutical industries, pointed out

> South Africa is getting the text-book treatment reserved for countries – particularly in the Third World where there is less trade muscle – who refuse to play the international pharmaceutical game. The companies have a well-deserved reputation for overbearing behaviour.[12]

By the beginning of 1998 an estimated 150 US companies had returned to South Africa following the abolition of sanctions although the major US pension funds that disinvested had not reinvested. According to the Investor Responsibility Research Centre (IRRC) – the organisation which played a key role in persuading US companies to disinvest from South Africa during the 1980s – US investment in South Africa had surpassed the levels which prevailed during the apartheid era and US companies had been entering and expanding their operations in South Africa at nearly double the rate of firms from all other investor countries combined and estimated that US companies held about US$10 billion worth of stakes in South Africa. Much of this investment represented re-entry. For example, by 1990 214 of 324 US companies which had investments in South Africa in 1981 had withdrawn so that investments plunged to $700 million and this outflow had contributed significantly to the abandonment of apartheid under President de Klerk. Since 1994 President Bill Clinton had designated South Africa as one of the world's top ten emerging markets. According to the IRRC the number of US companies with investments in South Africa had risen from 104 in 1991 to 296 in early 1998.[13]

12
Industry

Manufacturing accounts for just under a quarter of South Africa's GDP and provides employment for about 14 per cent of the labour force. The principal manufactures are food and beverages, soaps, paints, pharamaceuticals, refined petroleum, iron and steel, transport equipment, metal products, non-electrical machinery, paper and paper products, and construction. South Africa has become a substantial arms producer and arms now make an important contribution to exports. South Africa is also the leading world producer of oil from coal (through its SASOL plants) and these provide approximately half the country's petroleum products. The industrial sector is the most advanced and sophisticated on the African continent.

The end of apartheid and the emergence of a majority-rule government in 1994 faced the sector with a series of challenges that it was only beginning to grapple with – and then by no means always effectively – by 1999. On the plus side South African industries were free to expand their activities into the rest of Africa and some were quick to take the opportunity to do so. At the same time global companies, freed of former inhibitions about investing in South Africa, were entering the market either as new competitors or as potential partners able to provide additional investment funds. The major companies which had been unable to expand outside South Africa, because of exchange controls, now looked for investment opportunities beyond the continent where success would give them greater development potential at home. On the other hand, the sector could no longer enjoy the protection that had been provided by isolation while the new political situation meant it also had to contend with far stronger unions and implement policies of black empowerment whose long-term contribution to the economy would, nonetheless, be offset by short-term extra costs.

Air transport faced immediate prospects for expansion with South African Airways (SAA) developing into one of the world's fastest growing carriers. In 1995 its capitalisation value lay between R2.13 billion and R2.29 billion, while forecasts suggested that international passenger traffic to South Africa would increase by 50 per cent by 1998. If SAA was to meet such forecasts adequately and become an important international carrier it needed to expand and upgrade its fleet. The case for SAA expansion was clearcut and it would soon seek international partners to inject new finances and know-how into its operations. Elsewhere, arguments about expanded activities were more complex. Anglo-American, for example, rejected government charges (voiced by Cyril Ramophosa) that Anglo's dominance kept international investors out of South Africa. The chairman of Anglo American Industrial Corporation, Leslie Boyd, said that the Anglo group of companies had entered into joint ventures with Daewoo, Ford, ICI, SCA, Bechtel, Alcatel, ABB, CPC and Tubemakers of Australia and that, apart from ICI, these were all new partnerships. He suggested that 'We believe the reason foreign investors have not come is that they have a look here and realise that there are no easy pickings, that our business sector is sophisticated and First World and our companies competitive.'[1]

The competitive capabilities of South African companies were examined in 1995 by Chu-San-Ren, a Japanese industry consultancy service, whose representative Takeyuki Furuhashi found how hard companies were trying to solve problems and upgrade the level of their competitiveness on world markets. There was, he found a preoccupation with the idea of being 'world class' companies. Many of the problems concerned the democratisation of the work place, rapid product changes or shorter delivery times. As the Japanese consultant pointed out his own country's postwar resurgence began when they implemented their Reconstruction and Development Programme after the Second World War and had to struggle to achieve a consensus from the major interest groups in the country.

Industrial adjustment to a whole range of new circumstances was an essential part of the scene during the Mandela years, including new opportunities to invest outwards, the possible choice of new partners as international business – warily – moved back into South Africa, and a new relationship between management and labour. New investments, however, were often handicapped by a shortage of skills, a legacy from the past, as bottlenecks were created by lack of skilled workers. As the textile industry discovered during its expansion and investment in new machinery during 1995–96, extensive training programmes were needed throughout the industry while in most cases the skills required for operating the new machines demanded computer literacy and mechanical abilities which were scarce even in Europe. South African exporters needed to examine the potential of the SADC market on their doorstep and the Latin American market as well as their more traditional European markets. In 1996 only about 10 per cent of the R10 billion textile industry output was exported although its export target was 30–40 per cent of total output.

According to Zav Rustomjee, the director general of the department of trade and industry, South Africa's return to the world economy meant an end to local manufacturers who depended upon low value-added production and government handouts. He said: 'We want to move from a low-wage low-consumption economy to a high-wage, high-consumption one.' His department had been trying since 1994 to encourage the manufacturing sector to shift from producing low-value added goods to focusing instead upon high-tech products. As Rustomjee pointed out:

> Because of tariff protection during the period of isolation, firms produced everything, sometimes without much attention to quality. They could do that because they could charge anything and consumers paid higher prices.

Most importantly, he pointed out,

> Apartheid was instrumental in driving down wage costs by hammering unions. But this can no longer be done. We cannot sustain firms based on low wages.

What was needed was a shift in mindset.[2]

The ministry of trade and industry's industrial participation programme (IPP) aimed to create an additional R15 billion of revenue over the five years to 2002, including the generation of R3 billion of foreign investments, R8 billion of exports and the creation of 6000 jobs. The IPP claimed considerable success in the first year of its operation (1996–97) in attracting and completing contracts with multinationals. As its director Vassie Ponsamy claimed

> It is all about multinationals putting together a package as a prerequisite to being awarded the tender. We look at principles of sustainability and mutual benefits. ... We also look at global integration. We are stressing export bias. The domestic market is largely saturated

and overtraded. We are looking at production runs that will make sense: domestic-led projects with a strong export bias.[3]

The outward movement of major companies was signalled in July 1997 by Iscor and EL Bateman which had contracted to build a US$100 million steel mill in Saudi Arabia which could secure exports worth US$90 million a year for the steel group's Saldanha plant. The companies had made the agreement with Saudi Arabia's Al-Shamrany and would supply the plant, once completed, with 260 000 tons of hot rolled coil a year. The deal represented a major gain for Iscor which had made exports central to its strategy. Saldanha Bay, meanwhile, was being developed as a centre of the steel industry with the construction of the Saldanha Steel project. A new plant, Duferco Steel Processing, represented a R850 million joint venture between the Industrial Development Corporation (IDC) and the Swiss steel trading company Duferco. The plant was expected to come into full production in June 2000. South Africa reckons it is well placed to service the world steel export business since it is located between the American–European markets and those of the Far East. The IDC, which is financing the project, has also invested in a training scheme to make sure that the requisite skills are available on the West Coast. The initiative has the support of the labour and trade and industry departments.

In February 1998 Iscor reported moves to invest R400 million in a copper and cobalt project at Kamoto in the Democratic Republic of Congo. Here the company was clearly involved in a risk venture since the outlook for the Congo during 1998 became increasingly uncertain as more and more of the Congo's neighbours intervened on one or other side in that country's civil war. The steel giants became involved in arguments with both Russia and the USA over allegations of dumped steel imports. In April the South African Iron and Steel Institute launched an action against cheap imports of steel plate, hot-rolled sheet and coil from Russia and Ukraine and demanded an initial duty of 80 per cent on the price of imports. At the same time four US steel producers and the US Steelworkers Union filed actions in the USA against dumping in America of steel by Columbus Stainless which is a member of the South African Iron and Steel Institute. In 1997 US action had forced Iscor and Highveld to abandon sales of steel plate to the USA and Iscor had conceded that it had a two-tier pricing system, with higher prices for home sales than for exports.

Iscor decided in May 1998 to close two plants at its Vanderbijl-park complex with the loss of 6000 jobs, although the company said the closure would not affect the complex's annual production of 3.6 million tons of flat steel. The two plants which dated from the 1950s had become technically and commercially unviable. Iscor saw the USA and Britain as its main international competitors. If it was to compete in the big league Iscor would have to modernise and keep pace with its rivals.

Iscor, which was privatised during the last days of the apartheid era, had a long way to go to modernise its practices. The announcement of 6000 job losses as part of a rationalisation programme outraged the National Union of Metalworkers of South Africa (NUMSA). The company employs more than 40 000 workers and has an annual turnover of R12 billion. It was attacked by domestic steel consumers for its restructuring programme that aims to make the steel giant globally competitive. The trouble, as Dorbyl which is Iscor's largest domestic customer, argued, Iscor is a monopoly and this made it very difficult to control its behaviour in relation to the domestic market.[4] Iscor's managing director, Louis van Niekerk, defended the rationalisation programme, partly on the grounds that the Asian economic crisis had depressed the global steel market and partly on the grounds that South Africa's steel producers had been shut out of the international arena for decades because of apartheid and now had to struggle to compete internationally. Comparisons with the global steel market make gloomy reading, for whereas steel industry employment in South Africa over two decades had fallen by 40 per cent, the decline in the European Union over the same period was 65 per cent.

Growth potential for major companies may depend in equal part upon seizing opportunities for expansion outside South Africa and meeting new demands that the end of apartheid has presented within the country. Eskom, the national electricity utility which became incorporated during 1999 is in this category. During 1997, for example, it connected 274 000 new houses to the electricity grid and claimed to be on track to meet its RDP commitment of 1.75 million connections by the year 2000. However, with 2.4 million households electrified between 1991 and 1997 the easy expansion was over as it became more expensive to electrify homes – especially in remote areas – and ensure sustainable delivery. The Eskom Amendment Bill to turn Eskom into a corporation was passed during June 1998. The responsible minister, Stella Sigcau, said the government was committed to ensuring the bill would not lead to job losses or higher electricity costs while the ownership of Eskom's reserves and other assets would remain vested in the state. The main trade union bodies – Cosatu, Numsa and Num – argued that the change would put electricity prices 'beyond the reach of the poor'. As the Cosatu deputy secretary-general Zwelinzima Vavi said: 'The state will no longer provide electricity but will regulate or make the laws that govern electricity. This we view as the biggest change of heart from government.' The move was part of a wider ongoing process whereby South African industry and government together came to terms with the realities of competition in a globalised economy.

A price war began on airline routes to London at the beginning of 1998 with SAA slashing prices so as to compete with Virgin Atlantic. The London route had become keenly competitive with European and North African airlines making a range of offers to attract business. Alliance Air, a joint venture between SAA and the national airways of Tanzania and Uganda, was expanding its network but in the process coming into conflict with Kenya Airways and its equity partner KLM Dutch Airlines. Alliance announced its intention of taking over Air Rwanda operations. By the late 1990s SAA was placing greater emphasis upon developing routes within the African continent although, at the same time, working to consolidate its foothold in the European market so as to boost European trade and tourism with South Africa. In April 1998 Singapore Airlines sought to become SAA's strategic equity partner; Singapore Airlines saw South Africa as a springboard into the rest of Africa and South America. Then Lufthansa announced an interest in acquiring a stake in SAA. An optimistic Singapore Airlines general manager, Abdul Rashid Mordifi, said that South Africa was well placed to become an international hub for air and sea transport. Such prospects are, no doubt, exciting for the new South Africa as it struggles to emerge from the mindsets of isolation and apartheid yet, at the same time, SAA faces increasing pressures to rationalise and privatise to enable it to compete effectively in an exceptionally cut-throat sector of the international travel business. Its cargo division also sought an equity partner from outside South Africa. By October 1998 SAA sought deals to promote greater co-operation with Lufthansa, Swissair and Singapore Airlines with British Airways in the wings, each seeking a stake in the South African national carrier. Such international interest in a South African business represented a welcome sign of the changed times.

In 1998 South African Breweries (SAB) ranked as the world's fourth biggest brewery; it had breweries in ten African countries, five European countries and China, and was one of the continent's few entirely homegrown multinationals. It enjoys virtual total dominance of its home market in South Africa while its offshore interests account for 40 per cent of annual production. It seeks to expand its operations in Europe, Russia, India and elsewhere in Asia. There is a huge potential beer market in Africa (600 million), the only drawback being the low level of most incomes. Part of SAB strategy is, in its market jargon, to make its products more affordable (cheaper beer). Apart from offshore brewing SAB exports 20 per cent of its domestic production to virtually every non-Muslim sub-Saharan country with its leading brand, Castle lager, growing 17 per cent a year between 1990 and 1996.[5] During 1998 SAB stepped up its policy of off-loading its non-beer interests so as to concentrate on its core business. Late in 1998 SAB, which was then the second biggest company by market value on the Johannesburg Stock Exchange (JSE), decided to move its primary listing from the JSE to the London Stock Exchange, a move that would make it easier to raise the money from international investors that it required to fund planned expansion into China and Eastern Europe. SAB was finally listed on the London Stock Exchange at the beginning of March 1999. The company then faced the issue of whether or not to acquire a world brand (name) to enable it to compete successfully with other top brewers which each have one.

One unlooked for result of the political and economic changes in South Africa was a rapid increase in the number of black South Africans travelling overseas. Thus, the committee looking at the development needs of South African airports which thought the growth in international travel would continue at 15 per cent a year before levelling off at six per cent did not take into account this new group of air travellers. Instead, the sales marketing system found that the rate of travel into and out of South Africa was doubling every year and the South African reservation system, Galileo, needed to expand its operations into neighbouring countries. Foreign visitors entering South Africa through its three main international airports in April 1995 had increased by 124 per cent over April 1994. Such figures drew attention to the need for rapid improvement in the structure and practices of South Africa's tourist industry. The country possesses immense tourist attractions yet during the period of isolation and especially from 1985 onwards, as violence mounted, tourists, other than relatives, tended to avoid South Africa. As a result, the industry declined in efficiency while taking for granted a flow of visitors, especially from Britain, who had relatives and friends in the country. It became apparent after 1994 that the industry needed a radical overhaul.

A survey conducted in Cape Town – the premier tourist destination – during May 1995 found that visitors complained of the poor condition and dirtiness of public transport, poor service at nights and weekends and unhelpful staff. Visitors were unimpressed by attractions such as the castle or museums and complained of exorbitant prices for lunch at wine estates. Other complaints covered drivers, traffic, street children, beggars, air pollution, litter, poor service, low standards of eating places, dirty beaches, local attitudes to visitors, and lack of safety and security, and though some of these complaints could hardly be blamed upon the industry what came across clearly was a sense that no one was interested in visitors. Those questioned were first from South Africa (24 per cent), then Britain (15 per cent) while other large groups came from the Republic of China (Taiwan), Germany and Australia. The range of complaints was sufficient to suggest that a great deal could be done to make South Africa more attractive as a tourist destination.

In addition, South Africa offered a new venue for international conferences of a kind that had not been held there for many years. It hosted the UNCTAD (WTO) conference in 1996 and the biennial Commonwealth Conference in 1998 and if it is to compete successfully in this lucrative business needs to upgrade the facilities it offers. South Africa also hosted the 1995 rugby World Cup. The South Africa Tourism Board (Satour) revealed that visitors in 1990 numbered 498 712, rising to 521 257 in 1991, 559 913 in 1992, 618 508 in 1993, 704 630 in 1994 and, were expected to pass the one million mark in 1995.[6] Whereas in 1985 South Africa ranked 55th as a world tourist destination by 1994 it had climbed to 29th place. The Cape, in particular, began to work at its tourist possibilities during 1995 and, all-round, has the most varied attractions to offer. The tourist industry was set to become the Cape's most important generator of new jobs and, according to the minister responsible for tourism, Lampie Fick, could increase the number of visitors – it is already the country's most important tourist destination – by an additional 450 000 visitors a year. According to the minister the industry was set to overtake agriculture, fisheries and industry as the Western Cape's most important source of revenue and jobs. Should the Cape succeed in attracting an extra 450 000 overseas tourists they would create an additional 40 000 jobs. According to tourist experts every 30 tourists create one formal job (such as hotel workers) and two informal jobs (such as fleamarket operators). While tourism has become the biggest industry in the world it ranks fourth as a contributor to the South African economy. The isolation of the apartheid years which inhibited tourism is now a thing of the past, but violence and security (or its lack) present a major problem for the future. People will not travel where they believe they will be at risk.

Three years later, in May 1998, the chairman of the South African Association of Trainers, Consultants and Service Providers to the Hospitality Industry (Satchi), Colin Grimsell, reported that the South

African tourist industry was growing three times faster than the world average and that there were 110 new hotels and resort developments in the pipeline.[7] During 1997 an estimated 5.4 million tourists visited South Africa: of these 1.5 million were from overseas and 3.9 million from other parts of Africa. Satour hoped to attract 2.5 million overseas visitors by the year 2000.[8] The most interesting aspect of the above figures is that more than double the number of overseas visitors to South Africa came from the African continent itself (they were also estimated to spend more per day than either British or German visitors) and, as with so many other industrial and business developments, it is upon its own continent that South Africa should concentrate its attention.

13
The Mining Sector

South Africa is a major storehouse of minerals and these have long constituted the lead sector in the economy. Mining now contributes under nine per cent to GDP and only employs three per cent of the labour force. Gold, diamonds, coal and the platinum group of metals dominate the sector, and for many years gold has been the most important mineral contributing 50 per cent, and sometimes more, of total world output. Now, however, gold production is in serious decline while changes in world economic patterns mean that its future as a reserve to back up national currencies is less certain. Diamonds are also in decline and South Africa has fallen from first to fifth place as a world producer. On the other hand, since 1945 South Africa has become an increasingly important producer of a wider range of other minerals which include uranium, platinum, nickel, copper, coal, antimony, vanadium, asbestos, iron ore, fluorspar, chromium, manganese and limestone, as well as some other minerals on a lesser scale. Altogether, South Africa is a major producer of 14 of the world's principal minerals. The sector has always been volatile, depending upon world demand and the state of the export markets that South Africa supplies.

Control of the mining sector was crucial to the apartheid state which, for example, encouraged migrant labour to come to South Africa to work in its mines at the expense of local labour, so as to ensure that too strong a mining trade union movement did not emerge. In 1995, two mining houses reversed the labour policy of 100 years when they concluded agreements with the National Union of Mineworkers (NUM) so as to allow mineworkers to bring their families to live with them in mining towns. Both Gengold and the Johannesburg Consolidated Investment Company (JCI) decided to give workers a choice between living in single-sex hostels and building or buying their own homes. Both the mining houses and the union would approach the government to assist mineworkers obtain access to state housing subsidies. According to the Gengold agreement 'Foreign nationals will be assisted to obtain citizenship to be able to participate in … housing initiatives.'[1] These agreements represented a major break with a past that was both colonial and racist in its attitudes toward mineworkers.

But the mining sector now faces major changes as the old mines run out of easily accesible gold and the days of cheap migrant labour become a thing of the past. South Africa's market share of gold has dropped from 70 to 25 per cent and from being the world's lowest-cost producer its gold mines have now become the most expensive to run. The impact of these changes spreads beyond South Africa and for tiny neighbouring Lesotho, which for years has depended upon remittances home from its men working in South Africa's mines, the outlook is grim, for the country has little or no industry of its own. Over the ten years to 1995 the gold industry shed 168 000 jobs and, it is predicted, will shed another 100 000 jobs by 2005. As conditions change so the National Union of Mineworkers has demanded an upgrading of working practices and 'multi-skilling' so that, for example, the same worker can be responsible for four jobs rather than just one. Yet, whatever new working conditions are introduced, changes will only prolong the lives of the mines for gold – and other minerals – are wasting assets. The decline of the mining industry must have a knock-on effect through the economy as a whole since, economists estimate, for every one job lost in the mining industry six are lost in support industries while each job supports an average of 10 dependents, whether in South Africa itself, or in neighbouring countries such as Lesotho or Mozambique.

There are similar worries in the diamond industry where South Africa's predominance has long since passed and though De Beers maintains a brave front it is fighting against growing pressures from Russia and Australia that could bring to an end the long reign of the world's most successful cartel, the De Beers controlled Central Selling Organization. Russia for years has been selling the CSO only a part of its production and the size of its diamond stockpile is unknown.

At least there is no prospect of coal stocks running out and in 1995 SASOL announced details of a R635 million plan to enter the coal export market by expanding the capacity at its Twistdraal Colliery. SASOL has become a shareholder in the Richards Bay Coal Terminal (RBCT) which is the largest coal terminal in the world, and one of the most efficient, with a capacity to handle 60 million tons a year.

According to SASOL's general manager, Johan de Vos, SASOL has vast coal reserves which it can exploit once it finds suitable markets and, as he said of its export project: 'The export project will create 400 new jobs, earn R370-million in foreign exchange and contribute about R130-million to the gross geographic product of the Eastern Transvaal.'[2] South Africa currently produces about 185 million tons of coal a year and 84 per cent of this is mined by three major companies – Amcoal, Ingwe and SASOL.

The opening up of the South African economy to the world provided new opportunities for the mining houses to obtain quotes on the London Stock Exchange and seek finances overseas for new mining ventures. Gencor, Anglo American's old Afrikaner rival, moved to London in 1997 although in the end it was Billiton, the metals and minerals group which it had purchased from Shell in 1994, that obtained a placing on the LSE. Billiton held Gencor's non-South African interests in gold, platinum, copper, tin and zinc. In mid-1996, Randgold sought to raise £100 million in London to develop its gold mine in Mali. The Anglo American Corporation has interests outside South Africa that reach to Australia, Canada and Russia, while its sister company, De Beers, still controls the world diamond market. Yet much of the buoyant mood of mid-1997 had evaporated early in 1998 as the mining industry was hit by the slowdown in Asia since a great part of the demand for South Africa's minerals comes from that region. Industrial minerals – coal, steel, aluminium, copper, ferroalloys, uranium and the platinum group – were most at risk since these had been in high demand in the rapidly growing Asian economies. In 1997 South Africa exported 63 million tons of coal worth R8.8 billion and much of that went to Asia, with Japan and South Korea as major customers.

The complex workings of Anglo American have often baffled analysts and its importance in the superstructure of mining and industry in South Africa cannot be exaggerated. Freed of the monetary restraints imposed under the apartheid system, it was to be expected that Anglo American would look increasingly outwards for further expansion. In 1996 it acquired Tiny Rowland's 5.9 per cent stake in Lonrho while also securing first right of refusal on chief executive Dieter Bock's 18.5 per cent stake. Its interest was in Lonrho's African mining operations which covered gold, platinum and coal, and in 1995 had contributed 103 million in profits on a turnover of 439 million. Ashanti, the Ghanaian gold producer in which Lonrho had a 41 per cent stake, produced 26 tons of gold in 1995 while Lonrho's gold mines in Zimbabwe produced a further 177 000 ounces of gold. Anglo, by contrast, produced 237 tons from its seven huge mines to the southwest of Johannesburg. However, at the same time Lonrho was carrying out a merger of its platinum interests in South Africa with Gencor, that would make them a match for Anglo's Rustenburg Platinum which produced 1.8 million ounces in 1995. Later, in 1998, Anglo exchanged some of its newly acquired Lonrho assets with JCI for the HJ Joel goldmine. It was part of an endless game of asset swapping at which Anglo American is a past master; a game that keeps it on top of the complex African mining world.

Through its sister company De Beers, Anglo produces some 27 million carats of diamonds a year from mines in South Africa, Namibia and Botswana, and during the 1990s has begun to expand its diamond prospecting further north into other parts of Africa including Senegal, Burkina Faso, Zambia and Tanzania. It has substantial interests in Zimbabwe, and has invested $250 million in a gold development in Mali while it is relooking at the huge if declining copper business, in Zambia in which it once had the largest stake. Even so, the vast bulk of Anglo's capital expenditure programme remains focused upon its South African interests. At the same time, keeping abreast of the new political climate in South Africa, Anglo decided to sell the greater part of its stake in the industrial and media group, Johnnic, to black investors. The deal, which was worth R1.5 billion, was between Anglo American and the new National Empowerment Consortium (NEC) which represented some 50 black groups. NEC took a 47.7 per cent stake in Johnnic. The Anglo decision to sell to black investors was reminiscent of its 1964 decision to sell its General Mining (what became Gencor) to Afrikaner businesspeople. Anglo has always demonstrated a shrewd sense of what is politically necessary at any given time.

When Anglo American sold some of its mines to assist the process of black empowerment early in 1998, the move did not meet with immediate or easy approval from the National Union of Mineworkers. In a deal worth R38.3 million, Anglo sold six Vaal Reefs marginal shafts to the black mining group, African Rainbow Minerals (ARM); however, James Motlatsi, the NUM president, said the deal was not black empowerment at all, for the transaction meant the loss of more than 3000 mining jobs. 'We believe Anglo American is running away from its social responsibility by transferring the assets to another company' he said, although Bobby Godsell, Vaal Reefs chair, described the deal as 'a clear advance for the involvement of black South Africans, not only in the ownership of gold mining assets but in their management. More importantly, it broadened a partnership between two mining companies, one black and the other white-led.'[3] However, Anglo would retain ownership of the core gold assets and operations at Vaal Reefs.

In the renamed Democratic Republic of the Congo, Anglo signed a consortium deal with that country's state-owned mining company Gécamines to mine in the Kolwezi area. This brought it into conflict with the US company American Mineral Fields (AMF) which promptly sued Anglo on the grounds that it had interfered with its contracts by offering to pay the Congo government tens of millions of dollars to squeeze out the American company. Gécamines, however, said that AMF never had exploitation rights to the copper tailings in Kolwezi. The Kolwezi mine workings hold about 1.44 million tons of copper and 275 000 tons of cobalt, together worth about $10 billion.

During October 1998 Anglo American unveiled a plan to bring all its assets under the control of a single company and transfer its main stock exchange listing from Johannesburg to London. The move was seen as a psychological blow to South Africa's economy as the country works to make a fresh impact upon the international business scene. The stock market valuation of Anglo American, at about £6 billion, would ensure that it became a member of the FTSE 100 index of leading companies. The new company unites Anglo's South African activities with its operations in the rest of the world. Anglo American and Minorco, the Luxembourg-based company which controlled most Anglo operations outside South Africa, come together while De Beers will own 40 per cent of the new company, and the Oppenheimer family nine per cent. Anglo American chairman, Julian Ogilvie Thompson, said the move would end the financial structures that had been imposed on Anglo by apartheid. The news caused consternation in South Africa where it was seen as a snub to President Mandela and a blow to the Johannesburg Stock Exchange, even though Anglo is to retain a secondary listing on the JSE. Thompson argued that the London listing would give Anglo American access to new sources of capital and allow it to exploit new business opportunities elsewhere in the world. The combined assets of the new group – Anglo American and Minorco – were estimated at about £8.8 billion.

Given the history of Anglo American, which has been identified for nearly a century with the mining structures upon which the South African economy has been based, the move from Johannesburg to London, as soon as it was possible for the company to do so after the end of the apartheid era, could only be seen as a wounding blow to the new South Africa, especially as two-thirds of its assets remain in South Africa. Anglo American's huge success as a conglomerate – and the wealth the Anglo companies and the Oppenheimer family control – have been achieved on a basis of South African gold and diamonds, and the labour of thousands of South African blacks who were ruthlessly wage-exploited by the apartheid system from which Anglo greatly benefited. The National Union of Mineworkers (NUM) described the Anglo American move to list on the London Stock Exchange as 'passing a vote of no confidence in the economy of South Africa and its government'. The union noted the growing trend of big companies including Billiton and Old Mutual to opt for offshore listing. As Gwede Mantashe, the general secretary of NUM, said:

> We are unhappy about the move because it is sending the wrong signals. Why should international investors be excited about coming to South Africa when all our major companies are going to have their primary listings in London?

By choosing to optimise share value Anglo was

shifting from creating jobs.[4]

However, the move was seen in a different light by Nicky Oppenheimer, deputy non-executive chairman of Anglo:

> This is a great day for Anglo and a great day for South Africa. I understand the concerns that this may be perceived as Anglo abandoning ship, but this is simply not true. We see this deal as South Africa going out into the world. We need to compete and there is absolute understanding by the government of this.[5]

The effect of the move would be to make the new Anglo into a British company and the existing South African Anglo into a wholly-owned subsidiary. Whatever the financial justifications for the move, its political message was an uncomfortable one for the new South Africa, even though the government put a brave face on what could only be seen as a blow to all the efforts it had made since 1994 to reassure business. There was, too, something strangely 'colonial' in Anglo running to London instead of remaining in Johannesburg where its principal assets lie.

In January 1998, Nicky Oppenheimer became chairman of De Beers, which mines half the world's diamonds and sells three-quarters of them. In his first speech as chair, he said plans to disentangle De Beers's activities from those of Anglo would sharpen the focus of the company: 'We do not think of anything but diamonds. The new De Beers will be focused as never before on the success of the world diamond industry.' His most pressing task is to maintain the cartel whose existence has long been crucial to the prices and profits of the diamond business. De Beers' stakes in the diamond mines of Botswana and Namibia which between them now produce a third of the world's diamonds gives the company apparently vast powers, but it is facing new and tough competition. The Argyle mine in western Australia quit the CSO in 1996, claiming it could do better outside the cartel, and two rival companies, Broken Hill Proprietary of Australia and Rio Tinto are opening new diamond mines in Canada. These developments suggest that the long reign of De Beers in control of the world diamond business could be coming to an end.

In December 1998, De Beers (as well as the Belgian government) was accused of failing to enforce UN sanctions against the rebel UNITA movement in Angola which finances itself by selling diamonds from areas of the country that it controls. According to the human rights group, Global Witness, De Beers had contributed to the continuation of the civil war in Angola by consistently purchasing diamonds from UNITA-controlled territory. Between 1992 (when UNITA resumed the civil war despite the UN-brokered peace) and 1998 UNITA obtained an estimated minimum revenue of $3.72 billion from the sale of diamonds. De Beers denied the accusation and claimed it only purchased Angolan rough diamonds when accompanied by an Angolan government certificate of origin.

In keeping with the spirit of the new South Africa, De Beers sold a 24 per cent stake in its Marsfontein joint venture to the black-owned New Diamond Corporation (NDC) for less than half its real value, at least according to analysts; it had sold the stake for R100 million to the NDC and other empowerment partners. It valued its remaining 60 per cent stake in Marsfontein at R200 million. However, other valuations suggest the mine is worth between R400 million and R700 million and that the pipe being mined is one of the richest in living memory.

Gold, long the barometer of the South African economy, suffered its worst year of production in 1994 when output dropped below 600 tons for the first time since 1958. The fall was blamed upon low productivity, labour unrest and diminishing cost competitiveness but, given the political background at the time, this was perhaps hardly surprising. Prophets of gloom were plentiful, with Dr Aiden Edwards of Mintek predicting that up to a third of South Africa's mines could close within five years. He said: 'The only way to remain profitable is to work the high-grade deposits only, which will shorten the life of a mine.' At the same time, Gencor, which is the fourth largest gold producer in the world, was looking at other African countries and further afield for future expansion of its goldmining operations. Gencor chairman, Brian Gilbertson, said the company was broadening its horizons to include different types of gold deposits elsewhere in the world; mainly smaller, shallower and easier to mine deposits in Turkey, South America, Ghana and Indonesia. Other mining companies were increasing their activities outside South Africa. Anglo American, with gold mines in Namibia and Mali, was also prospecting in Botswana, Senegal, Cote d'Ivoire, Niger, Ghana, Burkina Faso, Tanzania and Kenya. The message was clear enough: the mining companies were determined to spread their activities outside South Africa. Partly, this reflected the new political and economic realities; and partly, it was a natural reaction to the decline in easily available gold that was taking place in South Africa itself.

In October 1997, two of South Africa's largest mining houses, Gold Fields and Gencor, announced plans to merge their gold mines in a R17 billion deal to create the world's largest gold company. The merger combined some of the largest gold reserves in the country with some of the lowest cost producers. The new company would be called Goldco. The company would rival Anglo American in terms of its gold assets. Yet, despite such moves which were seen as a prelude to enhancing gold production, the mood of the mid-1990s was pessimistic because it was becoming increasingly clear that central banks and the financial markets were beginning to see gold as obsolete, while some governments were either selling their gold reserves or contemplating doing so. Should this trend continue South Africa will be the greatest loser and it was against this background that Deputy President Thabo Mbeki held discussions with European central bankers at the World Economic Forum early in 1998; South Africa had asked the European Union central banks to clarify their plans for gold reserves so as to cut speculation that was undermining the gold price. After the meeting Mbeki was able to tell a news conference:

> The level of confidence in gold as a store of value continues. ... It would be recognised as a problem if people say 'let us offload', but nobody is saying that. Even with regard to the new European (Central) Bank, gold will continue to be part of what backs the euro.[6]

The poor price of gold had adverse effects upon the workforce with more than 50000 jobs being lost in 1997 and 13000 in January 1998.

James Motlatsi, president of NUM, slammed the mining houses for 'taking advantage of the gold price (as) the reality of the matter was that they were reorganising themselves under the pretext of a gold price crisis.'[7] NUM called for a gold mining summit. As the major mining houses reorganised – whether because of the fall in gold prices or for other reasons – they were certain to meet growing opposition from an increasingly suspicious and militant trade union movement. At the end of February 1998, however, an accord was reached between the government, the mining companies and the unions under which a major review of the gold industry would be carried out to take account of such issues as state assistance to loss-making mines, the implementation of a social plan to lessen the impact of job losses, and finding suitable alternatives to job cuts, such as tighter cost controls and improved productivity. As the president of the Chamber of Mines, Bobby Godsell, said, the accord struck a balance between 'the harsh commercial realities of companies losing money and their need to cut labour' and the emphasis of the NUM on the 'profound effects of retrenchments on workers and their families.'[8] The state of the industry – from an employment point of view – could be gauged in terms of the fall in gold mine employees between 1986 when there were approximately 530 000 and 1997 when that figure had dropped to 320 000. The newly established Gold Crisis Committee (GCC) faced a formidable task in balancing the demands of an increasingly fearful labour force and the determination of the mining companies to retrench. The gold summit at the end of February 1998 averted a NUM strike and brokered a stay of execution for mining jobs. More important for the future, was the question of what power it would wield if gold prices continued to fall and the costs of extraction continued to rise.

In a radical move (radical for a mining house) to obtain black support Anglogold, which is the world's largest gold producer, appointed two high profile black executives to its board. These were Don Ncube, the chairman of Real African Investments, and James Motlatsi, president of the National Union of Mineworkers. Although aware that he would be criticised for 'selling out' to management, Motlatsi defended his acceptance of a place on the board of Anglogold and argued that it would be for the good of the industry as a whole. It is unlikely that such black representation on the board of a premier mining company would have come so quickly, despite pressures for black empowerment, had there not been a major crisis in the gold industry. It took place, moreover, at a time when the reverberations of the collapse of JCI which, in a major black empowerment deal, had come under black management in the person of Mzi Khumalo and was posing awkward questions about the success of the black empowerment policy. At the end of 1996 JCI shares were worth R46; a year later they had dropped to R36.50.

The JCI deal had represented a chance for black business to prove itself; instead, a number of things went wrong and did so in the course of a single year. Anglo American had received much praise for leading moves towards black empowerment with the JCI deal, even if it did make a profit of 140 million out of it. The collapse of JCI led Jimmy Manyi, the managing director of the Black Management Forum, to admit that it was a body blow for black economic empowerment and may retard a process that many blacks argue is already far too slow. Mr Manyi said the disaster highlighted the need for a commission to look at empowerment. 'There is no real black empowerment in South Africa' he said; 'A few individuals are enriching themselves but there is no trickle-down effect.' The JCI collapse may serve a useful purpose because it focused attention upon a process – black empowerment – that was far more of a political sleight of hand than an economic reality. Tony Twine, an economist with Econometrix, argued that lack of education, training and business experience were in part to blame for the slow pace of black empowerment but went on to pinpoint the core problem: white business, like all other bastions of white privilege, was dragging its heels. No group willingly surrenders the powers and privileges it holds, whatever it claims in public. The real solution was to expand the economy and for the government to ensure that black business got the greater part of the expansion. And that, almost certainly, will be what happens in the long run.

14
Finances

Despite the huge adjustments that South Africa has been forced to make during the 1990s – the end of apartheid and the coming of majority rule, international diffidence at risking large stakes in South Africa which, all too often, takes the form of a 'wait and see' response to calls for investment, the demands for black empowerment, and the impact of the Asian economic crisis – the rand and the economy have remained remarkably strong. Confidence in a country's ability to do things is often as important as the actual ability itself. One sign of this confidence was the rapid growth of the African Merchant Bank (AMB) which by late 1997 sought a listing on the JSE. The AMB was established in April 1995 with a R7 million investment from New Africa Investments Limited (Nail) and by October 1997 had raised its primary capital base to R500 million. As its chief executive, Rob Dow, explained, 'In each of its three financial years, AMB has posted substantial growth in earnings, focusing on expanding its business activities organically, without resorting to acquisitions.' Nail holds a 48 per cent interest in AMB, the American investment and merchant bank Donaldson Lufkin and Jenrette (DLJ), holds 15 per cent, management and staff hold 12 per cent while the rest is held by institutions. DLJ provides training and access to research and, by agreement with Nail, its merchant and investment banking activities in southern Africa would be conducted through AMB for a period of three years. AMB raised more than R6 billion in its first three years of operation for some 60 black business groups. In April 1998 AMB was granted investment grade credit ratings by Fitch IBCA which awarded A2 and BBB + ratings for AMB's short-term domestic debt obligations. Fitch IBCA said the ratings indicated that AMB had a strong capacity for timely payment in the short term and adequate capacity for timely repayment in the longer term.

Beginning in 1995 the Reserve Bank started to take black South Africans into senior positions although the process was slow and uneven. Transformation, as it is called, has been far from easy and, for example, in August 1997 the governor, Chris Stals, told the bank's 1800 staff that efforts had to be redoubled to make significant progress. Over three years the black workforce grew from 23.2 per cent to 32.1 per cent while the number of blacks in the bank's three top job categories rose from 13 to 36. It is such figures as these that demonstrate the slow rate of the transformation process that, nonetheless, is taking place. It is a question, at last, of South Africa beginning to make full use of all its people, no matter from which sections of society they come. Levers to assist the process of transformation include requiring managers who wish to take enhanced early retirement first to hire, and train a black person at a suitable level within that manager's department. As X. P. Guma found when he entered the bank in 1995, his Afrikaner colleagues made a point of sending him memos in Afrikaans which he did not understand; he said if they insisted on doing so he would reply in Xhosa. Movement in this vital area of human relations remains far too slow but the turnround will gather pace as more blacks reach senior positions.

In May 1998, Sanlam, South Africa's leading insurance company, decided to link with Genbel Securities (Gensec) to create an R18 billion asset management group. The combined group would become one of the six largest financial services companies in South Africa with R190 billion of assets under management. One reason that prompted the deal was the reshaping taking place of South Africa's financial services sector both in the country and offshore. Meanwhile, Old Mutual Investments had contributed funding worth more than R2.3 billion for black economic empowerment transactions since 1996 and claimed that investment returns on such black portfolio investments over two years exceeded 35 per cent a year, an indication of the new – black controlled-money – that is altering the face of the economy. Fund manager, Derrick Msibi, said Old Mutual had invested R521 million in 12 structured finance deals involving 15 black business groups that had bought into companies such as Johnnic, Avis, Forbes, Bidvest and Fedics. The group had invested more than R1 billion in listed black-owned companies.

The banking sector grew phenomenally during 1997–98 with a spate of mergers pushing the banking index up nearly 50 per cent in the first four months of 1998. Just how significant for general growth these mergers would prove remained to be seen. In May 1998, Lloyds of London opened a branch in South Africa, which by then was its ninth largest overseas market (and by far the largest in Africa) with a 1997 turnover in insurance premiums of R691 million. In July 1997, Tito Mboweni, the young minister of labour, was appointed as the first black head of the Reserve Bank and though leading companies including Anglo American, Nedcor and Standard Bank welcomed his appointment, there were fears – many of them clearly reflecting racial and political concerns rather than financial doubts – that his appointment would have a negative impact upon that elusive quality 'confidence' which is so readily and so often raised whenever inroads are made into the South African white power base. He was to shadow Chris Stals for a year before taking over.

Early in 1995 the JSE was included in the International Finance Corporation (IFC) Emerging Market indices and this sparked off a demand for South African equities. South Africa was included in the IFC indices from the beginning of April 1995 with a weighting of about 12 per cent in the Global Index and 23 per cent in the Investable Index. By mid-year, according to Adrian Allardice of Old Mutual, offshore managers (of unit trusts) had become net buyers of South African shares and were extending their interest from blue chip shares to second-tier stock. Africa represents the last of the emerging markets. Much of it is underdeveloped and of little interest to foreign investors. The exception is South Africa which is the world's fifth largest emerging market. Some of South Africa's leading companies should not be rated as emerging – they are world class – but the economy in terms of GDP and per capita income is an emerging one according to World Bank and IMF criteria. Offshore investors in South African funds may well see these as a starting point for investment elsewhere in Africa and especially in the countries of the Southern African region such as Angola, Botswana, Mozambique, Namibia and Zimbabwe, each of which has substantial resources awaiting development, provided that a relatively permanent peace can be achieved in the area, and especially in Angola. As yet, global funds have only 5 to 10 per cent of their assets in Africa, and most of these are in South Africa which, as a result, is in a potentially strong position to invest outwards into the rest of the continent.

By early 1998 it had become apparent that the Asian economic crisis had only marginally affected the South African economy which remained remarkably buoyant despite world gloom and by the end of February 1998 the JSE share index had achieved a new high with share prices roughly doubling between March 1997 and March 1998. Given the usual gloom about the state of the economy and the problems

South Africa faces that constantly emanates from Johannesburg this was a remarkable performance. In April 1998 the JSE all-share index passed 8000 for the first time; this was ascribed to huge and growing foreign interest. According to dealers, the JSE looked attractive to outsiders for several reasons: the market had generally under-performed world markets over the previous two or three years and had recovered quickly from the Asian crisis. Moreover, the economic fundamentals looked sound. The government appeared committed to its conservative macroeconomic policy, while producer inflation at 2.5 per cent was low.

During late 1997 and into 1998 the South African JSE became the favourite attraction for foreign investments seeking a niche in developing markets; it had survived the Asian crisis and, generally, was prospering although portfolio investments in the stock exchange can be withdrawn as quickly as they can be deposited. The South African market was important as the only one on the continent that attracted sizeable foreign investment. It did so for a number of reasons: because operations are conducted in English, the world business language with particular appeal to Britain and the USA, which are the two most likely sources of new investment from the West; because communications are efficient; the government stable; and the long-term investment prospects are encouraging. What also became apparent in 1998 was the interest of a growing number of black South Africans in the JSE as a place to invest their money and increase their wealth with a number of new black millionaires emerging. And in 1997, for example, the Women Investment Portfolio Holdings sought to raise R40 million by means of a public offer of 20 million shares at 200c; over 11 million shares were taken up. The demutualisation of both Sanlam and Old Mutual in 1998 was expected to raise the market capitalisation of the JSE by an estimated R80 billion with a consequent increase in South Africa's weighting in emerging market indices, such as the International Finance Corporation index, from 12.5 to 14.4 per cent. In turn, this was expected to attract more foreign investment. When Sanlam made its debut on the JSE in December 1998 it had a market capitalisation of R15.7 billion which put the company up in the JSE top 20 companies by size.

However, the excitement about a booming JSE was tempered by the fact that a number of major companies sought to have their primary listings transferred to the London Stock Exchange, a move that was seen as wounding to the JSE and, even more, to the *amour propre* of the new government. In February 1999, Trevor Manuel, the finance minister, indicated that applications for listing in London would in no sense be automatic. Approval for listing in London had already been given to four leading South African companies – Anglo American, Billiton, Old Mutual and South African Breweries – each of which was able to make a convincing case in terms of its actual or potential international status – for a London listing. On the other hand, exchange control regulations mean the minister's permission has to be obtained and Trevor Manuel made plain that he was not interested in allowing a major migration of some of the country's most dynamic companies to the LSE. Billiton, which was the first company to achieve a London listing, found that its position in the listing was far from an easy one to maintain and that it almost dropped out of the FTSE 100 within a short time of its listing though it managed to avoid this by a late rally. Nonetheless, the attractions of the LSE, where more than 500 foreign companies are listed, remains great and London financiers, despite Manuel's reluctance, believe that before long up to 40 per cent of the JSE's market capital could be listed in London which, on a daily basis, at $11.4 billion, trades double the value of international shares than are traded in New York.[1]

These moves to London raise difficult political and psychological questions for the South African government. They were certainly not expected when the international community welcomed back South Africa into its ranks in 1994. Just why companies should take this step is open to debate. One reason advanced is that these major companies, which are all white-controlled, are doing so for fear of future political and economic uncertainty. Given the endless predictions about future uncertainty that were made once the initial euphoria of 1994/95 had worn off, this is hardly surprising. On the other hand, the groups that have moved argue they want to raise their international profiles so as to improve their chances of obtaining the hard currency they need for global expansion. Both arguments have a place but if South Africa is to deal successfully with its myriad problems at home, it will be most likely to do so if its economy is expanding and creating additional wealth and this, in turn, will be helped if its major companies can turn themselves into highly profitable international ones, always providing that, at a later date, they do not move offshore altogether.

South Africa's outward thrust was also reflected in 1998 by its decision to increase its share in the African Development Bank (ADB) by as much as six times. This move revealed a new confidence in the Bank as a driving force in the 'African Renaissance' which Thabo Mbeki has proclaimed. The South African pledge amounts to a further contribution of US$1.31 billion. The move, which increases South Africa's holding in the Bank from one per cent to six per cent, came after reforms leading to better management had been put in place following a two-year overhaul that had weeded out much of the deadwood that had given the bank a name for inefficiency and cronyism.[2] Gill Marcus, South Africa's deputy finance minister, described the move as 'not just in the interests of South Africa, it is part and parcel of our obligations as an African country. Any renaissance starts at home. The issues facing the continent face us: the poverty index, the have and have-nots divide' she said. And a further boost for South Africa came with the decision of the Bank to approve the introduction of the rand as the first African currency to be used for its disbursements. South Africa joined Botswana as the second African country to make contributions to the group's soft loan fund, the African Development Fund. The South African assumption of a higher role in the Bank underscored its commitment to play a vital part in the economic revival of the continent.

In its 1998 report the Development Bank of South Africa claimed to have nearly doubled its loans over the preceding year to R4.3 billion enabling 20 000 new jobs to be created after it had disbursed R2.2 billion for infrastructural projects, while a further 34 000 jobs were expected to be created as a result of projects approved during the year. The increase in the bank's activities had been achieved during a period of massive transformation. The bank's chief executive, Ian Goldin, said that these results showed 'that there is not a conflict between productivity and transformation. This past year has been a story of enormous growth within a transformation context.' During the period under review the bank had pursued an aggressive policy of affirmative action which resulted in the number of black and women managers increasing by 83 per cent. Although the transformation process had been tough and had caused tensions it had gone reasonably well. In addition to this programme inside South Africa, the bank had extended its reach outside the country with loans of nearly R2 billion for projects in Southern African Development Community (SADC) countries which by then accounted for 17 per cent of the bank's loans. Speaking on the occasion of the release of the Bank's Report, Deputy President Thabo Mbeki said:

As one of the primary funding agents of infrastructure in the Southern African Development Community region, the bank's role is pivotal. It must act as a catalyst to mobilise international and private sector funding for investment in infrastructure in the area.[3]

The state of an economy is reflected through its banking and stock-broking systems and in 1998, against complex international and internal problems, those of South Africa appeared to be refreshingly buoyant.

15
Agriculture

Although agriculture contributes less than five per cent to GDP its importance for the economy as a whole can hardly be exaggerated. The sector employs 13 per cent of the labour force. South Africa is both self-sufficient in food and a substantial food exporter, though in drought years it faces a shortfall in maize, the staple crop. Agricultural products account for seven per cent of exports and include beef, a surplus of maize in good years, fruit and vegetables. Cape wines have long been famous and with the end of apartheid these were recapturing their place in the world as a major export. South Africa has rich offshore fisheries with an annual catch in excess of 500 000 mt and fish make an important contribution to exports. Farming is inextricably wound into the history of the Dutch at the Cape and, until very recently, the Boers or Afrikaners have seen themselves, first and foremost, as farmers. Land, its possession and working, lay at the centre of Afrikaner politics. Today, despite huge changes in the Afrikaner community and the move of many Afrikaners into business and other occupations remote from the land, farming remains at the emotional core of Afrikanerdom. Disputes about land may last longer and be more politically damaging to the new South Africa than many of the other problems of adjustment that have to be faced.

The low subsistence wages and poor conditions of black farmworkers have long been notorious and it was inevitable that land reform would rate high on the ANC agenda after the 1994 election. In mid-1995 the Cabinet passed and gazetted for public comment the Land Reform (Labour Tenants) Bill; it became an immediate target of attack by white farmers for, unlike other land reform measures, it provided for land to be expropriated from the owners of 'labour farms'. These were large estates found in southeastern Transvaal and the northern areas of

141

KwaZulu-Natal round Newcastle where some 40000 black families lived and provided their labour in return for small patches of land for subsistence farming. The relationship between white farmers and black labourers epitomised everything that was wrong with the old system: for the blacks a form of harsh and inescapable bondage to the white farmers.

Commercial farms, almost all owned by whites and a majority of these Afrikaners, provide the only means of survival for between five and six million of the poorest people in the countryside. The hard right in South Africa argues that only white farmers can produce the food the country needs. But the majority, however reluctantly, know that change must come and that their unfettered control of the land is a thing of the past: land reform and redistribution is inevitable as is a change in the labour laws and the rights of small tenants. At a meeting of white farmers in Newcastle during July 1995, many of whom were members of the far right Afrikaner Weerstandsbeweging (AWB), despite defiant rhetoric there was a sense that change had to come and, as the right-wing leader of Resistance Against Communism, Eddie von Maltitz, said, 'They want to give this approach a chance to work. We want to try and help this Hanekom (Derek Hanekom, Minister for Land Affairs) and to become players in the game. We'll keep our eye on the ball because if we don't, we know we'll lose it.'[1]

One aspect of agriculture through the years of apartheid was the system of marketing schemes that ensured a flow of food and prevented violent price fluctuations so that food shortages or price hikes did not become a political issue. Marketing control meant stable prices for producers and consumers. The schemes became entrenched as a safeguard against the country's unpredictable climate and harsh (arid) farming conditions. However, as at the beginning of 1998 the system was ended and South Africa instead must face the far more volatile price movements that are both an automatic and necessary part of an open, free market system. Under an open system farmers will sell to the best market and should the whole of Southern Africa face a drought then demands from neighbouring countries such as Botswana or Zimbabwe could result in the staple crop of maize being exported to those destinations if the price offered were high enough – unless the price also went up sharply in South Africa itself or the government intervened. The 1997/98 season produced a bumper maize crop of 8.5 million tons. For 1998/99 the crop was estimated at 6.86 million tons – 2.8 million tons of yellow maize and 4.06 tons of white maize. This average crop would meet domestic needs which are between 6- and 7-million tons. There is not much margin however and the region is subject to periodic droughts, the population is increasing, and the acceptance of market forces rather than a controlled marketing system must make the future of this staple crop more volatile.

At Sydney, Australia, in April 1998, South Africa joined the Cairns Group as its fifteenth member. The group consists of countries prepared to battle with the world's economic powers in order to secure free trade in agricultural products; their main targets are Europe and Japan which protect their own highly subsidized farmers, and the USA. The South African minister of agriculture, Derek Hanekom, described the Cairns Group as revolutionary and said that South Africa's role in it must be central since it was the only African member. He said: 'We're lobbying against subsidies, including export subsidies, and to strengthen our case, we need not only to stand together as a club but to target food importing countries.'[2] The Cairns Group consists of middle powers such as Canada, Australia, New Zealand, food exporters in Southeast Asia – Malaysia, Thailand and Indonesia – a bloc of South American countries and some poor countries such as Fiji and the Philippines, so that South Africa found itself in good company. As Tim Fisher, Australia's deputy prime minister, said 'We're looking to South Africa to play a very useful role of forming a conduit into Africa.' Hanekom announced his intention to lobby the SADC countries to push for freer agricultural trade. South Africa and its new partners face a hard fight if they are to change the existing system. Subsidies in the OECD countries to uncompetitive farmers are estimated at US$280 billion a year which represents a huge financial and political hurdle to overcome if any system of freer agricultural trade is to be achieved. The top three targets for the group, in order, are, the EU with its Common Agricultural Policy, the USA and Japan. The United States, for example, is adept at creating trade barriers in the form of sanitary measures which set hygiene standards that control food and plant imports, but in real terms protect their farmers from unwelcome competition.

In the meantime, following the deregulation of the country's fruit export business, South Africa itself at once became a target country for the major food multinationals. Dole, the largest US fruit and vegetable importer into Europe and Japan, moved quickly in 1998 to establish itself in South Africa where it aimed to secure 25 per cent of the country's multi-billion rand deciduous, citrus and sub-tropical fruit production. Dole operates in 85 countries and has an annual turnover of approximately US$4.3 billion. The arrival of Dole in South Africa represented a major challenege to the country's main fruit exporters, Unifruco and Outspan, although both insisted they would hold onto a substantial part of their markets. Dole, however, will provide fruit producers with a formidable alternative outlet to the formerly entrenched South African organisations. Dole, which concentrates upon supplying supermarket needs, brings much-needed competition into South Africa where, during the apartheid years, many forms of institutionalised protection made major companies complacent about their market shares. As Benoit Galland, the managing director of Dole South Africa, said: 'The fact that we are setting up a company in South Africa highlights our long-term commitment to sourcing southern African fruit to meet market needs.' Such corporate-speak represents a new challenge to a South Africa that must adjust to a globalized market. In November 1998 Unifruco and Outspan announced that they were merging to form a single marketer for South Africa's fruit; it was a move to achieve economies of scale in a new more competitive market and to meet the growing competition from independent newcomers, including Dole and Del Monte from the United States, that had arrived in South Africa since deregulation had brought an end to single-channel export marketing.

Moves by President Mugabe of Zimbabwe to redistribute white-owned farms produced acrimonious debate and threats from international donors, highlighting the dangers of a poorly conceived land reform policy. In South Africa Derek Hanekom, responsible for land affairs, responded to events in Zimbabwe by defending the government's approach to the problem:

> Our redistrution policy distinguishes us from most countries which also suffered land dispossessions in their histories. But the two biggest threats to existing landowners are the absence of any land reform programme – and an ill-conceived policy. In South Africa, I believe, we have circumvented both these threats by devising a rational, implementable programme.[3]

The South African programme consists of three broad elements: the restitution of land taken (post-1913) from its former owners as a result of race-based legislation; redistribution of land to the landless and needy by the state according to market-related prices and principles; and reform of land tenure so that the occupation rights of labour tenants and farmworkers are protected. Claims had to be lodged with the Land Claims court by the end of 1998. The process is slow, fraught with emotional and political dangers – and essential to the long-term well-being of the country.

In mid-1998 President Mandela warned that only a fair redistribution of land to its former black owners would guarantee peace in post-apartheid South Africa. He was speaking at a ceremony in KwaZulu-Natal to mark the return of more than 600 000 hectares of land to former black owners. The ceremony included handing back land to about 85 black households whose land had been appropriated during the apartheid era. Mandela said: 'Our land reform programme helps redress the injustices of apartheid. It fosters national reconciliation and stability. It also underpins economic growth and improves house-hold welfare and food security.' The whites still own most of the best land in South Africa. They make up only 13 per cent of the population but control over 70 per cent of the land.[4] By 1998 about 23 000 cases had been lodged with the Land Commission demanding restitution of land rights while up to 400 000 hectares of land had been redistributed back to nearly a quarter of a million former black owners. The government was careful not to enter into confrontation with the white landowners.

Yet confrontation lies close to the surface in rural areas where vio-lence and the murders of white farmers have threatened any smooth changeover in agricultural policy. During 1998, for example, 15 white people in remote areas were murdered over six weeks, leading President Mandela to meet with his security chiefs to address white fears. George Fivaz, the national police chief, designated two senior officers to co-ordinate a rural protection plan while urging white farmers not to take the law into their own hands. On the other hand, there remained deep black resentment that four years after the 1994 elections little in fact had changed on the land and farm labourers still only received R20 or less in pay a month and were subject to corporal punishment. Moreover, according to the Pan Africanist Congress white farmers accentuated anger in rural communities by hiring cheap labour from Zimbabwe and Mozambique. Attacks on farms were believed to be motivated more by bitterness than greed, for in most cases nothing was stolen in the isolated attacks. White farmers claimed that the attacks were politically inspired although the government said the attacks were simply criminal. The political motive seemed more likely to be true since many farmers had evicted thousands of tenants in advance of new legislation to give farm workers tenure rights.[5] The land question brings into confrontation two elements in South Africa that are farthest apart from each other: white farmers who had long been among the most ardent supporters of the apartheid system; and the black farm labourers and their dependents who have long been the largest group of the poorest people in the country. It will take years before the land problem is equitably resolved.

Some white farmers decided to leave the new South Africa and trek north to farm elsewhere on the black continent. Given the history of South Africa and the nineteenth-century trek from the Cape by the Boers to escape British rule – and all that followed from that trek as they established their Republics of the Orange Free State and Transvaal – the 1990s spectacle of Afrikaner farmers seeking permission to carry out a modern trek into countries such as Zaire had about it all the elements of tragi-comedy. Four African countries – Angola, Mozambique, Uganda and Zaire (later the Democratic Republic of Congo) – were willing to exploit the farming experience of Afrikaner farmers to help feed populations that had been ravaged by wars or other ills. According to retired General Constand Viljoen who led a pioneering mission to Zaire in March 1995, 'This (the movement north of Afrikaner farmers) can serve as a catalyst to promote cooperation in southern Africa, around a common aim instead of the negative ideological differences of the past.' The General, leader of the right-wing Freedom Front, had already been on a similar mission to Mozambique. The object, to be supported by government agreements, was to grant land leases for 44 years to about 2000 Afrikaners. Another leader of this unlikely Afrikaner migrant movement, Hans Herbst, visited Uganda; reporting back, he said 'The people is lovingful. It rains a lot there. There is open space for South African farmers who know anything about agriculture.' According to Mr Herbst 14 farm families from his district in Transvaal were prepared to go to Uganda. The ironies of this development were startling. That Afrikaner farmers should be welcomed in Mozambique at a time when it was just recovering from a brutal civil war which had been carefully fostered by South Africa was bizarre enough, especially as the Speaker of the South African Parliament had just made an official apology to that country for the damage done to it during the RENAMO war. That they should be interested in trekking farther north to Zaire or Uganda represented a new kind of colonialism whose contradictions did not appear to bother the Afrikaners proposing such moves. Perhaps they did not even understand that there were contradictions inherent in such a move.

Nonetheless, the move north gathered a certain momentum during 1995. Dries Bruwer, the president of the Transvaal Agricultural Union, said the leaders of the scheme had established a forum to deal with the logisitics of moving, while a South African Chamber for Agriculture in Africa (SACAA) was created in July 1995. The would-be migrants claimed support from business and Bruwer said: 'The businessmen know our economy won't survive if we don't establish some kind of RDP in southern Africa'; a sentiment that could be seen as a forerunner of Thabo Mbeki's later vision of a renaissance for Africa. President Mandela supported the idea and had appointed General Constand Viljoen as his emissary to Africa. In August 1995 the white farmer trek began when 20 families – the first of 300 – flew to Congo (Brazzaville) to begin a new life. Arrangements were made by SADC and the Congo government and the farmers were to be settled in the Niare valley between the seaport of Pointe Noire and the capital Brazzaville. Other groups were due to settle in Zaire and Mozambique. The Congo settlers had obtained 99 year leases on their properties from the Congo government. The move had been worked out between Congolese officials, the South African government and SADC. The organiser of this move to Congo, Johan van der Westhuizen, said 'We believe in the next year about 100 to 120 farmers will be leaving for the Congo.' He added that South African farmers who were tired of bad rains and high farming costs (and, possibly, no longer quiescent blacks) believed they faced a better future in the Congo where there was high rainfall and large tracts of available fertile land. According to Congo's ambassador to South Africa, Manu Mahoungou, his country could benefit from the South African farmers. 'South African farmers are among the best in the world, and their contributions will be their know-how, technology … their contribution will be of very great importance.'[6]

A report in *The Star* of May 1998[7] suggested that the white farmers who had trekked under the Mozagrius scheme to a remote part of Mozambique's Niassa Province in 1997 were bringing a green revolution to the area. The chairman of the group, Antonio Muacorica, claimed that in just one year of operation the farmers, who had joined with a group of 10 local farmers, had succeeded in more than doubling the yields of maize per hectare. They had also improved the yields of crops such as millet, wheat, sugar beans and soya. They had earned foreign exchange for Mozambique with exports to Malawi worth US$110 000. The group had been selected from 200 Mozambicans and 50 South Africans. Each farmer was allocated 1500 hectares of land and seed capital to the value of R50 000 at commercial interest rates. Total investment in the project, after a year, stood at R1.3 million. The Mozambican government had allocated 220 000 hectares of land to the project of which 160 000 hectares had been taken up. The farmers had boosted development in a huge, sparsely populated province. Each farmer employed about 50 people.

If these farm projects work, not just in the first few years of enthusi-asm but over a longer term, they could be seen as a welcome South African export. Yet the idea is full of contradictions. Apart from the neocolonialism that is so clearly a part of the whole trekking venture, why are these farmers trekking away from the new South Africa? If they want to assist an African renaissance, why not in South Africa itself? If they can work in partnership with black Mozambicans, why not in partnership with black South Africans? If they are leaving the country in which for so long they have been part of the ruling minor-ity because they cannot face living in a black-ruled South Africa, just what kind of values will they take into the countries to the north? If it is escapism they seek then, no doubt, President Mandela was wise to let them go.

16
Foreign Policy I: Britain, the Commonwealth and the European Union

At Westminster Abbey, in May 1994, following the elections of the previous April which had resulted in Nelson Mandela becoming the first black president of his country, a grand service was held to commemorate the return of South Africa to the Commonwealth. The occasion, attended by Queen Elizabeth the Queen Mother, was a classic example of British establishment hypocrisy: South Africa was welcomed back as though it had been the prodigal son while Britain, by implication, had done nothing of which to be ashamed. In fact, the opposite was the case. When in 1910, still in her imperial heyday, Britain gave the new Union of South Africa self-government on a par with that already enjoyed by her other Dominions – Australia, Canada and New Zealand – she carefully obfuscated the question of political rights for the black majority in the full knowledge that the white minority had no intention whatsoever of sharing power. In the decades that followed and through the long years of apartheid, Britain, almost always, came down on the side of the white racist minority, helping to safeguard it from growing world anger after 1948 as apartheid was applied to every aspect of South African life.

During the crisis years of apartheid, Britain was always more concerned to safeguard its interests in South Africa than to exert the considerable pressure which the existence of those interests gave it, as a lever to alter the conditions that put the interests at risk in the first place. As Lynda Chalker, junior minister at the Foreign Office in 1988 with responsibility for southern Africa, said in defence of Britain's extensive involvement in South Africa at that time: 'You do not convert a country to Christianity by withdrawing the missionaries.' There was little evidence, however, to suggest that the missionaries had ever been more than nominally active in pursuing conversion. Throughout her eleven years as Britain's Prime Minister, Margaret Thatcher opposed the imposition of any sanctions upon South Africa in order to exert pressure against apartheid and as Frene Ginwala (later the Speaker of the South African Parliament) argued:

> Nothing could better illustrate the political perspectives of those governments which oppose sanctions than their new-found concern with the suffering of blacks in South Africa which they use to justify continued support for Pretoria. This argument is hypocritical, presumptuous and racist. Are we supposed to believe that Mrs Thatcher, for one, is unaware that blacks have been suffering for decades because of apartheid and are suffering even now?[1]

Once the changeover had occurred and Nelson Mandela had become President, Britain wasted no time in acknowledging the new leadership, almost as though London had long been fighting valiantly alongside the ANC to bring about change in South Africa. In March 1995 the Queen went on a state visit to South Africa. It was the first visit by a British monarch since 1947 when the Queen, as Princess Elizabeth, had accompanied George VI on his visit shortly after the end of World War II. On that occasion George VI had referred to the problems South Africa faced when he said:

> Adjusting from day-to-day the progress of a white population of well over 2 million with that of a far greater number of other peoples, very different in race and background ... .There is no easy formula for the wise discharge of this formidable task.[2]

A year later, when Dr Malan and the National Party came to power, the formula chosen was apartheid.

At the beginning of the Queen's visit the Deputy President, Thabo Mbeki, said 'Her visit is a sign of the strength of relations between this country and the United Kingdom.' Later the Queen formally welcomed South Africa back into the Commonwealth, appointed Nelson Mandela to the Order of Merit, and praised the spirit of compromise with which he had guided South Africa to peace and freedom. President Mandela reciprocated by making the Queen a member of the South African Order of Good Hope. What, perhaps, was extraordinary on this occasion and later, was the way in which Mandela spoke with such warmth of Britain and made plain how he – and his government – valued the two-way relationship. He behaved as though no blame should attach to Britain for the apartheid years that earlier British policies had ensured would come about.

As South Africa grappled with its problems of transition and adjustment, the need to attract foreign investment was given high priority and here the British connexion was of great importance. Apart from old imperial ties, language and a large white population of direct British descent, Britain had always been the country's principal trading partner and a major source of investment. Moreover, South Africa needed a sympathetic ally in the European Union whose trade and investment represent a vital part of Pretoria's outward strategy. Britain and South Africa had signed an investment and protection agreement in 1995, when Mandela visited Britain. This agreement was renegotiated in May 1998. In September 1998 the British consul-general in South Africa, Nick McInnes, outlined the extent of the two-way economic relationship between the two countries and emphasized that Britain was South Africa's largest trading partner. In 1997 British exports to South Africa were worth £1.7 billion (R11bn), while South African exports to Britain came to £1.3 billion, to make Britain, by far, South Africa's largest export market. When invisible earnings were also taken into account two-way trade was worth in excess of £5 billion. In addition, Britain was by far the largest investor in South Africa with investments worth more than £10 billion. Mr McInnes said that South Africa was one of Britain's target markets in terms of trade promotion:

> Several British companies, aware that they cannot compete in certain countries because of the high cost of manufacturing in Britain, are looking at South Africa as a base for manufacturing goods for export to markets as far afield as south America and south-east Asia. So there could be a surge in British investment in South Africa in the months and years ahead.[3]

Britain's Prime Minister, Tony Blair, visited South Africa in January 1999, in another move to promote closer relations between the two countries. Mr Blair asked President Mandela (he had already done so at the Edinburgh Commonwealth Heads of Government summit of October 1997) to use his good offices to persuade Colonel Gaddafi to handover for trial in The Hague the two Libyan officials suspected of planting the bomb on the Pan Am flight which exploded over Lockerbie in 1988. When, in April 1999, the two Libyans were finally sent to stand trial in a Scottish Court constituted in The Hague, they went in considerable part because Mandela had persuaded President

Gaddafi that they would receive a fair trial. The Blair visit was important since both sides see Anglo–South African relations as critical to their respective interests. Primarily, Britain is interested in South Africa as an export market while South Africa sees Britain as a main source of inward investment. Tony Blair spent a good deal of his time getting to know Thabo Mbeki who was expected to succeed Mandela as President of South Africa following elections in mid-1999. These meetings were important to both men.

Demands for apologies for the misdeeds of past governments became something of a political vogue during the 1990s and on arrival in South Africa Blair faced demands from the Afrikaner community for an apology for the deaths of thousands of women and children in British concentration camps set up during the Anglo–Boer War at the turn of the century when between 20 000 and 26 000 Boer civilians died in the camps from typhoid, dysentery, enteric fever and other diseases. Three quarters of the victims had been children. The demands highlighted the longstanding and complex relationship between the two countries. Mr Blair's visit was mainly concerned with trade, including an arms deal, and investment.

The return of South Africa to the Commonwealth after more than 30 years absence gave the association a major boost. The one African country with substantial international clout led by a man who had become a world revered figure, South Africa brought a sense of rejuvenation to the Commonwealth which, for years, had been neglected by Britain and seen as a fighting ground for arguments about sanctions against apartheid. At the Auckland, New Zealand, Commonwealth Summit of November 1995 two developments, one good, one bad, each included a special South African contribution. Mozambique, the first state that had never been a British colony, was admitted to the Commonwealth as a full member. This was in recognition of its role during the 1980s as a frontline state, the fact that it was surrounded by southern African Commonwealth countries, including the newly rejoined South Africa, and because of especially strong pleading by South Africa that it should be allowed to join. The admission of this new member certainly gave a fillip to Commonwealth optimists.

Unfortunately, a crisis arose over Nigeria whose military ruler, General Sani Abacha, deliberately defied the Commonwealth by having the anti-government activists, Ken Saro-Wiwa and his colleagues, executed in Port Harcourt prison as Commonwealth leaders assembled in New Zealand. President Mandela who had argued for quiet diplomacy rather than tougher sanctions against Abacha found that his approach was brutally ignored by the Nigerian leader. The event did considerable damage to Mandela's image and raised questions about his and the Commonwealth's determination to take tough action. It was a lesson in the limits of influence. Mandela, whose healing style had done so much for transition in South Africa, had assumed wrongly (or his advisers had) that a 'softly softly' approach would work with Abacha. It did not and Mandela's failure signalled the limits that could be achieved by reason when not backed by more tangible pressures. It was a lesson that Mandela had yet to appreciate as he was to discover two years later in relation to Laurent Kabila in Zaire. However, despite this debacle, the return of South Africa to the Commonwealth was a welcome plus for the association and a source of added influence for South Africa.

The European Union, the world's largest trading bloc which has moved into a position of economic equality with the USA, is of immense importance to South Africa. Apart from Britain, Germany, Italy, the Netherlands, Spain and Portugal are each important trading partners while access to the EU market is essential to South Africa's trade expansion. In 1995, on his visit to South Africa, the then German Chancellor Helmut Kohl had promised that Germany would help South Africa build up its economy. In fact not a great deal of either investment or enhanced interest had followed. Although in 1997 German direct foreign investment world-wide came to DM50.5 billion, only DM200 million of this found its way to South Africa and that represented a drop of 40 per cent from the investment figure for 1996. According to the South African German Chamber of Commerce, local German business interest in South Africa nearly halved during 1998 with more than half all German business, and especially small and medium-sized firms, holding negative views about South Africa. A survey showed that confidence had slipped from 86 per cent in 1997 to 48 per cent in 1998. Germany is a top investor in South Africa's automotive, electronic and pharmaceutical sectors while the 168 companies surveyed employed 42 000 people. Such findings are bound to be discouraging and South Africa must get used to combating the familiar list of arguments advanced by Western business: that confidence depends upon the elimination of violence, absence of corruption, high standards in the civil service and a number of other demands which, if they were all met, would turn South Africa into a paragon of states. At the same time, Pretoria learnt over years of bargaining just how tough the European Union could be and just how little sentiment counts in the economic world.

After a long battle in the South Africa–Europe negotiations, the EU finally agreed that affirmative action criteria should be allowed to apply in tenders for the supply of computers and other equipment for the South African parliament: preference would be given to black tenderers or tenderers involved in subcontracting or partnership agreements with black entrepreneurs. This small but important victory was in relation to the EU's R85 million programme for support services to parliament.[4] Its significance lay in the fact that economic programmes of any kind always have a social and political aspect to them and this fact should not be ignored, especially as the EU, by far the stronger partner in the two-way negotiations, has in its Common Agricultural Policy (CAP) by far the largest social-political-economic programme in the world.

As South Africa discovered, the proposed free trade agreement with the EU would only become a reality if it was prepared to accept a range of exceptions which at one stage included the EU suggestion that 46 per cent of South Africa's agricultural exports should be excluded. At the beginning of 1998 a June deadline had been set for reaching agreement. South Africa, insisting that its agricultural products should be given better access to the European market, found itself up against a European stonewall. During February 1998 South Africa threatened to pull out of the talks unless the EU offer was improved. According to Elias Links, the South African ambassador to the EU, and Bahle Sibisi, the chief director for trade relations in the department of trade and industry, the EU offers were disappointingly protectionist and placed much of the adjustment burden upon South Africa. That was certainly in keeping with the EU approach which has always sought to maintain maximum protection for its own markets while insisting upon maximum penetration of the world's weaker, developing markets. South Africa, however, showed no inclination to clinch a quick deal. Although, at this stage in the negotiations (February 1998), 76 per cent of South Africa's exports to the EU would be free of duty, about six per cent of its total trade, or 46 per cent of its agricultural trade, would be excluded from the tariff cuts. Thus, it was proposed that tariffs on products where South Africa had the greatest export potential, such as vegetables, fruit, meat and some wines, would only be cut between the fourth and tenth year and in some cases not until the twelfth year. It was in this area (agriculture) that South Africa's social and political concerns for its important farming sector exactly mirrored EU concerns, through CAP, for its own highly protected farming sector.

South Africa found some important European allies in its fight to obtain better access to the EU for its agricultural exports. A group of European parliamentarians supported South Africa's attempt to ensure that its trade agreement with the EU would deliver growth, development and job creation in South Africa. Alex Smith, one of the European parliamentarians who visited South Africa in 1997, had written to Joao de Deus Pinheiro, the European Commissioner responsible for the negotiations with South Africa, complaining that the existing trade regime discriminated against South Africa at the cost of thousands of jobs and that, for example, thousands of workers had been paid off from canning factories because high subsidies to European farmers as well as tariffs make South African products uncompetitive both in Europe and at home. As Alex Smith said in his submission to the Commissioner: 'We would hope to see a significant improvement in the market arrangements for South African agricultural exports (including canned fruit), and expect a comprehensive resolution of the problems created by the export of subsidised EU food products.'[5] He pointed out that canned and fresh deciduous fruit which South Africa had long exported to Europe now faced customs duties of up to 21 per cent while subsidised European canned products such as tomatoes could enter South Africa at prices way below the cost of producing them locally.

South Africa's tough stance against the EU's original mandate that had listed products to be excluded from a free trade area drew further concessions from the EU in March 1998. The EU offered to include 30 industrial products and 480 farm goods in its list of South African exports that could enter the EU tariff-free. The list included some ferro-alloys, wines, spirits and certain dairy products. The result would be to raise the list of South African tariff-free imports to the EU from 90 per cent to 94 per cent. Despite these concessions, about 46 per cent of farm goods were still excluded and these represented the mainstay of South Africa's export business to Europe.

Meanwhile, South Africa was beginning to examine the implications of a common European currency that was destined to come into effect in January 1999. European Monetary Union would lead to fundamental changes in international finance, trade and investment and, according to Gilles Rollet of ABN Amro South Africa, 'Africa might well become the next century's economic miracle and the economic integration occurring in Europe offers an interesting range of opportunities for this continent.' He suggested that the euro would come to rival the

US dollar.[6] In this, as in so many other respects, South Africa had to learn to adjust to a fast-changing international economic scene.

The South Africa–EU negotiations about a free trade agreement bogged down during May 1998 and so it was hoped that President Mandela, whom Britain's Prime Minister Tony Blair had invited to attend the EU Cardiff summit in June, would help to break the deadlock although, ostensibly, his visit was to enable him to say farewell to the European statesmen and women with whom he had been dealing. The 19th round of negotiations, due to take place on 11 and 12 June, would have to resolve seven key issues before the agreement could be concluded according to schedule although by then this looked increasingly unlikely. The seven outstanding issues concerned anti-dumping and countervailing measures, safeguards for South African industry during the implementation of any agreement, maritime transport, the South African government procurement policy, competition policy, intellectual property rights and agricultural policies. It was clear by this time that the EU was determined to obtain concessions for its politically powerful agricultural lobby; South Africa, on the other hand, was fighting a tough rearguard action to protect its own interests. It was also learning hard lessons about power. South Africa could not match the EU in terms of market power or access to information while its own lobby groups were simply not comparable to those of the European farming interests. The EU was using the negotiations with South Africa as a forerunner for further negotiations, later with the Southern African Development Community (SADC) and then the African, Caribbean and Pacific (ACP) countries for the successor to the Lomé Convention. As a result, South Africa was in the position of representing, in its negotiations with the EU, a far wider constituency than simply its own interests and it was beholden upon it not to make any concessions to the EU that subsequently could be used as a precedent for EU dealings with other, weaker economic groups.

At the June Cardiff summit EU leaders promised President Mandela that a trade deal between the EU and South Africa would be agreed by October. South Africa had been complaining that the EU was reneging on its political commitment to help it increase its share of world trade. But the summit promise, as subsequent events would demonstrate, was more of a goodwill gesture towards President Mandela than a true reflection of EU intentions. Both Britain's Tony Blair and Sweden's Prime Minister, Goran Persson, who were strong supporters of the South African position, were embarrassed at the lack of progress in the negotiations. As Mandela said, reflecting a statement by Michel

Camdessus, the managing director of the IMF, that European protective policies had hurt employment in Africa,

> Our position, and the position of Africa, seems to have been accepted by the IMF. The largest industrial countries have a large responsibility in particular to help Africa. ... They must phase out subsidies for agricultural exports.[7]

In mid-September, however, the EU widened the agenda under discussion by insisting that European fishermen should be given access to South African waters as the price for agreeing a new trade and aid framework for South Africa. Philip Lowe, the EU chief negotiator, warned that any deal had to be ratified by both the South African government and 'all 15 EU governments'. This, of course, represents yet another unfair card in the EU armoury for though South Africa negotiates with Brussels alone, in the end any agreement may be turned down because one of the 15 constituent governments refuses to ratify, in effect making any deal a one-to-fifteen arrangement. In addition, the EU insisted that South Africa phased out the use of the words 'port' and 'sherry' for its fortified wines. At the end of September, South Africa again suspended the talks. Commenting on the new EU line South Africa's ambassador to the EU, Elias Links, said: 'The position has been very hardline from their side. What we want is for the European Commission to come back with an improved agricultural offer. We were offered a fait accompli.' Bahle Sibisi of the Department of Trade made sharp criticism of the Brussels move to link a free trade accord to South Africa opening its waters to European fishing. 'It's not in our interest to open up fisheries resources in exchange for market access' he said, while the managing director of Sea Harvest in South Africa urged the EU not to exert such pressure over fishing quotas: 'It is straight blackmail and I would hate to see a natural resource like fish sacrificed.' The negotiations, once more, were at stalemate.[8] A new meeting to break the deadlock was then set for October between South Africa's trade and industry minister Alec Erwin and the EU commissioner João de Deus Pinheiro in South Africa.

No deal was achieved during the remaining months of 1998 while in December Graham Boyd of Warburg Dillon Read said that the advent of European Monetary Union in January 1999 would jeopardise South African exports, 31 per cent of which went to Europe, since preferential regional trade agreements facilitated intraregional trade while diverting it from other countries outside the region. On the other hand, Boyd suggested that EMU might work to the advantage of South African companies seeking to raise capital in Europe since a company 'which lists in London, moves its head office there and has its domicile there could be treated as falling within the European Union and therefore bypass trade restraints imposed by the EU on countries outside the region.'[9]

Agreement appeared to have been reached – subject to ratification – during February 1999 although full details were not made public. The EU had lowered its exclusion list of South African agricultural exports from 46 to 38 per cent so that over ten years the EU was committed to lower tariffs on 62 per cent of South Africa's agricultural exports. Free trade was to cover 'substantially all trade' – about 95 per cent – without excluding any sector while, in its turn, South Africa agreed to drop tariffs on 81 per cent of EU agricultural imports over 12 years. South Africa would also be able to export 60 000 tons of canned fruit at 'favourable conditions' to the EU and about 32 million litres of wine at 50 per cent rebates at the most favoured nation rate. However, five European countries rejected the deal as too favourable to South Africa; these were Spain, Portugal, France, Italy and Greece each of which is a major fruit exporter. The agreement, however, was still a long way from ratification.

What South Africa had learnt over more than three years of tortuous negotiations was that the EU would make no concessions, despite political promises of aiding the country to achieve a greater share of world trade markets, and that it had to be constantly vigilant and resist all the bullying tactics, at which the EU is expert. Throughout the negotiations South Africa had been approached by the EU as a potential threat to its protectionist policies rather than a Third World country which deserved special treatment. The experience should assist the new South Africa to come of age. The international trading world is a ruthless arena where any sign of weakness will be seized upon and exploited. Given the disparities in wealth and power between South Africa and the EU, the firm stance adopted by South Africa represented a welcome sign of political maturity. The EU, despite protestations to the contrary, is a powerful closed shop. South Africa must not allow itself to be bullied.

17
Foreign Policy II: The USA and Globalisation

The South African government which took power after the April 1994 elections was the recipient of much international goodwill. At the same time considerable naivety was displayed on both sides of the new equation, with the international community acting as though it expected South Africa to behave in a different fashion from other nation states in pursuit of their interests, and South Africa acting as though it believed that expressions of goodwill were synonymous with the actual interests that those who expressed such sentiments would pursue. A good deal of rapid learning had to follow as the new South Africa, and especially those responsible for its foreign policy, discovered how the world's powerbrokers would manipulate the government – if they were allowed to do so – for every advantage they could obtain.

The new South Africa emerged on the stage of the new world order which US President George Bush had proclaimed at the beginning of the decade. It discovered, quickly enough, how little the phrase meant. The end of the cold war had not resulted in any obvious reduction in arms; nor had the expected 'peace bonus' led to any improvement in the relationship between the rich North and the poor South. Indeed, almost every indicator suggested that the North–South disparities would become greater and that without the balance which the cold war had dictated the powerful would be even more arrogant in imposing their will on the weak. South Africa made an early gesture of goodwill to Namibia when, within a few months of the 1994 elections, it relieved that country of R400 million of debts incurred during the apartheid era and restored to it the port of Walvis Bay. On the other hand, the world made no comparable gesture towards South Africa which found itself saddled with nearly US$19 billion worth of debts incurred during the apartheid era, then equivalent to one third the annual budget. Economic studies, especially in the USA, described South Africa as one of the world's top ten emerging markets and as the gateway to a subcontinental market of a further 120 million people. Such prognostications indicated why the outside world would be interested in South Africa.

Meanwhile, the new democracy attempted peace mediation in war-torn Angola, intervened to reverse a coup in Lesotho and provided assistance to a Mozambique that was just emerging from 30 years of warfare. At the same time, having become a member of the Southern African Development Community (SADC), Pretoria endeavoured to persuade its neighbours (whom it had destabilised during the 1980s) that it now wanted to work closely with them for the good of the region as a whole and was rewarded by SADC mandating South Africa to lobby the international financial markets for direct financial investment in the region. As a new member of the Organisation of African Unity (OAU) South Africa made plain its desire to play a full role in continental affairs. It was a good beginning, earning the government an accolade from the US deputy assistant secretary for regional security affairs, Michael Lemmon, who was taking part in an African peace-keeping conference in Johannesburg. Mr Lemmon said that in its first year the Mandela government had done much to assist peacekeeping in the region: 'South Africa can potentially lend substantial moral and other support to conflict resolution in Africa. Its restructured military establishment has the potential to make significant contributions to peacekeeping operations.' At the same time, the South African deputy foreign minister Aziz Pahad said that his government was committed to do anything possible to find solutions to African conflicts and that Africa needed to develop a regional peacekeeping capacity.

Understandably, in terms of its apartheid past, the new government committed itself to pursue principles of human rights in its foreign policy, a laudable decision that rapidly brought it up against some of the most intractable problems in international affairs. What should it do about the blatantly anti-democratic policies pursued by its small neighbour Swaziland? And what line ought it to take in relation to the brutal dictatorship of Sani Abacha in Nigeria? The government discovered soon enough how pragmatic considerations of foreign policy and national interest, respecting the sovereignty of other states and exerting pressures upon brutal or dangerous regimes, create new and contradictory problems. As South Africa quickly found in relation to China, it could not have things both ways. Naive suggestions that Mandela might be able to engineer some form of 'dual recognition' of China and Taiwan had to be abandoned when China made plain that the opening of diplomatic rela-tions between the two countries would only take place once Pretoria's formal diplomatic relations with Taiwan had been severed. In September 1995 President Mandela was under pressure to intervene in the Comoros to reverse a mercenary-led coup whose personnel had been recruited in South Africa. It was an embarrassment that focused attention upon an exceptionally dangerous post-apartheid problem: how to control the out-of-work military personnel who were a legacy of the old South Africa.

The worst foreign policy setback for the government in its first 18 months concerned Nigeria. President Mandela had pursued a con-ciliatory approach to General Abacha, insisting upon quiet diplomacy rather than threats of sanctions, but after the execution of Saro-Wiwa and eight other activists by the Abacha regime on the eve of the Auckland Commonwealth conference, South Africa reversed its line and argued for tough sanctions. As one of Saro-Wiwa's lawyers suc-cinctly put the point in a letter to Mandela: 'Were quiet diplomacy pursued in South Africa ... I doubt you would be alive today.'[1]

By that time there were a good many indications that South Africa's foreign policy was less than coherent. On the one hand, and no doubt correctly, President Mandela saw himself as a conciliator and mediator. On the other hand, conciliation, mediation and peacekeeping require certain prerequisites which begin with an understanding of the nature of those whose policies are to be changed. There was a clear tendency in South Africa at this time to assume that Mandela, with his charisma and world-wide prestige, could be used almost anywhere as a mediator. It was not to be. South Africa's foreign policy was not helped by the lack-lustre character and capacity of Alfred Nzo, the foreign minister, whose appointment to this all-important post appeared to have been more in the nature of a reward for past services to the ANC than from an esti-mate of his ability adequately to discharge the role. Part of the problem lay in the fact that South Africa had been isolated for decades as an international pariah; then, when Mandela came to power, too much was expected both of his moral authority and of the country. As Glen Oosthuysen of the South African Institute of International Affairs said:

> Everyone has been looking to South Africa to play a bigger role in international affairs and to lead. But signs are that despite the moral gravitas of the President, the country is not ready to do so.[2]

One problem for South Africa, as for the South generally, is that most of the international media is controlled from the North; as a result,

South Africa is presented as the North wishes to see it rather than as it is. Thus, on the one hand during this early period, it was portrayed as uniquely special, bearing a moral responsibility enshrined in the person of Mandela that required it to behave differently from any other state. But then, when things went wrong, it was treated as though it had fallen from grace. The hypocrisy inherent in this attitude became apparent when Mandela insisted that he would not ignore the debts he considered the ANC owed to such figures as Cuba's Castro and Libya's Gaddafi, both of whom had supported the liberation struggle when the West was only too anxious to do nothing that would upset the white-controlled *status quo*. Having placed Mandela on a moral pedestal, the West demanded that he should behave without any reference to morality with regard to both Castro and Gaddafi because they happened to be Western hate figures. Western attitudes towards the new South Africa were designed, always and only, to ensure that it acted as a subordinate supporter of Western policies. Moreover, whenever the Mandela government demonstrated too much independence, Western media reaction was to raise the bogey of 'confidence', meaning of course that such South African actions put at risk the possibility of further Western investment.

The USA was the worst offender in this regard and came, quite soon after 1994, to be seen in Pretoria as both bullying and arrogant in its attitudes. A number of incidents gave the impression that Washington expected South Africa to accord to the USA a special right to interfere in its affairs. There was the question of the USA pressing charges and sanctions against the South African state company, Armscor, for its sanctions-busting activities during the apartheid era. In Pretoria this move was seen as a cynical attempt to prevent the sale of the Armscor attack helicopter. Then came pressure to reduce diplomatic and other contacts with Cuba and this was followed by denunciations of the deal whereby Iran would store its surplus oil in South Africa. There followed the incident of the shipload of frozen chickens with the US authorities trying to circumvent South African customs procedures and have the cargo offloaded at preferential duties. These incidents all occurred during 1995.

In his keynote address to the ANC congress of December 1997, Mandela complained that too much US assistance was being channelled through groups critical of the ANC government. He cited a Republican report in the US House of Representatives international affairs committee which charged that the USAID was pursuing its own political agenda in South Africa rather than assisting the government meet its reconstruction and development pledges. During March 1998, President Clinton visited South Africa as part of a wider tour of the continent and at a joint press conference with President Mandela in Cape Town was obliged to listen to his host say that he had invited Cuba's Fidel Castro and Iran's former president Hashemi Rafsanjani as guests to South Africa. 'I have also invited Gaddafi' he said 'because moral authority dictates that we should not abandon those who helped us in the darkest hour.'³ Mandela, in the moral role sometimes attributed to him by the Western media, lectured Clinton on the value of sitting down with enemies to talk peace – 'as the ANC had done with the old apartheid leaders'. The honours of the occasion were clearly Mandela's and though there was a great deal of temporary emotional hype, little of concrete value emerged from the visit, despite a typical Clinton rhetorical flourish when he said: 'America wants a strong South Africa. America needs a strong South Africa.'

American interests in South Africa, now that the end of the cold war had downgraded strategic considerations, were primarily commercial – trade and investment. Major US exports to South Africa were agricultural equipment, power generators, general industrial machinery, aircraft and motor vehicle parts, tractors and engines, electrical equipment and high technological equipment – office machines, computers and software – and medical and telecommunications parts. South Africa's main exports to the United States were metals, precious stones, non-ferrous metals, iron, steel, metalliferous ores, non-metallic mineral manufactures and an increasing amount of inorganic chemicals. In 1997 the US trade surplus with South Africa was US$500 million and US exports to South Africa that year stood at US$3 billion while US imports from South Africa were worth US$2.5 billion. South Africa was the thirty-sixth largest export market for the United States. At the end of 1996 direct US investment in South Africa stood at US$1.6 billion.

Speaking in May 1998 at a conference in Washington organised by the Open Source Systems, the South African national intelligence co-ordinator Linda Mti said:

A developed world lifestyle is not sustainable unless the developing world is kept poor. While the developed world continues the rape and pillage, the exploitation of the resources of the south and in our specific case of Africa, sustainable development cannot happen.⁴

Such strong words reflected, increasingly, South African disillusionment with the USA and its determined efforts to impose its own agenda upon South Africa. By September 1998 US business appeared to have become increasingly negative about South Africa, expressing

concerns about the management of the economic policy, labour productivity and relations, and crime and violence. A report of the
Responsibility Research Centre made these findings after surveying 343
US company executives. Respondents to the survey listed the changes
they wanted to see in South Africa. These included: an end to exchange
controls, a revision of the draft Employment Equity Bill, implementation of measures to combat crime and violence including reform of the
judiciary and police, scrapping the Medicines Act (passed earlier in the
year to provide cheap [non-US] medicine for the health service), and
increasing efforts at privatisation. The list was even more arrogant than
an IMF structural adjustment programme. As South Africa approached
its crucial 1999 elections, its relations with the world's only superpower could not be described as either easy or particularly friendly and
though many faults, whether of style or substance, could be laid at
Pretoria's door, the USA deserved the greater part of the blame. The
arrogance of power is never attractive and when such arrogance forms
the backdrop to deliberate bullying it becomes unpleasantly counter-
productive. South Africa had just emerged from the long trauma of the
apartheid years and it was unseemly, to put it no more strongly, for the
USA to try to force it into a subservient client mould with the implied
threat in the background that Pretoria needed the economic partnership offered by the USA more than it could afford to keep its own
national dignity.

Like everyone else, South Africa had to face the new challenges of
globalisation. At one level there is nothing new about globalisation
which is no more than the interdependence of societies according to
what their economies are capable of producing, a condition that was
expounded with admirable clarity by Adam Smith in *The Wealth of
Nations*. What was new in the 1990s and may well become the key to
changes in the early twenty-first century was the lessening degree of
control that governments were able to exercise over the process. The
realisation that this was so was beginning to frighten powerful governments of countries such as Germany with the third largest economy in
the world. South Africa, therefore, had to look at a reform process
which had already produced the greatest period of international economic expansion in history and was about to engulf the smaller,
weaker economies which had, until then, remained isolated in the
older pattern of economic relations in which governments believed
they controlled the levers of change.

As South Africa moved to become an integral part of a world market
it discovered how far it still had to develop in order to compete

effectively. A report by the World Economic Forum which measured 53 countries, ranked South Africa (in competitive terms) 42 below such countries as Vietnam.[5] Economic mismanagement under the apartheid government had been a weapon of political control which left a country poorly equipped to take on the world of the 1990s. Moreover, as South Africa soon realised, few rich countries carried out their promises of offering better access to the least developed countries despite the pledges they had given and as Pretoria discovered in the years of harsh negotiations with the EU. Faced with massive problems of transition and adjustment, South Africa also had to realise that while the advanced sectors of its economy represented by its major companies such as Anglo American would be sucked into the world economic system easily enough, the rest could just as easily be bypassed. A global system that was increasingly able to operate outside government control would also be able to operate without paying attention to large sections of the population that were poor and underemployed.

Celebrations were held in Geneva during May 1998 to mark 50 years of reducing trade barriers under the World Trade Organisation (WTO), the former UNCTAD. The celebrations provoked violent demonstrations by about 5000 people who blame free trade for increasing poverty and financial chaos in Asia and other parts of the world. Renato Ruggiero, the director general of the WTO, argued for greater efforts to help the least developed countries become more integrated into the mulitlateral trading system, while also calling for free trade to cover the export products of these countries. He said that WTO members should not underestimate 'the growing pressure of the multilateral trading system' to take account in trade discussions of social and political issues such as health, jobs and the environment.[6] The subject that Mr Ruggiero did not address was the protectionism of the powerful that is most obviously seen in the determination of the EU to safeguard its agricultural sectors. The major trading nations or groups constantly call for greater free trade in the world at large, and especially among developing nations, while endlessly finding reasons why their particular interest groups should be exempted. Addressing the WTO summit, President Mandela accepted the inevitable when he said: 'What happens in Switzerland affects South Africa the same day. It is a process we have to accept and adjust to.' The difficulty for South Africa, as for most other developing countries, is that acceptance of the inevitable does not also carry with it much ability to affect the way the inevitable develops.

South Africa hosted the 12th Non-Aligned Movement (NAM) summit of 113 nations in Durban early in September 1998. Thabo Mbeki, the Deputy President, and Alec Irwin, the trade and industry minister, set the tone by steering the summit towards economic questions. Mbeki challenged members of NAM to put their own houses in order, both economically and politically, so that they would have the credibility to challenge the hold the richer countries of the north have over the levers of world economic order. He said the single most important issue facing the summit was to find a way to restructure the world economy so that it addressed the needs of the developing world. He wanted a proper interaction between the developing world and the Group of Eight (G8) leading economies instead of the developing world, as at present, having to approach the G8 'as petitioners'.

South Africa had not only placed economics at the top of the NAM agenda but had also invited, for the first time, representatives of the United States, Britain, France, the EU and the G8 to attend. It was a bold move that met considerable criticism from other NAM members but South Africa was determined that the interests of the poor countries should be placed firmly on the agenda of the rich countries. Whether the move would bear any fruit was another question entirely. Back in the 1970s, then with Algeria in the lead, the Third World countries had proposed a New International Economic Order (NIEO) but this had met with short shrift from the rich nations which more or less ignored pressures for a NIEO altogether. Nonetheless, it was an important initiative for South Africa to put itself in the forefront of poor countries to argue their case with the rich.

The NAM communique, largely written by South Africa, included tough condemnation on the issue of nuclear disarmament which especially annoyed India (both India and Pakistan had detonated nuclear devices the previous May) whose Prime Minister Atal Bihari Vajpayee reacted angrily to Mandela's offer to help settle the Kashmir dispute with Pakistan. When it was suggested that this had damaged South African–Indian relations, Jackie Selebi, the South African director-general of foreign affairs, said 'If we cannot honestly say what we feel on issues of international concern like these without damaging relations, then that may be a sign that we have no relations at all', a clear indication that South Africa intended to speak its mind on important issues, even at the risk of offending putative allies. Referring to this and also to Mandela's attack upon the Israeli Prime Minister Benyamin Netanyahu, Selebi added:

> South Africa must become a normal country, and not a country made up in the minds of people and governments. South Africa

must be able to say that someone or some government is doing something wrong without having stock markets plunge. People must accept that we have critical views on issues and that these should not destroy relations with the countries we criticise.[7]

Foreign policy under Mandela was often, necessarily, about opening up new relations with countries that had either kept at arms length during the apartheid years or had a relationship which required to be changed to take account of the new reality of a democratic South Africa. Visits to Russia and China were mainly about greater trade opportunities, though in the case of China the issue of Taiwan also had to be resolved. The Asian crisis which brought a sudden halt to the rapid economic advance of the Asian 'tigers' sent warning tremors through South Africa at a time when it was being named as one of the world's most important developing countries and potential markets. Moreover, the Asian crisis came just when Pretoria had become excited at the obvious interest to invest in South Africa which was then being shown by Malaysia. In the case of Iran and the oil storage deal to which the USA took such exception, as well as the development of closer diplomatic and trade ties generally between the two countries, South Africa had to learn how to cope with the sheer vehemence of American objections to any independent policy which appeared to go against American interests.

Some initiatives, though ostensibly significant, were unlikely to have much impact for years to come. Thus, the formal endorsement by South Africa of the charter of the Indian Ocean Rim Association for Regional Cooperation (IOR-ARC) to promote economic liberalisation among the 47 Indian Ocean Rim (IOR) countries was optimistic in intent yet unlikely to produce much of substance. Indeed, for most of the IOR countries South African trade is peripheral, accounting for no more than 8.6 per cent of the total. That is not to say South Africa should not be involved but it should not place high expectations upon a new relationship with so wide ranging and disparate a group of countries. The new democratic South Africa found it had a great deal to learn about international relations and the relentless pressures that could be applied to force changes in its policies yet, despite obvious mistakes and some avoidable blunders, the government generally showed a tough and realistic appreciation of what it could and could not achieve.

18
Defence, the Arms Trade and Mercenaries

One of the top priorities faced by the new Mandela government in 1994 was to rearrange the country's defence establishment. The South African Defence Force (SADF) was one of the two instruments, (the South African Police was the other) employed by the former government to maintain white supremacy and keep apartheid in place. Almost by definition the white personnel of the SADF had believed in the apartheid system and many of its officers were understandably viewed with deep suspicion by the ANC. The new government had to proceed cautiously; it could not risk a revolt by the armed forces before it had obtained proper control. What is remarkable with hindsight is just how smoothly the government was able to carry through the process of integration.

By mid-1995 the acting chief of defence force staff, Lieutenant-General Siphiwe Nyanda, was able to claim that the new South African National Defence Force was being established despite problems with integration. He told the *Sunday Independent* that 'It would be naive with racism having been entrenched in society, [that] it would not have also been experienced in the defence force.'[1] At that time, July 1995, some 9383 former Umkhoto we Sizwe (MK) soldiers and 2154 Azanian People's Liberation Army (APLA) soldiers were undergoing bridging training while a further 13 000 MK and another 3800 APLA soldiers had still to be integrated before the process was completed. A month later the cabinet approved the immediate demobilisation of 10 000 MK and APLA soldiers and agreed the eventual rationalisation of 50 000 members of the new SANDF. The defence minister, Joe Modise, said that demobilisation and rationalisation would be completed by 1999 as the military cut back from a force of 135 000 to 75 000. The minister also said that the government was providing R225 million for gratuities for members of former political armies who opted for demobilisation. Overall, the government was in the process of carrying out the biggest military pruning exercise since the end of World War II, a sign that the country was no longer at war with itself.

In the meantime Joe Modise showed himself to be a tough lobbyist and by August 1997 had won a stiff battle in cabinet to spend substantial sums of money re-equipping the armed forces. Those opposed to such expenditure argued that the money should be allocated to schools and clinics. In the end Parliament endorsed plans to purchase four corvettes and four submarines for the navy as well as a range of other armaments. Britain, France, Germany and Spain then lined up to tender for the business and were followed by Italy which claimed to be at an unfair disadvantage because it had observed the United Nations arms boycott against South Africa while several of its competitors had been supplying arms throughout the embargo period. Military analysts supported the expenditure, at least on the grounds that most of the SANDF's equipment was in poor condition and that the navy's last purchase of warships had been a quarter-of-a-century earlier. Modise and the military had a good case since the defence budget only represented 1.6 per cent of the country's GDP as opposed to 4.5 per cent in 1989. By the beginning of 1998 the state arms procurement agency, Armscor, had drawn up a shortlist of potential suppliers for jet aircraft, submarines, corvettes, tanks and helicopters. The cabinet was expected to award the bids by May or June that year.

A row developed in May 1998 between the ministry of defence and the outgoing (white) head of the army. The British military advisory and training team (BMATT) had presented the ministry with a report in which it said that integration was no longer a priority for SANDF. However, the head of the army, Lieutenant-General Reginald Otto, claimed that the report represented a personal vendetta against him by the former BMATT team leader, Brigadier Paul Davis. The minister, Joe Modise, reacted tartly: 'The Minister wishes to place on record his highest regard for the integrity, objectivity and professionalism of both Brigadier Davis and the British team and profoundly regrets General Otto's unacceptable remarks.' The British team had been working to assist the process of integration since the elections of 1994. Otto was due to retire and hand over to his deputy, Major-General Gilbert Ramamo (a former member of the military wing of the ANC) in June 1998. At the same time General Georg Meiring, the head of SANDF, was also due to retire and hand control to Lieutenant-General Siphiwe Nyanda, so that the top two posts in the SANDF would be held by black South Africans for the first time. What the BMATT report had said which so angered the white commanders was that there had been a hardening of attitudes by the white officer corps towards the Non-Statutory Force (NSF) members (those coming from the former guerrilla movements) during the process of integration. Some 30 000 NSF members had been brought into the 90 000 strong SANDF which includes the army, navy, air force and medical corps and, as the report claimed: 'Very few room names, street names, flags, symbols, pictures or traditions come from the NSF. Thus many of the ex-NSF firmly feel they are being absorbed rather than integrated.'[2]

As the retrenchment of the armed forces' numbers gathered pace the parliamentary joint standing committee on defence questioned the wisdom of 'throwing out' about 24 000 trained soldiers. The committee chairman, Tony Yengeni, said that while it was accepted that military personnel costs should be cut by 40 per cent over three years, it should be understood that some soldiers possessed no other skills and faced little chance of obtaining civilian employment. Modise in his turn said it was imperative that those who left the army should be assisted to qualify for a new career. When he introduced the debate on his budget vote in May 1998, Joe Modise said that the SANDF then had 93 000 members of whom 70 per cent were black and 30 per cent white; however, only 29 per cent of officers were black (as opposed to 22 per cent in 1997). Of the 28 000 former MK and APLA members who had reported for integration only 7000 had opted to be demobilised with the majority electing to remain in the new SANDF and of these 1552 were officers. At a ceremony in Pretoria at the end of May which was attended by President Mandela and foreign military attaches, General Siphiwe Nyanda took command of the defence force from outgoing General Georg Meiring. In parliament Modise congratulated Nyanda on his historic appointment and expresssed his appreciation for Meiring's years of service and dedicated role in shaping the new defence force. The two occasions – military and parliamentary – marked a turning point for the new South Africa.

Real integration, however, still had a long way to go. Lecturing more than 250 top officers at the annual army conference in Pretoria (the subject was the need to speed up transformation) the Deputy Minister of Defence, Ronnie Kasrils, said there were 'disturbing signs of resistance to change'. He said the appointments of a black chief of SANDF and a black chief of the army, as well as black officers in charge of territorial commands, were not cosmetic. 'We have been compelled to make them as it is the only way we can bring about representivity in the armed forces. Five of the top ten army generals are black and this is extremely positive in anyone's terms and bodes well for real unity and partnership within the army' he said. He argued that the dominance of former members of the old SADF in the formation of the SANDF had given the impression that these officers were in charge of the new military while former liberation force personnel were on the outside looking in. His address which included details of white–black racist incidents was heard in silence but the minister got his point across and concluded: 'It takes one bad apple to ruin a reputation.'[3]

Parallel with the transformation of the armed services came the restructuring of the country's arms business which is the most advanced in Africa. In 1995 President Mandela established a commission of inquiry into the arms business under Judge Edwin Cameron who said that new criteria for the industry 'based, above all, on South Africa's commitment to democracy, human rights and international peace and security' were needed. The publication of the Cameron report coincided with a government decision to prohibit arms sales to Turkey because of its human rights abuses. The Cameron Commission confirmed that Armscor had deliberately misled the government about sales to the Middle East and recommended that the marketing manager and two of his superiors should be prosecuted for fraud and negligence. All three then resigned. The Commission recommended a comprehensive review of arms trade policy. The deputy defence minister, Ronnie Kasrils described the 'foul state' of the arms industry as the legacy of apartheid but said the government did not want to close down the industry because of the disadvantages of buying weapons from abroad.

A list was drawn up of 31 countries to be blacklisted by the South African arms industry. The secret list was leaked and published by the *Mail and Guardian*[4] in July 1995. The list banned any arms sales to 31 countries where for reasons of instability or human rights abuse it was considered arms would be misused; a further nine countries could only receive 'non-lethal' equipment; and 15 faced lighter sales restrictions. (In the last years of apartheid virtually any regime was encouraged to buy South African.) A debate was to follow between what was described as the 'peacenik' movement which in broad terms opposed the arms business and the arms lobby which now argued that the purchase of foreign arms, for the new SANDF, would assist the whole economy by engendering counter-trade based upon the size of arms procurements. The successful sellers of arms to South Africa would have to plough back a percentage of the total tender into local suppliers. The real argument centred upon the political future of the South African arms industry. This had been vastly increased during the apartheid years as the impact of effective arms sanctions increased, with the result that the Mandela government inherited an important industry with high export potential which, pragmatists knew, could play as significant a role in boosting the economy as any other industry.

In September 1997, a clear demonstration that the arms lobby had won the argument, South Africa was negotiating a multi-billion rand arms deal for Saudi Arabia to purchase between 70 and 80 G6 self-propelled artillery systems from Denel, the country's principal arms manufacturer. In the end the deal may be worth US$1.5 billion. The G6 is the world's only in-service self-propelled 155 mm howitzer set on a high-speed wheeled chassis and is ideal for sandy terrain.[5] Despite initial misgivings about the arms business which, inevitably in the new mood of 1994, was seen as immoral, in fact it grew steadily from 1994 onwards with civilian products made by the arms industry increasing to 50 per cent of the whole, and US$250 million worth of exports, 90 per cent of which were for foreign arms sales. The arms industry developed under apartheid was geared to produce almost anything the armed forces needed; as a result the Mandela government inherited the continent's largest and most developed defence industry employing 50 000. Its products had been used and tested in the wars in Angola, Mozambique, Namibia and some, indeed, in the 1991 Gulf War. In terms of both its own defence require-ments and the export business the government decided to keep and boost the arms business. In 1997 South Africa exported R572 million worth of heavy armaments to India but only R26.8 million worth to Pakistan. The defence ministry admitted that it had been obliged to choose between the two countries and India represented the more lucra-tive market. Altogether, arms exports for 1997 totalled R1.3 billion and markets included Uganda, the USA, Peru and the People's Republic of China. During these three years South Africa discovered the incompata-bilities inherent in pursuing an ethical foreign policy and selling arms. The success of the arms business was further enhanced in 1998 when it emerged that Denel was negotiating a workshare agreement with British Ordnance for a £100 million British Army order.

By late 1998 government plans to purchase R30 billion worth of foreign arms to update the armed forces was being condemned by pri-vate sector economists, and human rights and anti-war groups, but the government dismissed calls to go back on its plans to purchase military equipment from Europe and use the resources instead for its social pro-grammes. It argued that as a result of counter-trade the purchases would generate investment and create up to 65 000 jobs over seven years. South Africa found itself embroiled in the classic argument which, sooner or later, faces all arms producers and exporters; how to weigh social requirements and anti-war sentiments against a thriving arms industry that provides substantial employment and earns much needed export revenues. The arms industry won the argument.

At least South Africa could claim a modest slice of the high moral ground over the question of nuclear weapons. The country became a small nuclear power during the 1980s when, according to former President F. W. de Klerk, it had produced six bombs comparable in strength to that dropped on Hiroshima. The de Klerk government announced in the early 1990s that it was voluntarily destroying its nuclear arsenal and in September 1991, with the backing of the ANC, it signed the Nuclear Non-Proliferation Treaty under whose terms the International Atomic Energy Agency (IAEA) could verify the peaceful nature of South Africa's nuclear programme. In August 1994 the South African government adopted a policy of pursuing non-proliferation and disarmament in all its aspects.

The Mandela government had to deal with another highly complex and dangerous military problem: what to do about South African mercenary organisations operating elsewhere on the continent or beyond it and largely manned by military personnel who had been at the forefront of special units deployed to destabilise South Africa's neighbours during the last years of apartheid. The main such mercenary organisation, which attracted a good deal of attention internationally during the 1990s, was Executive Outcomes which had been set up in 1989. Executive Outcomes is an effective military advisory services organisation supplying mercenaries and other military assistance to independent African countries. It is largely staffed and led by white soldiers and by 1996 had become one of the best known private mercenary companies operating in the world. In Africa it had deployed combat units, made up of members of the former special forces which had been dissolved by the Mandela government, in both Angola and Sierra Leone. The question raised for the new South Africa by this high profile mercenary organisation was why the Mandela government would allow it to operate out of South Africa at all. In part the answer was almost certainly totally pragmatic: that it was better these highly trained and dangerous ex-regular forces should be employed as mercenaries outside the country than that they should be unemployed inside it. However, the official view upon Executive Outcomes was given by Kader Asmal, the minister of water resources who also chairs the national committee on the sale of arms. He argued as follows:

Our committee has decided that the correct way to approach this question was to accept that its (Executive Outcomes) activities should be given government approval. I think that the recruitment of personnel for or by a foreign military force should be regulated in the same way as the sale of arms. If an organisation seeks to sell its services to the legal government of another country, you regulate your permission according to the reality of the legitimacy of the government in question and according to its human rights and democratic record. I do not see any difference between the export of arms and that of advice and military services. They are the same thing.[6]

Whether allowing such a mercenary organisation to operate from South Africa (along with other such dubious mercenary companies such as the British Sandline or the American MPRI) will be conducive to greater peace and order in small countries, in Africa or elsewhere, remains to be seen. South Africa may well find that present pragmatism will assist the growth of a monster that is immoral in purpose and increasingly hard to control.

19
Springboard into Sub-Saharan Africa

Whatever South Africa's relations with the USA, Britain, the European Union or Asia, its future lies in Africa where its performance as the regional economic and political superpower will have a profound impact upon continental developments in the new century. Following the end of apartheid, foreign companies such as the Nissan Motor Company of Japan were not slow to see South Africa as a natural springboard for expansion into the African markets to the north and in this respect South Africa offers well developed infrastructural advantages, both as the largest potential trading partner in Africa for foreign companies and as the obvious starting point for their continent-wide commercial operations. When in August 1995 the Hong Kong Trade Development Council opened offices in Johannesburg, its chairman Dr Victor Fung described the country as the springboard for trade with the rest of southern Africa and the continent as a whole. In addition, Dr Fung suggested South Africa might also become the springboard for the sale of Hong Kong goods to the American and European markets since it enjoyed trade preferences with those countries. Asian interest in this potential South African role was especially marked immediately prior to the Asian economic crisis.

The sense of release experienced by South African business when apartheid came to an end was palpable; the country had been bottled up by a stifling system that had inhibited enterprise at home and prevented South African business operating in its natural markets to the north. Suddenly that changed and business looked outwards. Initially, the government was fearful that if it relaxed controls too much or too quickly there would be a haemmorhage of funds, but in July 1995 Chris Stals, governor of the Reserve Bank, decided to allow financial institutions to exchange assets with investors overseas. Pension funds, insurance companies and unit trusts were to be allowed to invest part of their assets overseas but only in exchange for overseas companies taking South African shares. Dr Stals said he was not yet ready to allow free capital movement.[1] Sanlam, the country's leading life assurance institution, led the way in arranging an asset swap, but was closely followed by Iscor whose Pension Fund announced a US$25 million swap with GT Management of London. These were limited exercises, however, and the principal criticism was that foreign counterpart assets would have to be locked into South Africa for a protracted period of time. Even so, both Middle Eastern and Japanese institutions showed interest in such swaps since they saw these giving them access to South Africa's highly illiquid equity market.

Meanwhile, a host of companies began to look at prospects to the north. Waltons, the office furniture company, sought acquisitions in Zimbabwe, while Energy Africa, in its first year as a listed oil and gas exploration and production company, developed its exploration interests in six sub-Saharan countries. In early 1998 International Chemical Producers (ICP) acquired the troubled Tanzanian (state-owned) Pyrethrum Processing and Marketing Company (TPPMC) for 630 billion Tanzanian shillings (R8.05 billion). Carson Holdings, the ethnic hair care and cosmetics manufacturer which doubled its sales to the rest of Africa during 1997, invested US$3 million in a Ghanaian operation. These, and other comparable companies, were relatively small operations but they were moving fast to seize new opportunities.

During 1998 Eskom, South Africa's electricity parastatal, looked at possible investments in Uganda, Rwanda, Tanzania and the Democratic Republic of Congo. It was interested in purchasing a share in the Uganda Electricity Board (UEB) when the Board was privatised. Eskom is the lowest-cost producer of electricity in the world; it made a net profit of US$300 million in 1997 and aimed to place 50 per cent of its investment outside South Africa over the ensuing five years with the emphasis upon sub-Saharan Africa.[2] In May 1998 Eskom made a commitment to rebuild the power infrastructure in the Democratic Republic of Congo with the long-term aim of receiving electricity from that country. Eskom technical experts would assist in restoring the huge Inga dam hydro-electric project on the Congo river and strengthen the transmission lines from Inga to South Africa. The Eskom operation would be paid for on a barter basis, electricity for services, since the Congo was in urgent need of money. Other companies were seeking deals in the USA or Europe.

In the year following the end of apartheid South African businesses made major investments in 19 African countries covering operations in aviation, breweries, electric power, hotels, mining, railways and ports, and telecommunications. In what one newspaper described as a new Great Trek, South African companies were taking over from American and European corporations which had become disillusioned with working conditions in Africa. Over 18 months to July 1995, for example, Protea Hotels (the continent's largest hotel management group) took over eight hotels in Malawi from British companies, as well as a tour operator and an airport catering company; in Botswana Protea won a contract to manage the Sheraton Hotel from the US chain, and beat a range of competitors to win contracts to manage a resort in Egypt and four hotels in Tanzania. The television company, Multichoice, over two years became Africa's biggest provider of pay TV channels broadcasting to 40 African countries up to and including Egypt. Standard Bank extended its operations to 14 African countries while mining companies rapidly expanded their exploration and other activities in West Africa (Burkina Faso, Cote d'Ivoire, Ghana, Guinea and Mali). South African Breweries established operations in Angola, Botswana, the Canary Islands, Tanzania, Zambia and Zimbabwe. South African Railways undertook to upgrade ports in Mozambique and South African Airways was busy developing ties with other African airways. And the end of apartheid had also brought a huge boost to South Africa's trade to the north. Such activity was creating a reverse process as an increasing number of trade delegations visited South Africa.

Uganda became a particular target for South African outward investment with as much as US$100 million being invested there over a few months at the beginning of 1998. The cellular phone company MTN launched Uganda's second telecommunications group with an investment of US$30 million at a time when MTN was also examining possibilities for expansion in the Democratic Republic of Congo, Eritrea, Swaziland, Tanzania and Zambia. Uganda, however, offered major growth potential with one of the lowest teledensities in Africa. MTN had been preceded into Uganda by South African Breweries which purchased a 40 per cent stake in Uganda's Nile Breweries for US$20 million while in 1997 the South African Bottling Company (Sabco) had invested US$35 million in two bottling facilities in Uganda. The South African power utility, Eskom was also looking at investment opportunities in Uganda and elsewhere. In January 1999 South African companies won two of the top three Ugandan investment awards; in the four years since 1994 South African investments in Uganda had risen from zero to US$280 million worth with some 29 licensed projects under-way that were expected to employ 3537 people.

Elsewhere in the East African region South African investors were look-ing for new opportunities. In Rwanda, where the government was trying to rebuild its shattered economy after the events of 1994, South African business was mainly interested in the telecommunications, energy and health sectors. In Tanzania the black empowerment company African Harvest invested in a new joint finance company, acquiring a 50 per cent stake in Vertex Financial Services. In Kenya South African Breweries opened a R240 million plant at Thika to end the longstanding beer monopoly of Kenya Breweries. Across the continent in Gabon South African construction expertise was working with American capital on major infrastructure projects worth an estimated $400 million. This rapid outward explosion of South African investment was a new phe-nomenon for a continent that had been largely sheltered from such South African attentions throughout the apartheid years and had looked, almost exclusively, to Europe for investment. It was as though a dam had suddenly burst allowing South African enterprises and capital to invade the huge hinterland that was their natural trading and investment target area. As this outward movement gathered pace it raised important ques-tions about South Africa's place in the troubled African continent.

In a thoughtful piece in the *Natal Witness*, Allister Sparks (the former editor of the *Rand Daily Mail*) posed the question whether South Africa could prosper in the midst of a sea of poverty in the world's most mar-ginalised continent. He suggested that the more successful economi-cally South Africa became the more people from poorer countries to the north of it would migrate south. He then formulated what should be the policy of the new South Africa.

> The only way is to help and stabilise the countries around us and so remove the cause of these great flows of political and economic refugees. But our government is not attempting that in any system-atic way. The philosophy of the moment is that we have too much to do at home, uplifting our own disadvantaged people and redress-ing the legacies of apartheid, to think of giving aid to anyone else. Charity must begin at home.
>
> There is, too, a sensitivity towards the neighbouring countries. There is the sense of a debt owed to them because of the heavy price they paid for supporting the ANC during the apartheid years, but it is coupled with a reluctance to appear arrogant or domineering as the continent's most powerful economy.[3]

South Africa has the capability to regenerate not just its own economy but those to the north of it and Allister Sparks' argument, which is a mixture of pragmatism, self-interest and idealism, is well-suited to both the economic needs and the political aspirations of the new South Africa. As the move to invest outwards gathered pace similar arguments were to be advanced: that South Africa could not really prosper unless her neighbours did so as well.

It suddenly became possible for South Africa to talk to neighbouring countries about tapping the waters of the Zambezi river to send waters from the river 1800 kilometres through a system of canals, pipelines and tunnels south to augment the Vaal river system which supplies the Gauteng industrial and residential complex. The scheme, which would also affect the parched western region of Zimbabwe and eastern Botswana, would cost billions of rands and provide thousands of jobs in all three countries. The project, if it is implemented, is thought to be the most ambitious of its kind in the world and would affect 10 per cent of the Zambezi waters. Such a grandiose three-nation development could not even have been discussed in apartheid times.

South Africa's first priority was to work out a *modus vivendi* with its immediate neighbours, the countries of the Southern African Development Community (SADC). Prior to the changes of 1990 these countries had constituted the frontline states that South Africa destabilised through the 1980s. Created in 1980 as the Southern African Development Co-ordinating Conference (SADCC) with the object of reducing its members' dependence upon South Africa, it transformed itself into the Southern African Development Community in 1992 and invited South Africa to join in 1994. As by far the strongest economy in SADC (as well as its former enemy) South Africa had to tread carefully. Speaking prior to the annual SADC summit in 1995, the South African Foreign Minister Alfred Nzo said that membership of SADC was the realisation of

> a dream South African democrats have had for a very long time. That dream is to participate as a good neighbour in the affairs not only of the region, but of Africa as a whole. South Africa is very anxious to contribute whatever it can to the stability of the region – economically, politically and security-wise. The SADC is an important vehicle for achieving that goal.[4]

But as President Mandela discovered in December 1995 when he attempted to produce a united SADC policy towards Nigeria (after the suspension of Nigeria from the Commonwealth at Auckland, New Zealand, that November) the other SADC members did not want to take any initiatives over Nigeria and he was forced to backpeddle.

Pretoria discovered quickly enough that the other SADC members were afraid that their small economies would be swamped by South Africa's large one and by 1998 the government was working on a comprehensive offer of market access for its SADC partners which would assist the move towards a free-trade agreement among the 14 members of SADC. The South African director of trade, Zavareh Rustomjee, said:

> We will (offer to) open up faster than the rest of the region, using the same principles we are following in our discussions with the European Union. ... The offer will be very comprehensive, though it might differ from country to country and from industry to industry.[5]

It was an irony for Pretoria that its SADC partners, in terms of their desire for access to its market, were in the same relationship to South Africa as it was to the European Union and the same kind of protectionist arguments were likely to surface. Other political arguments also surfaced during 1998 after the Democratic Republic of Congo collapsed into another civil war. Mandela advocated mediation and no military intervention but Zimbabwe, Angola and Namibia sent troops to aid the government of Laurent Kabila, a move that was retrospectively supported by SADC so as to preserve a doubtful unity. Then, in September 1998, South Africa did intervene with troops in Lesotho. It was unfortunate that Zimbabwe's President Robert Mugabe saw himself being overshadowed in SADC by President Mandela and as a consequence refused to contemplate a single SADC security policy since that, inevitably, would be dominated by South Africa. By the end of the year SADC was less than united: three of its members – Angola, Namibia and Zimbabwe – were firmly committed to supporting Kabila militarily, Angola in any case had reverted to another savage bout of civil war, and Lesotho was regarding South Africa with its old suspicions of 'big brother' from the apartheid era which had been renewed as a result of its intervention in September. Although South Africa was coming to see that regional security and regional prosperity were inseparable it was also learning the harsh problems that attend the role of a regional superpower.

Another problem for South Africa concerned its relations with its longstanding partners in the Southern African Customs Union (SACU) which had to renegotiate its 85 year old agreement in 1995. The other members of SACU – Botswana, Lesotho, Namibia and Swaziland – had been seen as economic prisoners of apartheid South Africa, which had manipulated the annual distribution of their joint customs and excise revenues as a weapon of political control. Lesotho, for example, had come to rely upon SACU for 60 per cent of its annual revenues. South Africa found that the other members of SADC believed they were being excluded from the advantages of SACU membership which they regarded as a trade cartel. A bitter row between South Africa and Zimbabwe about the latter's textile exports erupted in 1995 and threatened to develop into a trade war betwen the two countries. This did nothing to assist South Africa's acceptance in SADC. In the end such problems would be sorted out but the process posed a major quandary for Pretoria. On the one hand, South Africa would have to make concessions to its weaker partners; on the other hand, it could ill afford moves which would increase the flow of imports from neighbouring countries that in turn would put South African jobs at risk.

The five countries most immediately affected by South Africa's economic expansion are its old SACU partners – Namibia (which South Africa directly controlled in a colonial capacity until 1990), Botswana, Lesotho and Swaziland – and Mozambique. The Namibian economy depends upon mining, an agricultural sector largely controlled by white farmers, substantial offshore fisheries, a tiny industrial sector and tourism. It remains, overwhelmingly, dominated by South Africa which is the principal source of its imports and it will find it impossible to change this relationship into the foreseeable future. Since independence in 1990, however, Namibia has made two bids for greater independence of action from the all-pervasive influence of South Africa. In political terms it broke ranks with the Mandela policy over the Democratic Republic of the Congo when it sent a small military force to support Kabila in August 1998. And, even more important, in March 1998 when President Sam Nujoma was in Moscow he signed an agreement with Boris Yeltsin which gave the Russians a substantial partnership stake in Namibia's diamond mining sector, an area that formerly was exclusively controlled by De Beers. The March agreement allowed Russia's Almazy Rosii-Sakha (Alrosa), one of the biggest diamond companies in the world, to enter Namibia and form a joint venture with local diamond companies that will allow it to explore alluvial deposits along the Orange river, develop offshore diamond fields and prospect for other minerals. Russia has also moved into Angola, another former De Beers monopoly. At least the most lucrative aspect of the Namibian economy, its diamond mining sector, is no longer to be shared exclusively with South Africa. Namibia has little enough room in which to manoeuvre and in the new climate in the region expects to build good relations with South Africa. But it does not wish to be smothered by its giant neighbour and that, of course, will also be the problem for the other small or weak neighbours of South Africa.

Botswana's relations with South Africa since its independence in 1966 have provided an exemplary display of how a small weak state can maximise its freedom of action, while always recognizing the realities of its power and the limits beyond which it could not ignore the pressures of its neighbour. Botswana was also lucky in its mineral wealth – it came to replace South Africa as the continent's leading diamond producer – and the care with which its governments fostered the economy with the result that from the 1980s onwards the pula was at a premium over the rand. Cautious economic leadership under Seretse Khama and then Quett Masire ensured that Botswana built up its reserves and did not incur massive international debts over the 1970s and 1980s when most of Africa, disastrously, became heavily indebted with all too little to show for it. The end of apartheid has meant good instead of correct or strained relations with South Africa but it has not altered the economic imbalance between the two countries since, apart from its minerals and cattle Botswana has minimal industry, and grows only a small proportion of its food and remains heavily dependent upon its neighbour for the bulk of its imports.

Lesotho, an enclave entirely surrounded by South Africa, has had a far more turbulent relationship with its giant neighbour. Poverty has forced Lesotho into a position of massive dependence upon South Africa: the annual customs and excise payments from Lesotho's membership of SACU have usually accounted for more than 50 per cent of government revenues while remittances from Basotho working in South Africa have been the second major source of income. Both these sources of revenue were seen to be at risk or under review in the mid-1990s: SACU may well be changed to become less important as South Africa adjusts to its SADC partners while the numbers of Basotho able to work in South Africa may be drastically reduced as the Pretoria government seeks to deal with its own problems of massive unemployment. The huge Lesotho Highlands Water Project, designed to divert water from the Lesotho Highlands to water-scarce Gauteng which is costing R10 billion, is becoming increasingly controversial for both environmental reasons and because Lesotho may come to regret selling off the greater part of its one natural resource to its neighbour. The project will not be completed until well into the next century and royalty payments are expected to boost Lesotho's gross national product by between 4 and 5 per cent. The project was inaugurated by President Mandela and King Letsie III in January 1998 amid controversy in the wake of a report that suggested 75 per cent of the highland villagers affected by the water transfer scheme felt their standard of living had decreased since the start of the project and that compensation claims had been neglected. South Africa's water affairs minister, Kader Asmal, issued a statement saying he had directed that 'South Africa should go further than its treaty obligations, thus ensuring not only that no one would be worse off after the project but that all affected people would be better off.'[6] There was, however, always something 'colonial' about the scheme, a tiny, desperately poor country selling the greater part of its one important asset to its giant neighbour, just as there has always been something distinctly colonial in the whole relationship of Lesotho to South Africa.

This colonial relationship was borne out in September 1998 when South African troops went into Lesotho to restore law and order in Maseru in the wake of violent protests against the government over alleged election fraud. The intervention hardly brought credit to South Africa. Protests against election fraud on behalf of the Lesotho government had been continuous since May and escalated in September when there were reports of an attempted mutiny within the Lesotho armed forces. In the face of continuing deterioration of law and order, about 600 South African troops entered Lesotho on 22 September to meet unexpectedly strong resistance from both dissident members of the Lesotho Defence Force (LDF) and civilians who saw the South Africans as foreign invaders; it took the poorly trained members of the SANDF two days to get control of the three strategic points where the violence was centred – the LDF barracks, the Royal Palace and the Katse Dam. By the time the fighting was over a total of 114 people had been killed – nine South African soldiers, 58 members of the LDF and 47 civilians. The intervention had been requested by the Lesotho Prime Minister, Bethuel Pakalitha Mosisili, without reference to King Letsie III whom he described as 'part of the problem'. There was widespread burning and looting in Maseru and South Africa was criticised for sending an inadequate force in the first place. Later it sent another 450 troops and these were joined by 300 from Botswana to make the intervention a more authentic SADC one rather than simply South African. By 28 September about 1000 of the 1800 rebels had surrendered while more than 4000 refugees had crossed into South Africa as well as a majority of the country's expatriate population. During October 1998 the ruling Lesotho Congress for Democracy (LCD) and the opposition parties agreed to hold new elections by March 2000. If South Africa is to become the principal peacekeeper in the region it will need to give greater thought to the manner of its interventions as well as the forces necessary to minimalise violence and casualties. In the event the South Africans were seen more as agents of old-fashioned imperialism by 'big brother' than as saviours.

Swaziland, the smallest of the enclave or SACU territories, has a reasonable economy which has enabled it to be far less dependent upon South Africa than Lesotho; it is also one of the most conservative countries on the African continent. When in August 1995 King Mswati III went on a four-day official visit to South Africa there were fears that the occasion would be marred because of South African unhappiness at the lack of democracy in Swaziland. The South African department of foreign affairs saw the visit as part of South Africa's efforts to 'consolidate relations in the region' after the demise of apartheid. It was expected that Mandela would exert pressure upon the young king to move towards a more democratic system. The country was subject to particular criticisms from the South African labour movement with James Motlatsi, the president of the National Union of Mineworkers, attacking the Swazi authorities for harassment of trade unions and denying them basic rights. Swaziland, an anomaly in modern Africa, is ruled by a system of traditional authority which was imposed by Mswati III's father, King Sobhuza II, who died in 1982. As with Botswana and Lesotho, Swaziland is heavily dependent upon its neighbour for trade and investment though with far fewer Swazis working in South Africa. After a bitter battle between rival South African companies, MTN won the sole cellular phone licence for Swaziland in May 1998.

After decades of bitter confrontation between South Africa and Mozambique the climate suddenly changed as the civil war in Mozambique and apartheid in South Africa were brought to an end in the early 1990s. Prior to those events South Africa had supported the Portuguese during the long nationalist war from 1963 to 1975 and then, from 1980 onwards, had supported the Resistência Nacional Mocambicana (RENAMO) in its brutal and destructive war against the FRELIMO government. In the 1990s, however, South Africa has collaborated with the Mozambican authorities in searching for guerrilla arms caches and the two governments have reactivated joint projects that should work to the benefit of both countries. The largest of these concerned the rehabilitation of the giant Cabora Bassa dam which was originally constructed by the Portuguese to provide electricity for South Africa. During the civil war RENAMO destroyed some 1400 pylons carrying power lines along 800 kilometres to South Africa, but these were back in place by 1997. Then came the 'trek' of Afrikaner farmers to work farms at Lichinga, a remote northern area of Mozambique. The aim was to help create an agricultural infrastructure: there is plenty of fertile land but an almost total lack of skills or equipment to benefit from it. These, it is hoped, will be supplied by the Afrikaner 'trekkers'. However, this migration of white farmers into Mozambique needs to be carefully monitored by South Africa since the local peasants were quick to complain that the land was being sold to white colonialists which was hardly what FRELIMO fought the Portuguese colonialists to bring about. By 1996, in Maputo and along the adjacent coast, South African tourists were again in evidence as they had not been for the previous 25 years.

There has been a massive movement of South African business into Mozambique which began before the end of apartheid, with South African companies vying to purchase Mozambican industries as the government pursued its new policy of privatisation. Early in 1995 South African Breweries purchased a 70 per cent stake in Mozambique's two state-owned breweries in a R51 million deal. Other deals quickly followed. In 1997 the South African Industrial Development Corporation (IDC) signed an agreement with the government of Mozambique to set in motion the construction of a 3.5 million ton a year steel plant at Maputo. Finance for the project would come from USA, EU and South African investors and the plant would use gas from the Pande gas field, which was being developed by the US-based energy multinational Enron, and magnetite iron ore from Phalaborwa in South Africa. South African companies, alone or in collaboration with US and European interests, were only too eager to move into Mozambique whose postwar reconstruction needs coincided with the adoption of a free market philosophy. There is a suspicion, however, that companies rushing into Mozambique, which is so poor that it must find it hard to resist any incomer with finances to invest, are treating the country as a base that will supply cheap labour for production whose benefits largely go elsewhere and a parallel might be drawn between South Africa and Mozambique and the development of the North American Free Trade Agreement (NAFTA) between the USA and Mexico.

Other problems, however, are of a different kind. An estimated 150 000 would-be migrants attempt to cross into South Africa every year from Mozambique and are turned back for they are seen as a menace to the South African economy which faces its own massive problems of unemployment. South Africa has between 30 and 40 per cent unemployment and an estimated two to four million illegal immigrants who work for a pittance. At the same time it is seen as a land of opportunity to many thousands of even poorer people in surrounding territories and though the migrants are turned back they come again and again. The South African government would like to help but has realities of its own to face. As Mandela has said:

> These countries gave us a base and asylum, food and resources during our struggle. Now we are free we cannot treat them as hostile people. But welcoming illegal immigrants will aggravate our unemployment. We have to find a balance.[7]

In a gesture to the past President Mandela promised to reopen an investigation into the death of the Mozambique President Samora Machel in 1986 when his plane crashed on the Mozambique–South African border. Neither side believed the explanation of the apartheid government that the crash had been due to pilot error.

Development corridors became the fashion in South Africa during the 1990s and one such proposal – the Lubombo corridor – would create a growth area of regional cooperation between South Africa, Mozambique and Swaziland. The initiative was launched in 1998 to include the Greater St Lucia Wetland park in northern KwaZulu-Natal which was expected to attract R600 million of investment and create 2000 jobs. The park would be part of a package development scheme extending to the Indian Ocean coast of Mozambique; it will include a 156 kilometre road between Hluhluwe in South Africa and Ponta do Ora in Mozambique and embrace some 78 tourist projects in the area. An estimated 75 000 people within five kilometres of the road would gain access to social services such as schools and clinics. As the Swazi minister for economic planning and development, Albert Shabangu, said: 'This will be a test case for forging regional economic cooperation and will involve the creation of synergies and a uniform approach to economic development.'[8]

The largest private investment in Mozambique was that led by Billiton to construct a US$1.35 billion Mozal aluminium smelter in Mozambique close to Maputo on the Maputo Corridor. According to Billiton the project would provide a powerful boost to Mozambique's economy by developing the industrial base and export potential of the region. Billiton would be the largest shareholder in the project at

47 per cent worth US$245 million, Japan's Mitsubishi would hold 25 per cent (US$130 million), the Industrial Development Corporation 24 per cent at US$125 million and the government of Mozambique 4 per cent (US$20 million). Since everything was to happen inside Mozambique that country's share seemed modest and raised the question which always arises when a powerful economy invests in a weak one: how much is the deal of genuine two-way advantage to the investors and Mozambique and how much does it represent exploitation. There are other resources awaiting development in Mozambique; they will only get off the ground with the aid of massive injections of outside capital and South Africa is the first and most obvious source of both the capital and the expertise needed for such developments. The inevitable temptation for South African business will be to move into Mozambique and strike bargains that its impoverished government cannot refuse but which could be so one-sided as to turn Mozambique into an economic appendage of its powerful neighbour. This may well be the pattern over the next decades.

During the crisis over SADC intervention in the Democratic Republic of the Congo in 1998 Mozambique and South Africa drew closer together with Mozambique firmly suporting the South African decision not to intervene militarily. This decision led to bitter recriminations against Mozambique by both Angola and Zimbabwe; they had intervened with troops to support Kabila and they accused Mozambique of ingratitude, especially Zimbabwe which had provided substantial numbers of troops to assist the FRELIMO government fight RENAMO through the 1980s. More important, Mozambique's support for the South African position was seen as marking a definite shift by Maputo into the South African orbit. The split in SADC over the Congo crisis raised difficult questions about the Community's future viability. Mozambique, however, was signalling clearly where it believed its interests to lie: with South Africa.

The development of the Maputo Corridor between Gauteng, Mpumalanga and Maputo was given high priority in 1997 when work on the toll-road link got underway. The Maputo Corridor was the largest, most significant infrastructural project of its kind in Africa: it included the upgrading of the road from Witbank to the South Africa–Mozambique border at Komatipoort, the creation of a single border post to service both countries which will straddle the international border in a neutral zone, the upgrading of the railway line to Maputo, a new stretch of road in Mozambique to shorten the distance from the border to Maputo by 50 kilometres, the improvement and dredging of Maputo harbour. The project was expected to cost about R35 billion. To encourage development along the corridor was an essential aspect of the whole project. Such developments included the Mozal aluminium smelter outside Maputo, a number of other industrial projects, the settlement of a number of small farmers and new tourism projects, as well as the provision of services for those living along the line of the development.

In May 1998, on the other side of the continent, the presidents of Botswana and Namibia met on their joint border at a ceremony to open the new trans-Kalahari highway which will link Walvis Bay on the Atlantic with Maputo on the Indian Ocean to complete what has become known as the Walvis Bay–Botswana–Gauteng–Maputo development corridor. The western stretch of the highway will cut the distance from Walvis Bay to Gauteng, the industrial heartland of South Africa, by 400 kilometres. The effects of this trans-Africa development could only be calculated in 1998 but they would undoubtedly have a profound impact upon the movement of goods between the four countries concerned – Namibia, Botswana, South Africa and Mozambique – with South Africa at the hub. For example, it seemed probable that Botswana would switch its beef exports from Cape Town to Maputo, to cut travel times in half while Maputo harbour estimated a rapid increase in goods to be handled.

According to an article in the *Sunday Independent*[9] 'The Maputo Development Corridor shows an understanding of economic imperatives. South Africa cannot expand its markets if the states around it remain among the poorest in the world. And it cannot control illegal immigration if the citizens of those countries lack opportunities at home.' An indication of its knock-on effects could be seen in 1997 when the Mpumalanga government, with Gencor and the Development Bank, drew up a list of 91 projects worth R5 billion that would create between 35 000 and 40 000 sustainable jobs. On 6 June 1998 President Mandela and President Chissano of Mozambique met at Ressano Garcia for the official launch of the Maputo Corridor, a joint South African–Mozambican venture that will benefit the people on both sides of the border. Mandela said:

> As we co-operated in our struggle for liberation, we are now joining hands to improve the lives of our people. Already the corridor is inspiring similar projects elsewhere. It has helped set a trend that is changing the face of our region and making a reality of our dream of development through co-operation.

Hopefully, the single border post was seen as the prototype for others on South Africa's borders with Botswana, Namibia and Zimbabwe. Euphoria about the opportunities offered by this joint venture needed to be tempered by caution, especially on the Mozambique side. South African companies were busy snapping up concessions for the rebuilding of Maputo harbour and infrastructure and, as a representative of the Maputo Development Corridor Company, Dave Arkwright, said: 'Mozambicans are concessioning their prime infrastructure, their lifeline, to private developers. There are voices of dissension.'[10]

Another infrastructural development to link South Africa with her northern neighbours was put in motion during 1997 and completed during 1998: this was the Trans Africa Railway Corporation link from Johannesburg to Kampala in Uganda. It consisted largely of rationalising a railway system that covered South Africa, Botswana, Zimbabwe, Zambia, Tanzania, Kenya and Uganda in which the railway gauges differ so that transshipment points, the most important being that at Kidatu in Tanzania, had to be created or improved. The system is expected to open up new northern markets for the members of SADC and, for South Africa, bring mineral rich areas in Tanzania closer for exploitation.

Such developments are exciting and hold out great promise of increased trade and prosperity yet enthusiasm has to be tempered by other factors and, most notably, those of the political relations between the countries of the region. Thus, relations between South Africa and Zimbabwe since 1994 have ranged from the cool to the hostile. There were a number of reasons for this: the row during 1995 over Zimbabwe textile exports undercutting South African exports because Zimbabwe was ignoring the rules of origin; a plain personality clash between Mandela and Mugabe with the latter resenting the South African leader's greater charisma (and greater power base) in the councils of the SADC; and the split between the two countries over the approach to the civil war in the Democratic Republic of Congo in 1998. Despite these differences Zimbabwe is South Africa's largest trading partner in Africa.

Angola is potentially the richest country in SADC apart from South Africa and as early as 1994 Mandela attempted to mediate in the bitter and longstanding confrontation between the MPLA government of Eduardo dos Santos and the UNITA rebels led by Jonas Savimbi. He was stepping into a minefield. Apartheid South Africa supported UNITA throughout the 1980s as a means of destabilising what it saw as a Marxist state on its borders. During the 1990s Executive Outcomes has been hired by the Angolan government to assist in the recovery of diamond mining regions of Lunda Norte with De Beers at one stage being accused of dealing in diamonds produced by UNITA, though this they denied. During 1998 the civil war in Angola escalated with renewed ferocity and continued unabated into 1999. Until this confrontation, whose roots go back to the nationalist struggle against the Portuguese, has been resolved the viability of the SADC region and prospects for regional development will be severely curtailed.

Further north Zambia became a substantial recipient of new South African investments during the 1990s and in 1997 over half the total of US$272 million of investments in Zambia involved South African companies including a $50 million hotel complex at the Victoria Falls. More important, Anglo American which was already a major shareholder in Zambia Consolidated Copper Mines (ZCCM) was waiting for the Zambian government to carry out its privatisation plans so that it could recover a greater share of the copper and cobalt business that formerly it had largely controlled. Other South African companies were acquiring assets in Zambia as that country continued on its course of privatisation and Anglovaal Minerals (Avmin) set out to acquire the Nkana slag dumps and the Chambishi cobalt and acid plants from ZCCM. The copperbelt which straddles Zambia and the Shaba Province of the Democratic Republic of Congo remains one of the world's great mineral deposits containing about 34 per cent of the world's cobalt reserves and 40 per cent of its copper. South Africa, led by Anglo American, was determined to be – or return to being – a major player in the region. In any case, by 1999 as President Frederick Chiluba of Zambia pursued his policy of economic liberalisation, South Africa emerged as the biggest beneficiary. It was the largest investor in Zambia and its leading trade partner for both imports and exports, and expected to see a dramatic increase in its influence once Anglo American returned – as seemed certain – to running the most important of the Zambian copper mines.

Economic power in Southern Africa rests with South Africa. In 1995 its GNP stood at US$130 billion while the combined GNPs of its eleven SADC partners – Angola, Botswana, Lesotho, Malawi, Mauritius, Mozambique, Namibia, Swaziland, Tanzania, Zambia and Zimbabwe, plus the Democratic Republic of Congo (then still Zaire), only came to $39.5 billion. South Africa may tread softly in political terms, indeed it is vital that it should, but in trade and investment it already dominates the region and over the coming decades will do so to a far greater extent. This dominance, whatever South Africa's neighbours may think, will be inevitable. Given its huge strengths and advantages in relation to its neighbours South Africa must use its strength for the benefit of the region as a whole and not become (as did the United States in relation to Central and South America) a feared and resented 'big brother'. Its coming role will be far from easy to fulfil.

20
The Future

When World War II came to an end in 1945 the Union of South Africa, then a Dominion of the British Empire and Commonwealth, was ranked as a middle power with countries like Argentina and Canada, while its wartime leader, Field Marshall Jan Smuts, was the one South African politician who had become a world figure. He then played a significant role in formulating the Charter of the United Nations. Three years later, in 1948, Daniel Malan led the National Party to victory in the South African general elections and his government began at once to introduce apartheid laws to cover every aspect of South African life. From 1949 onwards, once a year, the General Assembly of the United Nations passed a resolution condemning apartheid and the word went into international usage as a term of political condemnation. The years between 1960 and 1961 marked South Africa's withdrawal – half forced, half chosen – into 'laager' or isolation. In February 1960 at Cape Town Britain's Prime Minister, Harold Macmillan, delivered his 'wind of change' speech whose message his white audience rejected. In March the Sharpeville massacre set off a new phase of repression that would last for 30 years. In 1961 white South Africans voted to make the country a Republic and South Africa left the Commonwealth. The period of high apartheid under prime ministers Hendrik Verwoerd and Balthazar Vorster followed and South Africa steadily became more isolated, more defiant of African and world opinion even as independence swept the African continent. In 1960 17 African colonies became independent; in 1963 the Organisation of African Unity was formed; and by 1965, when the white minority government of Ian Smith made its Unilateral Declaration of Independence (UDI) in Rhodesia, liberation struggles were already underway against the Portuguese in Angola and Mozambique, while South Africa was entrenching itself in its old League of Nations Mandate of South West Africa (Namibia) and refusing to recognize United Nations jurisdiction over it. Thus, by the mid-1960s South Africa was isolated on the African continent, cut off from black Africa to the north by a cordon of three white-controlled territories each of whose minorities were fighting rearguard actions, which were doomed to failure, to hold onto power. Ten years later, after a revolution in Lisbon, an exhausted Portugal withdrew from Africa, Angola and Mozambique became independent under Marxist or Marxist-inclined governments and then South Africa was convulsed by the 1976 Soweto uprising. The end of the decade saw the National Party wracked by the Muldergate scandal and Vorster was succeeded by P. W. Botha. During the 1980s, while President Botha tinkered with reforms at home, South Africa embarked upon a policy of destabilising its neighbours.

Botha's new constitution of 1983, designed to divide so that the whites could continue to rule, did not work and by 1985 the country was in turmoil with the level of violence rising to approach civil war dimensions. In July the US Chase Manhattan Bank sparked off a crisis by refusing to roll over South African short-term loans and was quickly followed by other banks. On 15 August, after a build-up that had raised expectations for change, Botha delivered his 'Rubicon' speech and produced nothing new. The effect was calamitous and the value of the rand fell by 60 per cent. The events of 1985 effectively signalled the end of apartheid which was simply no longer viable as a workable policy and when F. W. de Klerk became leader of the National Party and then President in 1989 he faced a situation in which only radical reform could prevent South Africa collapsing into chaos. The sequence of events from de Klerk's speech of 2 February 1990, when he unbanned the ANC, to the April 1994 elections – which brought the ANC to power under the presidency of Nelson Mandela, although initially leading a government of national unity – became the outstanding story of the early 1990s. The tasks facing the new government could be divided under four broad headings: healing the traumas of a society that had been run for generations on racially divisive lines; addressing the expectations and aspirations of the black majority and bringing about black empowerment; creating the extra wealth needed to finance the government's reforms; and restoring South Africa to its rightful place as a leader in Africa. In the five years 1994 to 1999 the Mandela government made some notable inroads into the array of problems it faced.

South African foreign policy may turn out to be the decisive factor that ensures the success of social and economic reforms at home. It is a matter of both wealth creation and continental leadership. When in 1994 South Africa was invited to join the Southern African Development Community and the Organisation of African Unity, and rejoin the Commonwealth, while also finding itself, once more, an acceptable business partner for the European Union and the United States, it discovered just how much it had lost touch with mainstream international politics. Remarkably, in the years from 1994 to 1999, South Africa came to terms with the realities of international pressures. President Mandela refused to allow the United States to bully South Africa over such issues as relations with Iran or Libya, while his economic team demonstrated admirable toughness in the long, tortuous negotiations with the European Union. Unsurprisingly, there were blunders in foreign affairs yet the most notable of these related to Africa rather than the wider world beyond. South Africa's 'softly softly' approach to Abacha's Nigeria in 1995 left Pretoria looking weak and foolish while Mandela's efforts to persuade Laurent Kabila to halt his victorious advance on Kinshasa in May 1997 and talk with the regime of Mobutu that was in the process of collapsing appeared downright naive. There was an element of wishful thinking about these and other attempts at foreign intervention based upon the mistaken, if understandable, belief that the reconciliation approach practised with such success by Mandela in the particular circumstances of South Africa could also be applied with equal success to quite different problems elsewhere on the continent. It was not to be. Mediation of conflicts should always be attempted but persuasion in international affairs needs to be supported by power, and the determination to exercise it, as well as charisma. And in this respect, it is plain, the new South Africa was inhibited by its past. Suddenly, the pariah state which had ruthlessly destabilised its weaker neighbours had turned into the regional superpower whose investment and assistance could be called upon to realise the 'African renaissance' which Thabo Mbeki has proclaimed and is determined to bring about. But if there is to be an African renaissance led by South Africa then Pretoria must learn to act as a regional superpower and force the pace, also learning at the same time that such a role will often make it highly unpopular.

With regard to the rich developed world of the European Union and the United States, South Africa has to pay enough attention to their selfish interests so as to attract to itself the trade and investment which are essential to increase its wealth. With regard to Africa, South Africa has to provide the kind of leadership that will resurrect the continent's self-respect, while also becoming the motor force for an economic revival that will raise Africa out of the doldrums in which it has been mired for too long. Both tasks will demand a high degree of leadership. Yet, the time could hardly be more appropriate, for the re-emergence of South Africa as an acceptable partner on the continent coincides with the collapse of European and American interest in an Africa which they have come to see as a hopeless mess.

Chester Crocker, the USA assistant secretary of state for African affairs, put the case for South Africa in an interview he gave to the Connecticut journal *Southern African Analysis and Advice*.[1] He argued that South Africa's economic dominance was unquestionable 'whether you measure it in terms of electricity generation or GDP per capita or size of the stock exchange' and he suggested that its role should be economic rather than military. 'South Africa cannot develop in isolation. As I travel the region I have a sense of the need for the South African private sector and the government to pull together and help with the development of the neighbourhood. Otherwise South Africa will be swamped demographically and then isolated.' Addressing the issue of investment realistically, Crocker said: 'Investors don't come because they suddenly see a country that is more democratic. They go where there is business to be done and there is a chance they will not suffer a reversal.' He also made the point that while South Africa was marginal to most major economies, it was not marginal to Britain, a point that both Pretoria and London should build upon. He concluded on a hard-headed note: 'I am realistic rather than optimistic. I do think that the worst days are behind us. There are a lot of possibilities, but it is pretty much up to Africans to grab those opportunities.'

In February 1999 Mandela addressed the final session of parliament as it opened in Cape Town before his retirement at the elections of 2 June 1999. He called for a 'new patriotism' to counter the enemies of reconciliation. He summed up five years of achievement since he had become the first democratically elected president of South Africa. He said: 'For a country that was the polecat of the world … the doors of the world have opened, precisely because of our success in achieving things that humanity as a whole holds dear. Of this we should be proud.' He went on to list the social and other achievements of his government. He conceded 'difficult areas' included crime, corruption and unemployment. His most telling statement, however, concerned the ending of apartheid attitudes. 'The critical act of reconciliation is the dismantling of what remains of apartheid practices and attitudes. Reconciliation, without this major step, will be transient, the ode of false hope on the lips of fools.'[2] Unfortunately, for this was Mandela's parliamentary swansong, the opposition whites of the National Party and Freedom Front showed no inclination to applaud the man who had done so much to make the new South Africa possible. At one point in his speech Mandela addressed them particularly and said: 'When I say Africans I mean everybody for whom the continent of Africa is their home.' Arguably, the worst tragedy for South Africa will be if the whites refuse to go the full course in reconciliation and behave as though, having formally abandoned apartheid, nothing else remains for them to do.

During the last two years of President Mandela's stewardship speculation about the character and intentions of his designated successor, Thabo Mbeki, mounted. Mbeki will have the task of leading South Africa into the twenty-first century when the glamour and excitement surrounding the emergence of the Rainbow Society or the New South Africa have worn off. Instead, he will face an array of potentially explosive problems with few prospects of real help from outside in overcoming them. If the whites determine to put into the New South Africa some of the energies that formerly they reserved for their own aggrandisement at the expense of the black majority then its prospects should be bright. If, on the other hand, they stand aside in bitterness because their privileged position has been eroded then Mbeki's task will be that much the harder. As we move into the twenty-first century South Africa has the chance to become the hope of a continent; whether or not it succeeds in this objective must depend upon the combined effort of all its peoples.

Notes

South African publications are indicated thus: (SA)

Introduction

1 *The Times* 27/06/96.
2 Tony Hawkins in *The Independent* 12/10/97.
3 *Sunday Times* 13/08/95.
4 *The Independent* 22/04/98.
5 *The Independent* 12/07/98.
6 *Finance Week* (SA) 18–24/12/97.

1 Setting the scene

1 *The Independent* 18/02/96.
2 *The Independent* 21/05/97.
3 Roy Hattersely in *The Observer* 31/08/97.
4 Ibid.

2 Racism

1 *The Independent* 11/04/95.
2 *The Star* (SA) 29/07/95.
3 *Sunday Times* (SA) 06/08/95.
4 *The Independent* 22/11/95.
5 *The Independent* 01/02/96.
6 Shaun Johnson in *Sunday Independent* 14/12/97.
7 *The Independent* 12/02/98.
8 Mary Brand in *The Independent* 28/02/98.

3 Truth and reconciliation

1 *The Observer* 30/10/94.
2 *The Independent* 21/02/95.
3 *The Observer* 26/02/95.
4 *The Independent* 16/03/96.
5 *The Independent* 02/12/95.
6 *The Independent* 12/10/96.
7 *The Observer* 03/11/96.
8 *The Independent* 22/11/96.
9 *The Independent* 31/10/98.

4 Politics

1 *The Independent* 22/12/94.
2 Ibid.
3 *The Independent* 04/05/95.

4   *The Star* (SA) 05/08/95.
5   *Sunday Times* (SA) 06/08/95.
6   Quoted in *The Star* (SA) 16/12/97.
7   Ibid.
8   *Daily Telegraph* 17/12/97.
9   *Mail and Guardian* (SA) 07/07/95.
10 *Business Report* (SA) 03/08/95.
11 *Sunday Times* (SA) 13/08/95.
12 *The Independent* 16/01/96.
13 *The Observer* 12/05/96.
14 *The Independent* 10/05/95.
15 *Cape Times* (SA) 21/08/95.
16 *Sunday Times, Business Times* (SA) 21/06/98.
17 *The Observer* 12/02/95.
18 *Cape Times* (SA) 24/07/95.
19 *The Sunday Independent* (SA) 31/05/98.

5   Problems and expectations

1   *The Independent* 17/12/94.
2   *Sunday Independent* (SA) 30/05/98.
3   *Sunday Times, Business Times* (SA) 07/06/98.
4   *Human Development Report 1998*, 'The new South Africa – ending apartheid in consumption' UNDP New York and Oxford University Press 1998, p. 56.
5   *Sunday Independent* (SA) 14/12/97.
6   *The Star* (SA) 26/05/98.
7   *The Independent* 16/06/98.
8   *The Independent* 08/03/95.
9   *Business Development* (SA) 22/05/98.
10 *Business Development* (SA) 15/05/98.
11 *Sunday Times, Business Times* (SA) 03/11/98.
12 Tom Nevin in *African Business* November 1998.

6   Mechanisms

1   *Star Business Report* (SA) 16/01/98.
2   *The Reconstruction and Development Programme*, African National Congress (ANC) 1994, Umanyano Publications, Johannesburg.
3   *Cape Times* (SA) 29/07/95.
4   *Financial Week* (SA) 18–24/12/97.
5   *Sunday Independent, Independent Business* (SA) 24/05/98.
6   *Business Report on Sunday* (SA) 18/10/98.
7   *The Star* (SA) 19/10/98.
8   *Business Report* (SA) 27/05/98.
9   Ibid.
10 *Business Report* (SA) 27/02/98.
11 *Business Report* (SA) 24/07/95.
12 *Sunday Independent Business* (SA) 19/10/97.

7 Labour and unemployment

1 *Cape Times* (SA) 11/08/95.
2 Ibid.
3 *Business Report* (SA) 07/04/98.
4 *Business Report* (SA) 07/05/98.
5 *Sunday Times, Business Times* (SA) 10/04/98.
6 *Sunday Independent, Independent Business* (SA) 26/04/98.
7 *Business Report* (SA) 18/05/98.
8 *The Star* (SA) 27/05/98.
9 *The Star* (SA) 28/05/98.
10 *Business Report on Sunday* (SA) 01/11/98.
11 *The Independent* 02/08/94.
12 *Sunday Independent, Independent Business* (SA) 17/05/98.
13 *Sunday Independent, Independent Business* (SA) 23/08/98.

8 Crime and violence

1 *Sunday Independent* (SA) 16/07/95.
2 Ibid.
3 *The Independent* 28/11/95.
4 *The Star* (SA) 27/05/98.
5 *The Independent* 10/07/95.

9 The economy

1 *The Reconstruction and Development Programme*, African National Congress, Umanyano Publications, Johannesburg 1994.
2 *The Independent* 20/03/95.
3 *The Standard* 04/08/95.
4 *Business Report* (SA) 08/08/95.
5 *Business Report* (SA) 01/03/98.
6 Ibid.
7 *Cape Times* (SA) 25/07/95.
8 *Sunday Independent* (SA) 06/08/95.
9 *Business Day* (SA) 02/02/98.

10 Catching up

1 *The Independent* 09/10/95.
2 *Business Day* (SA) 08/08/95.
3 *Sunday Times, Business Times* (SA) 26/04/98.
4 Ibid.
5 Ibid.
6 *Business Report* 10/03/98.
7 *Sunday Independent Business* 22/03/98.
8 *Business Report* 19/05/98.

11 Investment

1 *Business Day* (SA) 27/07/95.
2 *Business Report* (SA) 27/07/95.

3 *Sunday Business* (SA) 30/07/95.
4 *Sunday Times* (SA) 30/07/95.
5 *Business Day* (SA) 31/07/95.
6 *Citizen* (SA) 02/08/95.
7 *Mail and Guardian* (SA) 02/10/97.
8 *Sunday Independent Business* (SA) 08/03/98.
9 *Business Report* (SA) 07/05/98.
10 *Business Report* (SA) 15/09/98.
11 *The Independent* 11/07/96.
12 *The Independent* 08/10/97.
13 *Business Report* (SA) 02/02/98.

12 Industry

1 *Sunday Times* (SA) 13/08/95.
2 *Business Report* (SA) 20/05/98.
3 *Sunday Independent* 28/09/97.
4 *Sunday Independent, Independent Business* (SA) 24/05/98.
5 *Financial Mail* (SA) 30/01/98.
6 *Business Day* (SA) 31/07/95.
7 *Business Report* (SA) 20/03/98.
8 *Business Report* (SA) 95/05/98.

13 The mining sector

1 *Sunday Times* 06/08/95.
2 *Mail and Guardian* (SA) 23/08/95.
3 *Business Report* (SA) 16/01/98.
4 *Business Report* (SA) 16/10/98.
5 Ibid.
6 *Business Day* (SA) 02/02/98.
7 *Business Report* (SA) 12/02/98.
8 *Sunday Times, Business Times* (SA) 01/03/98.

14 Finances

1 *Sunday Times, Business Times* (SA) 21/02/99.
2 *Business Report* (SA) 29/05/98.
3 *Business Day* (SA) 03/08/98.

15 Agriculture

1 *Mail and Guardian* (SA) 07/07/95.
2 *Sunday Independent Business* (SA) 05/04/98.
3 *Financial Mail* (SA) 30/01/98.
4 *The Independent* 24/06/98.
5 *The Independent* 15/09/98.
6 *Citizen* (SA) 08/08/95.
7 *The Star* (SA) 22/05/98.

16 Foreign policy I: Britain, the Commonwealth and the European Union

1 Frene, Ginwala 'The Case for Sanctions' in *South Africa in Question,* James Currey, 1988, p. 105.
2 *The Independent* 18/03/95.
3 *Sunday Independent* (SA) 06/09/98.
4 *Business Report* (SA) 16/01/98.
5 *Business Report* (SA) 23/02/98.
6 *Business Report* (SA) 30/04/98.
7 *Business Report* (SA) 18/06/98.
8 *Sunday Times, Business Times* (SA) 20/09/98.
9 *Business Report* (SA) 03/12/98.

17 Foreign policy II: The USA and globalisation

1 *The Independent* 21/11/95.
2 Ibid.
3 *The Independent* 28/03/98.
4 *Business Day* (SA) 27/05/98.
5 *Business Day* (SA) 04/06/98.
6 *Business Report* (SA) 19/05/98.
7 *Business Report* (SA) 10/09/98.

18 Defence, the arms trade and mercenaries

1 *Sunday Independent* (SA) 23/07/95.
2 *Business Day* (SA) 22/05/98.
3 *The Star* (SA) 12/06/98.
4 *Mail and Guardian* (SA) 28/07/95.
5 *African Business December* 1997.
6 Quoted in *Le Monde Diplomatique.*

19 Springboard into sub-Saharan Africa

1 *The Nation* 14/07/95.
2 *Business Report* (SA) 18/05/98.
3 *Natal Witness* (SA) 09/08/95.
4 *Business Report* (SA) 22/08/95.
5 *Independent Business* (SA) 19/04/98.
6 *Business Day* (SA) 21/01/98.
7 *The Observer* 30/03/97.
8 *Business Report* (SA) 20/03/98.
9 *Sunday Independent* (SA) 02/06/98.
10 *Business Report* (SA) 28/08/98.

20 The future

1 Quoted in *Sunday Independent Business News* (SA) 19/10/97.
2 *The Independent* 06/02/99.

Index